T0380726

Denny McCartney

PICKING UP
THE PIECES

 **Trafford** www.trafford.com
PUBLISHING®
North America & international
toll-free: 1 888 232 4444 (USA & Canada)
fax: 812 355 4082

CONTENTS

CONTENTS

DEDICATION

This book was brought about as a means of giving credit to my wife Dorothy, daughter Maureen and son Murray for their invaluable support and encouragement during my career. Thought was also given to providing our grandchildren Colin and Denise Haddock and Nicholas, McKenzie and Lauren McCartney with some knowledge of the early days of aviation and the experiences of their grandfather as he mended and rescued the bent and broken "birds" that accident and error scattered over the remote reaches of North America.

top left; **Cessna 180, CF-KNG rebuilt in the basement of our home with the help of our 12 year old daughter Maureen, on the rivet gun.**
middle left; **Daughter Maureen**
bottom left; **Son Murray, my able assistant, with patched Super Cub CF-MTN ready for ferry flight from a strip on a B.C. coast inlet.**

ACKNOWLEDGMENT

My heartfelt thanks to my wife Dorothy for critiquing the stories, daughter Maureen for typing, Ed Hawkes for his encouragement and friendly push and the team of Jack Schofield and Danielle Letourneau for their professional guidance.

PREFACE

I like books because they rely on the wonderful theatre of the mind. I like this book because it opens the doors of that theatre and offers an opportunity for vicarious participation in a unique career that I would never, in a thousand years, have chosen for myself.

In the course of getting to know Denny McCartney I asked him what he did for a living. He replied that he specialized in the salvage of damaged aircraft, in detecting what caused them to be damaged and as an aviation insurance adjuster, providing a detailed report. So we had more than an interest in aviation in common: In the distant past, while in the air force, I had endured the experience of standing before a multi medaled, multi ringed authoritarian to admit that I had bent, bashed and broken parts of one of the King's flying appliances and had been saved from shame by a detailed report.

Our conversations were of the usual, around the

pool, kitchen table, back porch exchanges of yesterday's yarns. I found Denny's tale of wreckage rescues off the Arctic ice and tundra, from the remote bush of Canada's north and of coaxing reluctant engines to pull an aircraft across the top of the South American jungles, to be interesting accounts of ingenious problem solving and dedication to achieving a successful outcome. I urged him to get his story on record because nothing like it would ever be done again.

I get extra enjoyment from the stories because I set my imagination button to place me as part of Denny's crew – I am there. I recommend the device to all readers as Denny shares the stories of a few of the more than 800 aircraft he brought back from the "pile of junk" state to renewed utility. Turn the pages and join Denny as he tells of "Picking up the Pieces."

Ed Hawkes

Picking up the
Pieces

When the flames of a log fire are trying to reach the bottom of a carefully suspended coffee pot, and all the spooks in the world seem to be dancing with the Northern Lights under a moonless Arctic sky, someone, sometimes, is inspired to toss a philosophical thought into the conversation.

On one such occasion a companion observed that a life path was laid out for everyone and I was out there on the edge of the northern tree line listening to howls of the wolves because it was written; it was my fate.

Now I don't duck black cats or avoid walking under ladders. I became skeptical about mumbo jumbo while doing my puberty course as I sat expectantly under a clutch of mistletoe. It didn't work unless you count the big slurp I got from a wet-nosed cocker spaniel. But the comment about a life path has darted in and out of my mind over the years and now that the ring of the phone no longer signals a trip into the wilderness to collect a bent aircraft, it has prompted me to take a peek over my shoulder at how I got shunted onto such a strange line of work.

Shunted. Now there is a word that really meant

Denny McCartney with sad aircraft.

something in my growing up years. Every community in Western Canada that was a nodule on the rail system knew the meaning and sound of "shunt" in the twenties and thirties. Waking and sleeping hours were regularly and irregularly filled with the boom and bang of rail cars being shunted into sidings and lined up into trains. My home town, Port Coquitlam, was such a place.

Most of us who grew up in those communities, much like the box cars, waited and hoped to be shunted into a good paying job; preferably with the railroad. While I waited for the 'big' opportunity, I did all the usual kid jobs and as a teenager landed work with a shingle mill; a no brainer that required a strong back, stamina and enough alertness to retain possession of all your fingers.

Looking back, it was some kind of gymnasium. By humping thousands of pounds of cedar blocks I acquired the physical tools to tackle any and all kinds of manual labor, plus a determination to finish, no matter how tough the going got.

One day, before the machinery started up, I heard the sound of an engine coming from above the trees. I looked up to see an airplane soar across our clearing and dreams ignited by the Vancouver Sun's kid feature, Sun Ray Club, popped into my head. I resolved then and there to make my career in aviation.

I had entered every Sun Ray aircraft and flying contest even though I had never been near an airplane. I had read every story I could find about the adventures of World War One pilots; I had logged hundreds of hours of fantasy flights and the wondrous sight and sound of a flying machine riding high above the tree tops made the prospect of spending my life in a shingle mill seem like a prison sentence.

For the rest of the day an advertisement I had clipped from a magazine constantly nudged its way into my thoughts and when I got home after work I hunted it out. It offered a correspondence course on aircraft manufacturing and structural repairs through the Aero Industries Technical Institute in Los Angeles. I ordered the course and started monthly lessons and exams. I was on my way.

It wasn't easy. All day breaking my back and all evening breaking my brain. I struggled because I had never seen or handled most of the tools discussed in the lessons. But with the combination of my mother's encouragement and gentle prodding to keep me awake over the bookwork, I plowed through the program. Finally, in the spring of 1937 the last lesson and the last exam was completed and I was ready to tackle attendance at the Institute.

Funds were short and the family was working on a plan to save enough money to send me to California in the fall when tragedy struck. My brother was killed by a drunken driver. This sad event produced a small insurance payment and my mother and father dedicated the money to my education.

Bags were packed and Dad took me to New

Westminster where I boarded a bus bound for Los Angeles. A genuine bush bunny with a sophistication clock set at zero.

My seatmate for the long journey turned out to be a guardian angel. He gave me valuable advice on how to deal with new found friends and be careful in placing my trust. When we got off the bus in Los Angeles he took me straight to a bank and had me deposit my money so that I could draw on it as needed and not have it exposed to predators. We shook hands, wished each other good luck, and said goodbye. I have never seen him again but I'll remember him forever.

The Institute set me up in a boarding house owned by an ex-Ziegfield Follies chorus girl named Jerry McCamey who could have written the book on how to excel as a landlady. She and her husband Lewis took me into their extended family and made sure that I didn't get blinded by the bright lights or caught up in wild oats sowing adventures.

Jerry and Lewis kept their show biz connections. Phil Harris and his orchestra had played at their wedding and they were still part of that scene. People active in the movies and show business dropped into the kitchen at all hours. I was bedazzled. They took a lot of the rough edges off the boy from the bush. For my part, I had been brought up to help with kitchen and housework and they appreciated me pitching in.

The Aero Industries Institute was great. As the famous teacher Joseph Campbell advised, I had found my bliss. Every day at that school was sheer joy. It proved one sure thing to me; if you are interested you try harder. I can't claim to have had the top marks in high school but it was a different story at the college with my grades continually in the top end of the nineties.

Many of the instructors were experienced older technicians drawn from aircraft manufacturing plants such as Consolidated, Lockheed and Douglas. They spoke and demonstrated with knowledge that could only be gained from practical experience. As a result of exposure to the teachings of these pioneers in aviation technology, graduates of the Institute found quick employment in the aviation industry.

My last term at the Institute came to a close and almost coincidentally Canada declared war on Germany. I found myself in a strange category. All foreign students were deemed, by the nervous American bureaucrats, to be aliens who had to be listed and finger printed. I headed for home with my diploma shortly thereafter.

In Vancouver I presented myself to the R.C.A.F. recruiting office and gave them a problem. I was over qualified for enlistment as a trainee and they were in a muddle with the establishment of training facilities. Their quandary was whether to enlist instructors and give them commissions or non-commissioned rank or employ civilian instructors.

While they tussled with that I worked for Boeing Aircraft as a supervisor in several departments, met Dorothy Murray (better known as Dot) and was a member of the Royal Canadian Artillery

Reserve. When the commanding officer found out about my aviation training he asked what the H I was doing around guns and suggested that I offer my services to the Navy.

If they gave me a medical, I can't remember it. I was in, posted on loan to the Royal Navy Fleet Air Arm and transferred to England so fast my laundry didn't catch up to me for a month.

I was posted to a Baracuda torpedo and dive bomber squadron. The commanding officer was the famous Lieutenant Commander Carver, who zig-zagged his Swordfish aircraft through a wall of gunfire to slam a torpedo into the rudder of the German super battleship Bismark, turning the monster into crippled scow. He was a terrific squadron leader.

His incentive plan for mechanics consisted of one rule: If you worked on an aircraft you rode with the pilot who did the air test. I had more than a few hair raising experiences riding in the gunnery seat behind the fearless "cowboys" who put our work through the aerobatic wringer.

Close your eyes and picture yourself strapped into an aeroplane at five thousand feet, nose pointed straight down, headed for the ocean. At the last split second, the pilot pulls out of the dive, levels out and you look behind to see that the five bladed prop was leaving a deep trench in the water without touching it. .You only needed one flight to convince you that making sure your own work was the best you could do was an absolute must. I made it a lifetime commitment.

Suddenly, the war was over and the Royal Navy sent me back to the Canadian Navy. They must have sent the gremlins with me. A Denny McCartney file did not exist; the black hole in communications between the two navies had swallowed it.

Navy bureaucrats who couldn't or wouldn't cope punted me from base to base starting in Halifax and ending up in Esquimalt. I talked the Commanding Officer into sending me to H.M.C.S. Discovery in Vancouver. There, I found a smart clerk who unraveled the riddle, calculated that I had 122 days paid leave coming and sent me home to wait for orders. For all intents and purposes, I was out; just like all the other guys who were out looking for something to do.

Loaded with leave and back pay, I gathered up the gumption to ask Dorothy to marry me. She fell for my story and we headed for California on our honeymoon.

We had a great time. I was still an alien but the war had taught our American friends a thing or six about alienation. They put on their 'good neighbor' hats and greeted us like long lost cousins.

Jerry and Lewis, my pre-war landlords, who had always treated me as a favored member of the family, were especially hospitable. They were now located in Hollywood, wealthy and sadly showing the signs of hard work, hard play and advancing years. People of their special ilk should never grow old.

The honeymoon has lasted to this day but our

California holiday was soon over and it was back to Canada; back to meet the new world of life on civvy street.

Jim Spilsbury, now famous as one of Canada's pioneer radio and aviation entrepreneurs, had his Queen Charlotte Airlines up and flying. I landed a job working on his fleet of Supermarine Stranraers.

Jim treated his staff like a prairie harvesting crew; when winter set in he laid off everyone who didn't have a 'right now' job on the work bench. I eventually got cut and immediately joined Brisbane Aviation where Stan Sharpe operated a combination flying school, a maintenance training school, and aircraft repair shop.

It was a great place to work. We did everything. Included in our cutting edge experiences was the conversion of a Tiger Moth into a crop duster for Art Sellars of Skyway Air services in Langley. Johnny Johnson and I, under the guidance of master technician Hugh Thomas, did the complete job.

The Moth was Art's first crop duster and is currently a feature display in the museum in Langley, B.C. It was the signature aircraft that established Skyway as the nucleus for Conair Aviation, now known throughout the world for its outstanding ability to convert aircraft into super water bombers to battle forest fires.

Stan Sharpe had collected some of the most skilled people in the aviation industry to man Brisbane Aviation. Two of them, Elmer Tryon and Hugh Thomas were the best in the business. They buffed the rough edges off our skills and brought the best out of all who worked with them.

Elmer expanded my engine knowledge to include the 65 horse power light plane engine, rounding out my resume which already included larger engines up to the Rolls Royce Griffin used in the Navy. Hugh established my confidence to handle any kind of airframe and fuselage problem.

It was 1949 and Canada's western and northern wilderness beckoned to the new breed of adventurers who had honed flying skills in the war birds and acquired undauntable self confidence. Experienced fighter and bomber pilots became entrepreneurial bush pilots who needed experienced mechanics and technicians to keep them in the air.

The future looked very bright indeed for the McCartneys. So good, in fact, that Dot and I bought an empty lot and started building our present home and I mean started...right from the first pitch of the first spadeful of dirt into the wheel barrow. My ex navy friend, Al Warner brought his own shovel and together we excavated the basement - that was 1949.

In spite of the fact that I had more advanced training than most, I wasn't prevented from being out of work during several winter periods. Sadly enough, I had a lot of company in that regard as it was the practice for aviation businesses to reduce staffs at the end of the seasonal summer work.

Each winter month I was out of work I took a job on the water front as a longshoreman. That included cleaning the dirty bilge's of the 10,000 ton freighters and lining them for grain loading. It was very hard work for good pay at $1.38 per hour. Thankfully, Dot was working as an accountant and bookkeeper for a logging and sawmill company. We managed to keep our noses above the tide.

The aviation industry following the end of W.W.2 was in a pioneering stage of advancement following the economy with its ups and downs. I can, from a struggling experience in getting established in the industry after the war, speak with first hand knowledge of the trials and tribulations that faced so many in the relatively new industry.

The struggles with bureaucrats, monopolies and financial hardships faced in getting established in the flying business, especially in the north, is best described in The Max Ward Story, a recommended reading.

Brisbane was slowing down a bit and I was offered a steady position with the title of Superintendent of Maintenance at Bob Gayer's Associated Air Services. That was a good move for me and a big challenge to prove that they had not made a mistake in hiring me for that position.

We maintained a large number of aircraft for Associated Air Taxi, the flight portion of Bob Gayer's organization and a large number of outside machines operated by logging companies etc. Whenever an aircraft was damaged some distance out in the boondocks or sunk at the seaplane dock it became routine for me to hear, "Go get it Denny."

Eventually the Company passed its peak in the flying end of the business as did the dependent servicing department, and I had an offer from Ed Hanratty, Chief Engineer for Russ Baker's Central B.C. Airways. I was pleased and I guess, somewhat flattered by it and accepted the job. I was put in charge of the maintenance for the multi-engined aircraft that included the PBY-5 Cansos. Ed Hanratty, whose ability I respected very much, was my immediate boss.

Thanks to Russ Baker I got an early introduction to the wonderful Beaver. He bought the first Beaver manufactured by De Havilland. Its registration was CF- FHB and as is the case with most new models of aircraft, the manufacturer issued service bulletins from time to time for improvements. I remember having to add extra rivets all around the main bulkhead. I believe the aircraft is now in the Ottawa Aviation Museum – more about Beavers later.

Central B.C. Airways became part of a new company named Pacific Western Airlines Limited with a huge work load. I recall that one season I worked 10 hrs. on week days and 16 hrs. on week ends with no days off from early spring to late fall. Dick Laidman, then the president, appreciated my efforts to the point that he paid me overtime. An unheard of thing in those days. It paid for our first nice car.

I went to work for Jack McMahon of Western Airmotive in the capacity of chief engineer of maintenance and major repairs on private aircraft and others owned by various companies. A sub-company with the title Far West Aircraft Salvage was formed for the retrieval of accident damaged aircraft for insurance companies. I did quite a number of salvage jobs over a period of time in distant locations and started to build a reputation for success in that line of work.

Those early years were the beginning of a new era in B.C. Aviation. Air traffic in the northern latitudes was growing and the number of kites being involuntarily parked in remote parts of the wilderness was on the increase. Dot and I recognized this as an opportunity to start a business of our own. I was working long days in remote locations for other people so why not for us? In 1957, we formed Denny McCartney Ltd. We were soon doing most of the aircraft salvage assignments for the top two adjusting firms in Vancouver, namely J. Brouwer and Co. and Meredith, Allan and Robinson as well as James Taylor Company of Edmonton and Leo J. Lecler's Seattle office. Jim Redwood and Frank Wright of the Canadian office for the British Aviation Insurance Company were always very supportive.

My first big salvage job was Max Ward's Otter CF-GBY on Baffin Island. I considered that to be the turning point in my career. That was the beginning of true family involvement in the company, with Dot becoming the office manager operating out of our home while looking after two young ones and worrying about me when I was away patching up an aircraft that would be flown back with me on board.

Quite a number have suggested I write a book and observe that I had followed a very unusual road to retirement. They thought the work was unique and an account of some of the adventures would be of interest, not only to aviation folk, but to others who would never come any closer to a wilderness adventure than looking for a lost golf ball. So here, selected from more than eight hundred "prangs", are a few tales about:

"picking up the pieces"

Picking up the Pieces

As previously mentioned, the locations of the stories in Picking up the Pieces are scattered over the remote reaches of North America. I have included maps within a few chapters, but shown here is an overview of the area that I travelled over the years.

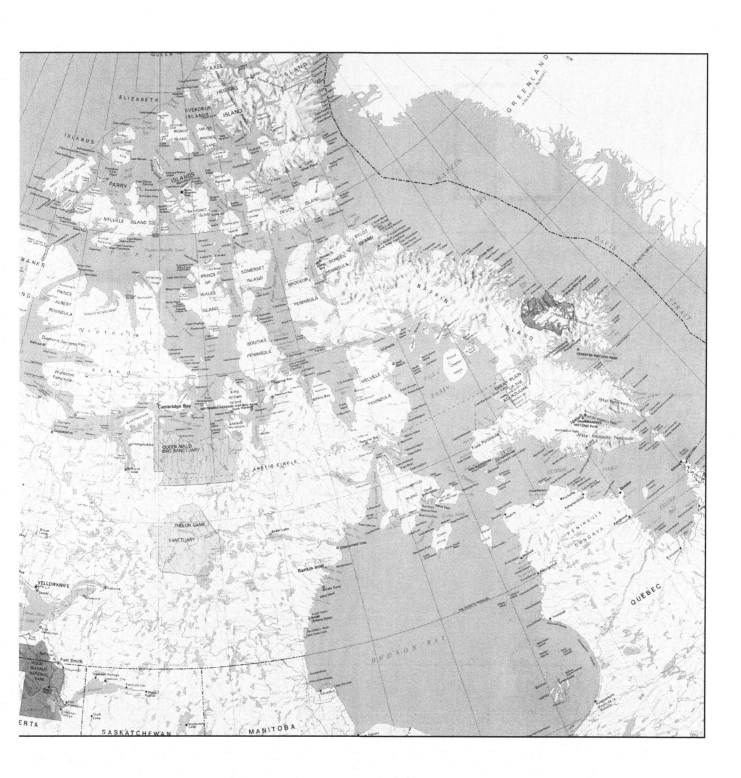

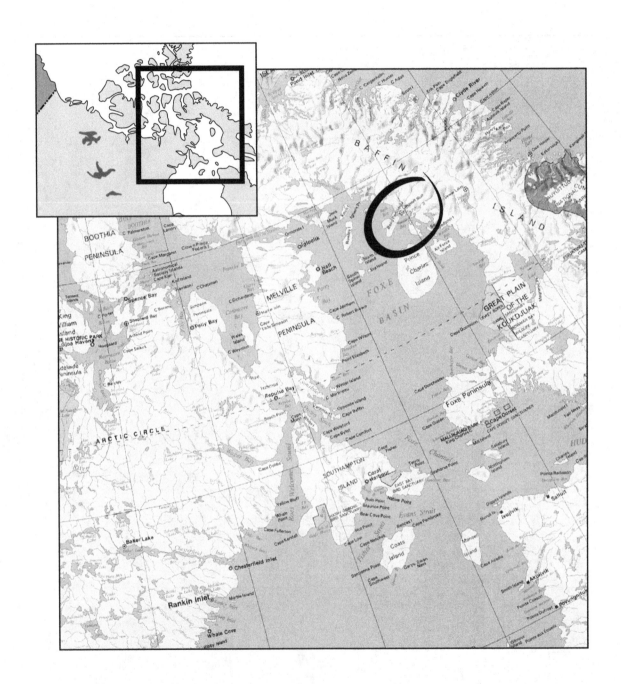

picking up the pieces

chapter one

Wardair Single Otter CF-GBY

A Baffin Island Challenge

This is the beginning of the all new "in our own business" adventure. Spring was turning into summer; the sky was alive with the sound of aircraft going somewhere and going nowhere; statistics showed that some of them were bound to have an accident – what more could an optimistic salvage expert expect? – We didn't have to wait long.

On the 3rd day of June 1958, while our shiny new phones still sat by the boxes they came in, I received a call from Seattle. Jack Mitchell, manager of the western office for Leo J. Leclerc Inc. of Montreal, an aircraft insurance adjusting company was on the line with a problem. He had some photos and information on a damaged de Havilland Otter aircraft located on Baffin Island, that he thought I would be interested in taking a look at. We were ecstatic - our first call and it was a biggy, not a ground looped ultra lite.

The machine was on a D.E.W. Line site at a base called Fox 4 near Baird Peninsula and directly north of Prince Charles Island in the Fox Basin. It not only seemed so far away, it was far away. We were in the south west corner of Canada and the damaged aircraft was diagonally across the continent in the north east corner, well north of the Arctic Circle.

For those with a foggy or blank recall of the early days of the Cold War, the Distant Early Warning Line, the D.E.W. Line, was conceived to give the Americans a chance to intercept any flying Russian Bears before they could bomb important targets in the United States.

As soon as daylight hours returned to the north in 1955, they began to build the D.E.W. Line by positioning a string of 50 tracking and control stations from Alaska to Greenland at about 70 degrees north latitude. The radar sites in Canada were on our Arctic coast and off shore islands.

There are some who claim the Line was outdated as soon as it was completed but there were the same whines about the Suez Canal. Like all pro-

jects of its kind there were reasons to criticize but there were many benefits and beneficiaries. The aviation industry boomed as a result of the huge air cargo and passenger loads required. And that gave Murphy and his Law a chance to put some business our way.

Now, back to Max Ward's ailing Otter. The photos showed extensive damage to the outboard section of the left wing, at a point about 6 to 8 feet from the tip, including the centre aileron bell crank area. At first glance, it looked as though explosives had damaged it. The swirling winds had blown the tip section up on to the top surface of the wing. There was also other major damage. The landing gear was in a snarl; the belly was torn out from near the camera hatch back to the tail and the main support assembly for the empennage (tail end) was crushed and torn beyond the possibility of making temporary repairs.

All this damage had been caused by a windstorm tearing the machine free of its tie downs and blowing it across the large rocks strewn over the rough parking area surrounding the air strip.

I was sure that Mitchell was going to ask me if the aircraft could be made fit for a ferry flight out of there. I took an optimistic approach and felt, based

Single Otter CF-GBY on Baffin Island N.W.T.

on the details in the enlarged photos, that it could be done. However, I had no hands-on work experience on the aircraft. It was a relatively new model and there were none in commercial use in B.C. However, the R.C.A.F. had a couple operating in the Vancouver area. I knew I would get a good briefing from their maintenance officer. Looking back, I find it hard to believe I was ever that cocky.

The serial number of the machine was 5. It was the fifth one built by de Havilland and was the first aircraft Max Ward had bought to form Wardair in 1953 and the first in commercial use in western Canada. It was a valuable asset to Max's fledgling airline and it represented a surefire reputation builder for our little company. I needed a couple of days to get some basic details and do a little serious thinking.

I had two top priority items in mind that had to be dealt with before I could honestly say I was ready to take on the job. The first was to confirm the availability of a good airframe technician. The other was to obtain complete details on the airframe structure in the areas of the damage.

My first choice for technician was Karl Frisk, an excellent airframe specialist. Fortune smiled. He was ready to go when I spoke to him about it and, needless to say, I was pretty happy about that.

Next stop the Royal Canadian Air Force base.

I met Gordon Brown who briefed me on the primary structure of our damaged areas and then had his men remove inspection panels for internal viewing. This was very helpful, particularly with regard to the left wing where we took accurate measurements of the webs of the spars between defined points. The locations of those points were determined from the photos by counting the rivets and ribs within the damaged areas. We would then be able to make up webs which, with extruded bulb angle material, temporary spar repairs could be made.

This close-up look at the healthy structure settled any doubts we had about rebuilding the damaged areas. We were confident we could make the wing flyable again. I was so grateful to Gord Brown for his help in my first major salvage operation.

An estimate on the approximate cost of the temporary repairs, made from photos only, plus transportation and ferry costs, was prepared and presented to adjuster Mitchell. He seemed quite satisfied with our proposal and readily accepted it.

It was not until much later that I learned we had been competing with some one in Eastern Canada who had planned to airfreight a new wing from Toronto to the accident site. That would have required a large aircraft with cargo doors. Such freighters were not always readily available in those days.

Charlie Smith, at that time, was the West Coast representative for the de Havilland Aircraft Company. He knew his business and was always willing and helpful. He was a great help to us by confirming the availability of parts and materials we would need. Charlie also told me who to contact at the factory and later I was to find out just how much his influence meant when I approached their finance department to arrange payment.

Karl and I checked and rechecked our requirements until we were satisfied. We were then ready to go. In the meantime, I had obtained clearances for access to the D.E.W. Line for both of us. It was fortunate that I had come to know Stan Rothwell quite well by doing the maintenance on his Beaver aircraft that he flew for the RCMP. A letter from him cleared the way.

I proceeded to de Havilland to procure the parts etc. and any information I could obtain from their engineers and technicians for our job. Later, I would meet Karl Frisk in Montreal for the trip north.

I was well received on my arrival at de Havilland, this made me feel good. However, when I explained what I had in mind for the temporary repairs and showed them the photos, I did not receive any encouragement on our plans for the wing repair. The Chief Design Engineer, Fred Buller, eventually told me that it could not be done safely because the wing type structure did not lend itself to such major temporary repairs.

Well, it was a sure thing that I did not have the training or knowledge of their design engineers but I was confident it could be successfully performed. Perhaps it was the structural and manufacturing training I had received from an aeronautical college in California that was subconsciously guiding me. Perhaps it was also some plain stubbornness that made me feel so sure that an adequately rein-

forced temporary repair could bring the wing back to its original strength.

I began to feel that I had a serious problem because I was not able to technically prove that our repair scheme was both practical and structurally safe. I also could not totally ignore the advice I had been given.

That was not the first or last time a manufacturer's aeronautical engineer would tell me that my plans for a temporary repair could not be satisfactorily performed. I realized of course that Mr Buller was in a delicate position. He could, by agreeing to our plans, place himself and De Havilland in an awkward position in the event that we had an accident.

I should mention that while I was seeking information, Fred Buller asked me to accompany him as he toured the plant checking various structures along the assembly line. His purpose was to show and explain to me some of the finer points in the design of the aircraft. That information proved to be invaluable in dealing with later problems.

Fred had another purpose. He questioned me at some length on the problems of salt-water corrosion. How did we combat it, what preventative measures did we take etc., etc.? Corrosion, has always been a continuous problem especially on seaplanes operating on coastal waters.

I felt good about being able to provide the factory's Engineering Department with proven facts from actual experience. I should mention that Fred Buller and Dick Hiscocks were the Engineers who

(both); Major Damage to left wing and its control surfaces.

designed the world renowned and famous de Havilland DHC2 Beaver aircraft.

It was in the afternoon of the next day that I was approached by a young liaison Engineer who said he was interested in my project and thought my plans had a lot of merit. He wanted me to meet someone to obtain another opinion. What a surprise that was. McCartney luck was at work.

My new found friend introduced me to a very busy Stress Engineer named Ed Krzehlik who was doing strain testing of the Caribou aircraft structure and he was kind enough not to use that as an excuse to say he was too busy to help me. After hearing my plans and while looking at our repair sketch and photos, said. "Your plans are good. What is the problem?" I was surprised, delighted

and shocked by his approach to what had been considered an impossibility.

It took a few seconds for me to get my head around what I had heard. I apologized for hesitating with my response, said I was deeply appreciative of his observations and said, "I don't have a problem with my plans but I do not have your training and knowledge to support them - could you give me suggestions on how to improve the presentation of my proposals."

He proceeded to mark out the wing loads on my sketch from the root end to the tip. He said, "There is not much load out in the damaged area. Your plans are good." He then wished me good luck and went on his way. I was close to getting airborne on the spot. "Your plans are good." - I was on cloud nine.

For those not familiar with aviation technology, wing loads are actually stress points that vary throughout the length of the wing.

I felt so relieved at getting such expert endorsement. It was like a bright light being turned on in a dark room. I told him how grateful I was for his help, we said our good-byes and I proceeded with renewed confidence. The knowledge obtained from Ed Krzehlik, previously of the Polish airforce, would prove to be invaluable in a number of future Otter wing bush repairs.

The next day I prepared to bring my visit to an end and get on my way. I went to their stores and presented my list of parts, fasteners, manuals etc. When I approached the finance office to make payment arrangements, I was told that through arrangements from their Vancouver office I would be given credit and an invoice would be sent to me.

I knew right then that Charlie Smith, also known as Charlie de Havilland, had helped me again. I was running close to the line financially on the job and the credit line he had set up was wonderful. I bought Arctic equipment such as Woods eider down sleeping bags and other northern items through Canadian Helicopters Ltd. It was wonderful to have such help. I then notified Karl Frisk to meet me in Montreal as previously planned.

We flew from there to Frobisher, now called Iqualit, Baffin Island and from there to Fox 4 D.E.W. site in a Beaver.

During that last portion of the flight two stops were made at small airstrips. It was at one of these spots that there seemed to be too long a delay in taking off so I asked the pilot what was holding us up. He said, "An Eskimo lady had a baby a short distance down the trail and will be along in a few minutes, then we'll be on our way."

The rest of her group had come on ahead of her. We didn't have to wait very long until we saw her coming up the trail, on her own, with her bundled up baby in the pouch of her Amauti (native parka with a pouch on the back for babies.) She wasn't dragging her feet either. Remarkable. There is a message there somewhere. The pilot had his priorities right. His patience was a demonstration of true northern spirit.

It was about June 20 when we arrived at the accident site. The sun remained high overhead all the time, going around the horizon line like one horse on a merry- go-round. Sunshine 24 hours a day.

The salt water surrounding the land was still ice covered with some surface water and slush. The short summer was approaching. An expanse of ice could be clearly seen from one end of the airstrip and farther out, a large, tall iceberg was sitting directly in the flight path.

Much of the area at higher elevations was flat topped, not at all like the mountains of B.C. The D.E.W. Line observation post was high above us on one of those tops. It reminded me of a castle in a nursery story with a winding road leading up to it.

We established our campsite and set up the tent near the damaged aircraft. It would be our home for a while so we made sure it gave us all the shelter available. That done, we inspected the damaged aircraft and set out a plan of attack.

Our first project dealt with a section of the left wing, from the tip, inboard to about the centre of the aileron and outer flap. It remained attached to the main portion of the wing by some of the remaining top surface skin, which had acted as a hinge with the wind blowing the broken section up on top of the main panel then back down into a hanging position.

The damage was now worse than shown in the photos. Continuous wind-induced hinge action appeared to have increased the damage. The destruction was a mass of broken metal such as an explosion might have left it. We cut off the broken end and all the torn fragments.

We could see that when all the broken and shattered metal was removed there would be a large opening or gap in both the front and the rear spars that would have to be bridged to join the two sections together as one again. There was a large amount of damage to the belly of the fuselage, the rear section supporting the tail assemblies was destroyed, the rudder, landing gear and right wing were also damaged.

The left wing was going to be the big challenge, and it being so high off the ground didn't help matters at all.

We needed a platform of some kind to work from

and we had not brought in any materials to build one, as we were counting on there being something around such as gas drums and or other items we could use. I had not received any information, through the investigating adjuster, on what was available on the site, that we might find useful. All we had been given were photos of the damage. Not his fault if we couldn't find on site resources. There are very few adjusters who would consider such necessities because their knowledge and experience does not follow along the lines of making repairs.

Fortunately, we were blessed with a little luck that is so needed at times. We found pieces of lumber, scattered around, apparently left over from construction of the runway and site. There were enough nails in the pieces to satisfy our needs as well.

The completed platform did not look like a construction engineer's dream but it was exactly what we needed. We extended its use by adding a few boards to form a support, it was actually a jig, to hold the broken-off piece in line with the main portion of the wing. The alignment of these sections had to be very accurate in all directions and this was done by eye.

We were satisfied that the aircraft couldn't move and alter the relationship of the wing to our wooden structure because the remaining mass of the torn out belly was resting solidly on the rocky ground.

The tip of the severed end contained the outer

hanger bracket for the aileron/flap hinge. Therefore we had to be very accurate in the measurement from it, inboard to the next hanger bracket for the centre hinge, otherwise the aileron/flap assembly, which was to arrive later, would not fit. In fact, we did not receive those units until after the wing repairs were nearly completed. It would have been so nice to have had them earlier to use as a guide or tool.

Karl Frisk and our Arctic precision built wing jig.

We worked together on the various problems until one man could carry on alone for a while. We tackled the worst problems first in case something drastic reared its ugly head, then we would have time to think about it while we worked on something else.

Karl continued on the wing when we had it secured in place and I started on another damaged area. He did a great job and I was fortunate in having him working with me. He is to aircraft metal, what Rembrandt was to paint. A true artist.

We had a very interesting break in our work one day. We could hear what, to me, sounded like seagulls as they circle over the Fraser River at fish spawning time. However it struck me as being strange. Seagulls over ice covered waters?

Looking out over the ice we quickly saw that the sounds were coming from teams of dogs pulling Komatiks (eastern Arctic sleighs) and heading for the shore below us. At the same time a young fellow from the D.E.W. site yelled, "LOOK, MY FRIENDS, MY FRIENDS." The Eskimos set up on the shore and we were to see much more of them in the next few days.

The Eastern Arctic sleigh dogs are not harnessed to the komotik in the same fashion as is done in the Western areas. Each dog is on a separate single line and the team fans out, in a very much broader fashion than the single line type harness wherein each dog follows the one in front of him. The Eskimos were able to do that in the eastern areas where there are no trees.

They had an interesting habit of working at scraping and cleaning sealskins during the hours that would normally be night time to us and slept during the day while we worked. Apparently they did it that way because their sleeping hours were warmer.

We worked long hours until we were tired then made supper and went to bed, slept until we awakened (no alarm) then back to work. The days were quite warm and we often had our shirts off but when it became breezy on went our shirts in a hurry.

One evening while we were having dinner with our backs to the tent entrance, I got that strange feeling that some one was watching us. I turned around and there were three Eskimos, in complete skin clothing, standing just inside the tent looking at us.

We offered them bread and butter and some tea, which they readily accepted. We gave them some more bread and butter as they had eaten the first lot so quickly. Apparently they were hungry. The leader of the group put the food inside his parka. Using few words and sign language I asked, "no eat?" He replied "Bebe" (French for baby). We had about half of a long sliced loaf of bread on the table. I looked at Karl and nodded toward our visitors, to whom he smiled and nodded yes, so I gave it to them. They nodded with a thank you smile and took off for their camp.

A couple of days later the same Eskimos again visited our camp. This time, I asked them if they had any polar bear skins. Two of them glanced at the leader who shook his head and said, "no bear"; the other two did the same. I was sure they were kidding me. Later I asked them again and they nodded yes and by sign language it was a small animal. I asked how much and the leader said. "sucre" (sugar). Using sign language I described a 10 lb. bag and received a yes nod with broad smiles, then off they went.

Well, we didn't have much sugar. So, what to do?

It was a nightly occurrence for a maintenance supervisor and a cook, from the D.E.W. site station, to visit us and we would have refreshments and coffee. The Supervisor would kid the cook by asking him to smell and taste the coffee and try to remember those qualities when he made their coffee in the morning. I told the cook I needed sugar and what for. Well, we did have some extra refreshment that he could use so a deal was struck.

The following evening the Eskimos were back, and with a polar bear skin. Rather surprisingly, the cook arrived at the same time with the sugar. He made no movement to give it to me. The Eskimo turned to the cook and made the exchange, then left.

I had an awful feeling that I had lost out but after slowly examining it he, while laughing, said "Here Denny, it is your skin, I was just having fun with you". He did however, tell me that it was a good hide in all respect and supported his statement by saying that he was in the fur business in Montreal prior to coming north. The long hair fur market had slowed down so he went on to the D.E.W. Line as a cook at very good pay.

We had pretty well completed the wing work with all the top and bottom metal skins on, when a maintenance man from the Line informed us that some one, a short distance away, wanted us to go and see him. We were having trouble at the time with a fitting and replied by saying we were too busy, which was the truth. He didn't take no for an answer and we said OK, we would go when we had solved our problem.

It turned out that it was Phil Lariviere of Montreal who had just come out from a salvage job back in the hills some distance from there. We had known of each other for some time and I had a lot of respect for him and his achievements.

There was no doubt in my mind that he had known it was I who was up there on the Wardair machine. Perhaps he had bid on the job also. I had no idea.

We greeted each other with, "at last we meet." He invited us to have a drink with him and we had a very enjoyable get together. After a while Lariviere wanted to know how we had repaired the wing, as he did not see an air compressor of any kind for riveting. That question surprised me, as it must have Karl too, from the look on his face.

We described the repair with the parts held together by using nuts and bolts, blind rivets, machine screws and metal screws. Lariviere seemed concerned about us using those instead of rivets. He said he was worried that we might not make it back to Vancouver safely. I must say he appeared quite genuinely worried about our safety. We invited him over to inspect the wing and see how we had done it but he declined. He did

say, however, that he would know if we didn't make it all the way. My reply was that all Canada would know very quickly.

I have had the pleasure of meeting Lariviere several times since then at aviation conventions and it was always pleasant. He was generally with a group and would say, "here comes trouble," then laugh.

During the repair of the wing we made the horrible discovery that the flap/aileron bellcrank (in layman terms, an arm-type hinge) was broken and the photos had not had sufficient detail to expose the failure. Also, I had not been provided with a written or verbal description of any of the damage.

Whether or not the Adjuster/surveyor had made any notes on it, I did not know and at first, a discovery such as that in any salvaging job is a bit of a shock but one does not dwell on it because you know you will find a solution and there are so many other known problems to deal with while you let it circle your subconscious.

By the time the wing was repaired, we decided that a bellcrank could be made up from scrap steel plating. We knew there was a shop up at the radar site so instead of labouring through with a hack saw, Karl went up to the shop and returned with a good hinge made from quarter inch boiler plate.

We wondered what the design engineers at de Havilland would think about it. The part was rough looking from using an acetylene cutting torch but it fit perfectly and the pressed in bearings from the old unit finished off a fine new part.

The wing repairs had just been completed when the new aileron/flap assembly arrived so we proceeded to install it. I was at the wing tip end. We lifted the assembly into place and I could not believe my eyes. Our measurements in the attachment of the wing outer section had been perfect.

It fit, as it would have on a new wing, I lowered it down again in disbelief and Karl asked what was wrong. I replied, "Nothing, but I couldn't believe it could fit so well." I had been prepared to use a little force on the wing tip hinge to line it up with the aileron fitting. We were both so pleased that we had attached the broken off wing section so accurately.

One day, the fellow who had first sighted the Eskimos coming across the ice on Komatiks, arrived at our camp somewhat shaken up. He had a story to tell, and it was a good one.

He had taken a short cut down to us, from the D.E.W. site on the mountaintop, by scrambling down the hillside and sometimes jumping down from one ledge to another. He said that he had come to a spot where he thought he could scramble down for a ways in soft dirt and rock. Looking down from the ledge he was on, he almost had heart failure. Below the next ledge he would be aiming for, was a polar bear lying down. He was fortunate that the bear was quite some distance below and he was able to go back up to the road. We would never know how hungry the bear was. The experience seemed to have shaken him up

 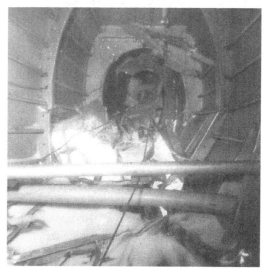

(left); Finished wing and patched pitot. (right); Extensive damage to rear half of aircraft.

quite well. Polar bears have something in common with seagulls, they are always hungry.

The fuselage belly repairs were major problems and time consuming. The tail wheel and supporting structure had been torn out and the large assembly forming the very end of the fuselage was destroyed. A replacement unit had been brought with us, which had to be installed to mount the tail wheel and to obtain ground clearance for the belly repairs. The horizontal stabilizers and elevators were strengthened and patched up after that. Ribs of the fuselage were repaired with bulb angle extrusion formed into curvatures by cutting notches in the upright legs and reinforcing them with thick metal sheeting. The belly had been torn open so badly at one point that one could walk on the snow for a few feet without touching the torn metal.

The repairs to the aircraft were nearing completion and we were satisfied that there would not be any unforeseen problems or surprises. I wired my wife Dot to obtain clearance and send a pilot - Either Jim McInnis or Ken Carlson. Both those fellows were well known to me for their flying ability and I hoped one was available. I received word that Ken Carlson was on his way.

He arrived in an aircraft flown by a pilot from Quebec, a very cheerful and friendly fellow. He was something of a joker as well. His approach to the airstrip had been made low over the water then up through a deep rock cut or channel and directly on to the strip.

As soon as he had his machine parked he went directly to the D.E.W. site phone and with his French accent, said to the radar operators, "I am here. You did not see me come, HA HA HA." He had flown under the radar and was apparently in the habit of doing that from time to time, to provoke the radar operators.

Well, the repairs were finally finished. Karl and I did separate double check inspections on the machine. The engine run-ups and taxi testing were completed to our satisfaction. We loaded our tools and other equipment into the aircraft, ready to fly away.

I think Karl was expecting a test flight to be done prior to our departure when I said. "Let's go and if the aircraft performs, as we expect it to, we will head west for home." He was as positive as I that nothing was overlooked. So, with a grin on his face, he climbed aboard and away we went. The aircraft performed very well in all respects and Ken Carlson had it well under control as I had expected he would.

I decided not to have a test flight on completion of the temporary repairs. The location was not favourable for making any more maneuvers than necessary, and extra fuel for such a flight was not available. Besides, when I told a pilot that the aircraft was ready and safe to fly, I expected him to believe me.

It was now July 4 and our first stop for fuel was at Shepherd Bay, south of Boothia Peninsula. We then continued a scenic tour along the Arctic coast of Canada to Cambridge Bay, a main base about mid point across the north coast. We could see lots of ice still in sheet form as well as much of it broken up, forming rough looking pack ice. Not a place for our hard work to fail.

The next leg of our flight was a long one south to Yellowknife, Wardair's home base where Max Ward greeted us with very complimentary remarks on our achievements. Little did I know that we would meet again shortly in a remote northern spot where he would do me a very great personal favour with his Bristol Freighter and at no charge either.

Max and I met several times again at aviation meetings. He was a true aviation man interested in our work and keen to find out what I had been doing in the salvage business since last meeting. I very much enjoyed those times.

Our flight continued with refueling stops at Fort St. John and Prince George, terminating at Vancouver where the aircraft was permanently repaired at Western Airmotive Ltd. with Karl in control of the work.

It had been a long flight in a temporarily repaired aircraft and it would not be any different today. It was also a trouble free flight and pilot Ken Carlson did an excellent job with a cheerful approach to it.

Mitchell arrived a couple of days after our return and met me with "Welcome home hero." Neither Karl nor myself thought of the job as having been as special as that, but it was nice to hear it coming from an insurance adjuster who had an aviation background, a rare qualification in those earlier days. And it carried another subliminal signal - more work would follow.

Later, I was so surprised and elated upon receiving congratulatory letters from Mr. W.R.Calder, Service Manager and Mr. D.L Buchanan, Sales Manager for de Havilland Aircraft of Canada Ltd.

Their letters were great ego builders for which I was very thankful. After all, that had been my first big salvage job. Many more followed, but that first one still stands out in my mind as a winner with Karl having a full share in it.

Max Ward, after a long hard struggle, made a name for himself in the air charter business. He would, as we saw later, lead the world in the highest quality charter flights around the globe.

It was gratifying to have played a small part in his successful rise to prominence.

Dot loved the polar bear skin.

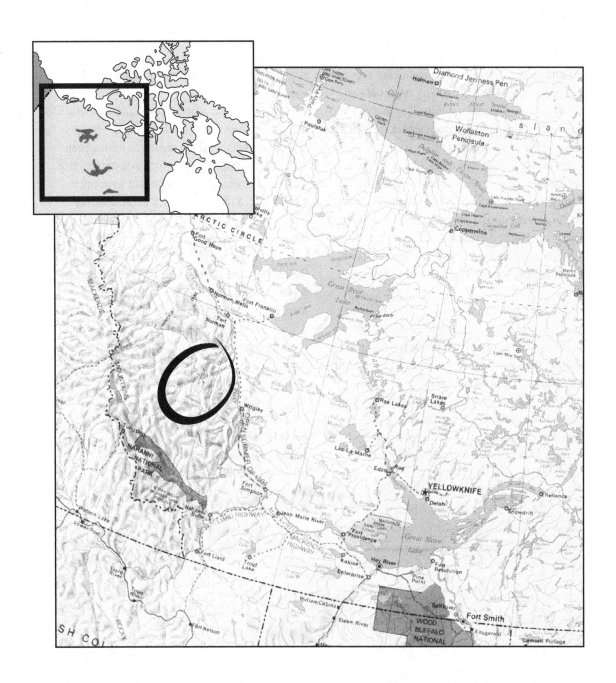

24   picking up the pieces

chapter two

Redstone River

A Harrowing Experience

When I look back on my many salvaging experiences the Redstone stands out as having been very close to a disaster. Not only in regards to the aircraft but for John Langdon and myself.

A de Havilland single engine Otter CF-LAP, of Gateway Aviation in Edmonton, had come to grief on a gravel bar in the Redstone River, Northwest Territories.

Phil Clayton, an insurance adjuster in Edmonton, had called to ask me to go up there and rescue the aircraft for a ferry flight out to a repair shop in Edmonton. He had received a preliminary report advising that the float plane had come to a stop on a gravel bar and the bottoms of the floats were damaged but no one had been able to tell him to what extent.

I didn't know where the Redstone was, but when Phil said it was in the Mackenzie Mountains and related its approximate latitude position with that of Norman Wells on the Mackenzie River, I envisioned a mountain river. That was quite correct, as I would find out later. Strange as it may seem, my file notes show that I had, at the onset, a deep concern about the precarious position of the aircraft.

I had grown up in an area near the mountains and knew how quickly a river could rise with heavy rains in its upper reaches. Phil had no information on how secure the aircraft was or would be with higher water and therefore, time was of the essence in preventing possible further damage or a complete loss. The problem was now mine and I had to get moving on it. Or else?

I had previously repaired floats (pontoons) that had been damaged in a similar manner. I therefore closed my eyes and tried to get some kind of a mental picture of the damage I should expect to find. The most vulnerable part of the bottoms, with the aircraft moving forward over gravel or rocks, is in the areas of the step compartments. The metal skins forward of there might have some rips in them as well.

A shipment of small sections of sheet metal, hand tools, metal screws and other miscellaneous items was made up and air freighted to Edmonton. Heavier equipment including a gasoline driven generator and chain block would be picked up in Edmonton or Norman Wells. Phil was a great help in confirming the availability of those items prior to my departure from Vancouver.

No time was lost in getting to Edmonton, then on to Norman Wells the next day, arriving about noon. The remainder of that day was spent collecting equipment that included a sledge hammer, heavy long steel rods, outboard motor and of course a spare propeller and shear pins to name a few things. Many of those items were obtained through the Water Resources, department of Transport, Forest Service, Northward Aviation and several individuals.

A single Otter would be ready to go to the Redstone in the early morning.

I must say that the Government Water Survey fellows were most helpful. They told me where I could find their aluminum boat, hidden on the riverbank, that we would need. In the meantime I located John Langdon, an Otter pilot, who agreed to go with me even though he had a back injury.

We loaded everything into a Northward Aviation Otter for an early start. I inquired about hiring a couple of good ax men and was told that Fort Norman, a short distance farther up the Mackenzie River, would have the men I needed. The Native Indian name for the Mackenzie is Deh Cho, the Big River. Within North and South America only the Mississippi and the Amazon Rivers exceed it in size and flow.

I had been led to believe that there was a shack near the accident site but there wasn't. So we would have to rent a tent as well as buy food from the Hudson Bay Post in Fort Norman. The flight to Fort Norman was a short one and as soon as we had landed and tied up at the dock I went directly to the Royal Canadian Mounted Police and the Administrator for the town, to see about hiring two Indian woodsmen.

I explained who I was and as much as I knew about the job ahead of me and why I needed a couple of helpers. I also explained what would be required of them and paid at the going local rate for such services. The men would have to provide their own bedrolls and an axe each. The authorities had two men in mind that were very reliable but I found they were not very fluent in English. Therefore I asked that an interpreter be asked to clearly explain every thing to them. Then no one was left in the dark about anything. I used that same procedure any time I needed Native help. It always developed a good atmosphere.

I then heard a story about an outfit from southern B.C. who had been through there earlier in the year with hydrofoil type boats. They had obtained local services then departed quickly without so much as a thank you or an offer to pay for assistance received. As a result of that, I may have been looked upon with suspicion but my straightforward approach must have cleared up any doubts or questions because there was no lack of enthusiasm to help me.

Float bottoms torn out. Frantic repairs through our first night. River rising.

In a couple of weeks it would be the longest day of the year. Also, we were positioned only a short distance south of the Arctic Circle with days of 24 hours daylight.

All was set and we took off for the Redstone and what turned out to be a new type of nerve-racking adventure. Indeed it was.

As we approached the river and flew up it, I could see that it was truly a fast flowing mountain stream with much white water. It's source was high in the Mackenzie Mountains and flowed generally northward, toward the mighty Mackenzie River that empties into the Arctic Ocean near Inuvik, N.W.T.

A nice landing was made on a stretch of smooth deep water, a little upstream from the Otter that sat forlornly on the rocks, just above the start of a stretch of fast white water. We tied up to shore at a spot used by Water Resources. The river was deep on that side with a steep shoreline, so our camp would have to be set up on the other side of the river, on flat ground near the stranded aircraft.

When we had finished unloading, the pilot waited until we had located the boat, set it in the water and checked the operation of the outboard motor. Then he left and we were on our own with two very willing and friendly Indians.

We moved everything across the river and made camp. A northern type lean-to of spruce trees and boughs for John and I. The Indians had the tent, which brought smiles to their faces and perhaps they wondered about those strange white men

from the south. I directed my attention to the aircraft, anxious to see what we had to be done. The damage was confined to the step areas of the float bottoms, the left was not as bad as the right but it was closer to the water's edge.

The aircraft was sitting on a large stretch of good-sized smooth rocks, some distance out from the high water shoreline mark and our camp. There were no signs of smaller stones or sand in that part of the river bed, which was a sign, that at times, the river must be high and fast to have washed them out.

I have always been interested in geology and while walking over the rock bed I gathered up a large handful of red stones and thought that might be why the river was named Redstone.

Little did I know that my assessment of the river as being, at times, a raging torrent, would soon be proven to be true. No time was lost in getting on with the repairs, and the patching on the left float, which was closest to the water's edge, was finished within a few hours. The damage to the right float was more complicated and we had to erect a tripod to lift and block it up so a drill motor could be used on its underside.

When our two assistants had finished setting up the camp, they went to work cutting spruce poles to build a corduroy road under the floats to skid and roll the aircraft to water when the repairs were completed. The trees were quite a distance away and they worked hard at it. John was working between helping the Indians and me.

So much of the patching was a one man job but removing the dozens of machine screws, which fastened the large access covers to the deck of the floats, was always time consuming and sometimes frustrating if the threads were rusted. That was John's job.

It was nearly midnight when we went to bed, but I had difficulty sleeping. My mind seemed to be working overtime on our problem. I was for some unknown reason, worried about something and I asked myself what it was. I didn't receive an answer.

I woke up wide-awake at about 1:30 a.m. The sky, as far as I could see, was a bright red and the old slogan, "Red sky in the morning is a sailor's warning," flashed through my head.

Otter in same location late following day. River rose over four feet in 24 hours.

That was it. Nothing was bugging my subconscious mind anymore. The sky condition had cleared that out by telling me that trouble was coming and I was about to find out just how true that saying was.

That did it. I got up and went straight to work. High water could spell sudden disaster. The mere thought of it gave me a chilling shiver.

Later on it started to rain lightly and I wondered how heavily it was raining in the headwaters of the river high up in that massive mountain and how long it would be until that water reached us.

The Water Resources boys had said that the river had been known to rise feet in 24 hours. We continued in steadily increasing heavy rain, desperately trying to finish the patching of the right float. The time was then about 4:30 a.m.

It had become difficult to use the electric drill, in the last stages of the repair. More space was needed to get the drill under the float and that was obtained by scooping out rocks to form a fairly deep depression in the gravel bar.

Water seeped into the excavation steadily so I'd scoop it out and have time to drill only two holes then repeat that procedure throughout the last portion of the patching. I would have been in great trouble if the drill had destroyed itself by shorting out from water contact and in that event, I would have provided an excellent grounding for an electric shock. I suppose it could be said that I had probably been a little nervous about such prospects. It certainly was a little disconcerting, to say the least, but thinking about the hazards wouldn't help, so we pushed on and had the patching done by about 8 am.

Fortunately, at that time, I didn't know that the patches would later be torn from that float with drastic results.

I was very wet from having to lie down on the job, so as to speak, so we stopped for breakfast and a little drying out. Then back to work, as quickly as possible, placing logs under the floats to build a road to the water. Using a jackall that resembles a long heavy car bumper jack, we tilted the machine forwards and backwards to get the logs in place.

We then drove long sturdy steel rods well down into the riverbed ahead of the aircraft. A heavy nylon rope bridal was attached to the floats, then with a chain block and engine power; the aircraft was turned and moved toward the water. It was painfully slow work and we were always mindful of being in front of the propeller and the possibility of the aircraft lurching forward at us.

The thickness of the logs varied considerably and sometimes a float bottom would stick on one, then move quickly in a turn. At the same time we were always concerned with the possibility of damage to the patches.

Relocating the steel rods for every advancement was no small chore either. A block of wood had to be clamped to a rod and the jackall was used to draw it upward until we could work it free by hand labour.

Heavy rain and strong winds continued all afternoon and by about 6 p.m. we had gone as far as we could on that project. The upriver wind was too strong to try putting the aircraft into the water. We would have to wait until, hopefully, the wind dropped and a small rise in the river level would be helpful. What wishful hoping that was.

We increased the weight of the aircraft on the corduroy road bed to assist the steel rod anchor system in holding the aircraft securely by stacking logs on the floats. I tried to get dried out to some degree by a campfire, then went to bed without any supper, too tired to eat.

I had been going steady since before 2 a.m. and with only 2 hours sleep prior to that time.

We woke up early next morning to a discouraging scene. The river had risen and spread out so much that it covered all the rock up to the high water shoreline edges near our camp. It was a raging torrent with tree trunks and roots racing down it.

The aircraft now looked like it was far out on the river but, thankfully, it seemed to be still well anchored with the water churning and whipping around the floats. I was so thankful that we had expected high water and had done everything possible to secure the plane.

There, I thought, as I stared at the raging mass of water, was exactly what I had told Phil could happen with a mountain river, when he first described the aircraft's position.

If we'd been one day late in getting on the job,

Mother Nature would have added the aircraft to her collection.

John and I tried to get on the aircraft by using the boat but no matter how we approached it we couldn't keep the boat alongside a pontoon long enough to get a good hold. We managed to grab onto the ventral fin at the tail end but couldn't hold on and we were swept down river.

We worked our way back by using the back eddies at the shore's edge, something I learned as a kid with my Indian dug out canoe. We then put on chest waders and made another attempt with sharp knives in hand to cut the waders open if they filled with water. Thinking back, it was a darned dangerous thing to do, but we were successful and climbed up on the floats.

We had not made any plans as to what we would do when we got on board, but after we had looked the situation over, we decided we should try to taxi out into deeper water and across to the tie up spot on the far bank.

It had stopped raining and we were afraid the water level would drop, leaving us in shallow water, over the gravel bar, to grind out the patches on the rocks if we attempted to taxi the aircraft out into the deep water. There was the possibility of having to wait for days and, just maybe, the water level might drop enough to allow us to continue with the corduroy road scheme. We could have also been hit with another deluge of rain.

Our biggest worry however, and the most nervous part of it all, at that time, was our fear that the steel rods, holding the aircraft from being swept down stream just might be pulled out or bent forward enough to let the bridle slip off. That would be the end.

There were too many negative factors out of which we had to make a positive decision. A weather report would have been a great help, but we couldn't get one and our weather observations were not at all encouraging.

It was agreed that we should try to get the aircraft tied up on the other side of the river. We hand pumped the float compartments, the repaired ones had, thank goodness, very little water in

Salvage crew. John Langdon and two Fort Norman Natives in front of our "home sweet home."

them. Then the large float top access covers were reinstalled with a few finger-tightened screws.

John started the engine and as soon as operating temperatures were obtained I moved the logs off the floats, into the river. Then the engine power was increased until the aircraft moved forward and the anchor bridal showed slackness.

John maintained the power and held the aircraft in position while I crawled out on each float in turn to the nose bollards and cut the bridal off. I would then work my way back along a float, past the screaming propeller that seemed so much closer each time. I told myself repeatedly that I would be all right so long as I kept my head down while skidding backwards on my stomach. As soon as I was finished and in the cabin, John advanced the throttle for full power.

We had moved forward a little and sideways into mid stream when a strong gust of wind coming up river caught the tail and swung us broadside to the river current. We started to go down the white water or rapids side ways and I recall screaming at John to kick it around and go down stream nose first. There was actually no reason to yell at him to do that because that was evidently what he was trying to do.

We were lucky, because the combination of engine power and the wind, which was now helping us, with it's full force on the large tail surface, the aircraft quickly responded and down the rapids we went, head first for approximately 2 miles.

A couple of times I felt and heard the float bot-

toms strike the river bed and I just knew that it would be the step areas making contact and the patches! It was enough to create a heart attack.

As soon as we were through the white water we had to try stopping the down stream run. There was no shore that we could drive the aircraft up on to, instead there was an embankment. Time after time, the noses of the floats were driven into the embankment in an attempt to slow us down and come to a stop. Finally, maximum engine power held both float noses against it as we slid side ways until the river pushed the back end of the floats down stream and John held the nose of the left float solidly against the embankment with engine power.

I scrambled out with rope, secured it to the float strut then climbed the bank, slipped into the water, out of it, up and over, on to the shore. The area was all rock with no standing trees so I tied the rope to the largest piece of drift wood I could handle and buried it with a mountain of the largest rocks I could run with and formed a dead man's anchor. That was still not good enough so, with bare hands, I dug a ditch through a high mound on top of the bank until the rope was flat on the ground. The river flooding, over the years, had built up a mound of soil and rock along the top of the embankment. That mound had acted as a lift on the anchored rope, pulling it up and outward as the aircraft tugged downward on it.

The engine power was slowly reduced and thankfully the aircraft stayed in position. More rocks were then piled in front of the dead man for good measure. As soon as the engine was shut off our last piece of rope was put on the nose bollard to secure the nose of the float snugly against the embankment.

It was the month of June but after the panic was over I felt a cold shiver. During our fight with Mother Nature, both of us knew that if we hadn't been able to stop the aircraft from being swept down the river we could have come to a fatal end.

A little farther down stream, maybe a quarter mile, the river changes direction in almost a 90-degree turn. I had heard that an aircraft, about a year earlier, had been swept down the river and met a horrible end by being completely destroyed on contact with that abrupt piece of property.

We were still deep in the woods so as to speak. What about the float bottoms?? Luckily the large access covers on the float tops had been rein-stalled with only a few lose screws and were easily removed, allowing us to do a quick internal inspection. The left float was OK but the right one, in the step compartment, the largest compartment in any float, was, as I had feared, damaged again. Some of our patched areas had been torn open.

The compartment was full to the level of the river and the rear portion of the float was nearly under the surface. Then almost steady hand bailing, using a cooking utensil from the aircraft's emergency kit, every half hour.

We had an awful night. It was a nightmare with almost continual bailing and to make matters worse, it snowed heavily all night. I was wet and cold, with no foul weather clothing and John was almost as badly off. We watched the right wing tip and when it was down, in line with a reference point across the river; it was time to bail the water out again. Added to our problem was the dropping of the river level, which tilted the right side of the aircraft toward the water because the nose of the left float was secured and resting on a piece of the embankment, above the water level. We were, because of a shortage of rope, unable to correct that problem very much.

We needed help and our time without it was running short.

During the night we frequently ran the engine for the cabin heater, to stop us from shivering for a bit. We had no dry wood anywhere near the aircraft to make a fire and we couldn't leave the machine to look for some. We were close to losing the Otter if we didn't get help.

While running the engine we made desperate radio calls to Norman Wells and Fort Simpson with no replies so a frantic May Day call was made for any one who heard us. Finally we received an answer from Coppermine on the Arctic Ocean. We told them we could not last much longer and to advise Norman Wells that we needed a Forestry portable gas driven fire pump and rope to be brought in by helicopter because the river was not safe for a floatplane. They in turn notified Norman Wells radio who had not heard our calls.

Later we were surprised to see the two Indians,

in the boat, with all our gear, pull into a backwash a short distance up ahead of us.

One of them said they had seen us go down the river and could hear the engine on the wind at night. They had come down to help us and had brought our dry clothing, food, tent, etc. They surely were a welcome sight.

I then asked them if they had eaten. Their reply was " NO. Food not ours, food yours."

That took me back a bit and I couldn't help saying, "you foolish fellows but darned honest

Rescue completed and now on Airplane Lake at Norman Wells. Aircraft flown out with Forestry fire pump spewing water out of float at full capacity during take-off.

Indians, white men not all that honest." That brought smiles to their faces and I said, "go make a fire and make some breakfast." They rushed off and soon had a fire going. Meantime, a fixed wing aircraft passed over us to confirm, we thought, the river condition, then left.

Not long after that a helicopter arrived with a pump and lots of rope. It was indeed, Christmas time in June. John and I immediately replaced the anchor rope with a longer one and using driftwood as poles, the left float was pried off the embankment face and the aircraft was then sitting level on the water.

Oh, what a relief. We had just finished bailing out the float so had a few minutes for breakfast by a hot fire.

It is impossible to find the words to describe that luxury and relief. The pilot, I think his name was Jim Durchie, had picked the pump up from an Andy Jacobson in Fort Norman. I think Andy's home was in Inuvik, and at the time, he was working for the Department of Forestry out of Fort Norman.

We lost no time in putting the pump to work and what a difference it made. Full throttle was needed to empty the full compartment. I then climbed down inside the compartment and could see that not only had the patches been torn off, but the metal leading into the forward compartment was also broken.

I made an attempt to slow down the leak by stuffing rags into the holes but the pressure, from the weight of the aircraft on the water, blew them back at me. It was no wonder that we had been bailing almost steadily.

We decided that the only way we could hope to keep the float empty enough to safely fly the aircraft off the river would be to secure the pump to the float deck and leave it running wide open. Otherwise the force of the float being driven through the water could fill the large compartment very quickly and add enough weight, approximately 1000 lbs., so as to prevent a take off or worse, cause an accident.

To make matters worse, the take off run would have to be up stream, at an angle across the river with no room to spare, every foot would be needed. The water was still high and fast. The wind coming up river would be on the tail, a critical and negative factor to say the least.

I had, in the meantime, asked the helicopter pilot to remain with us until the Otter had made its escape. I also had him bring the rest of our equipment down from our camp.

The Otter would leave with only John and no baggage.

We had the Indians take the boat about 20 miles down river to a camp called Catalina, where they were to wait for us. We then turned our attention to getting ready for the big event, getting the Otter into the air.

The Wajax fire pump was lashed to the float and its fuel tank to the cabin entrance steps. I was worried that operating might damage the pump

after the float was pumped dry so rigged up a wire for John to pull the switch off. I was also prepared to pay for the pump but as I found out later the unit had an automatic shut off.

We were all set and John ran the engine until all operating temperatures were obtained. Then as soon as there was a drop in that infernal up-river wind, he started moving out into the stream while we payed out a long rope, secured to the forward front fitting of the left float, to hold the aircraft nose into the fast water until the engine power took control. There was still a tail wind that John had to fight and he needed every thing in his favour that was available.

The fire pump was at full throttle. The aircraft reluctantly lifted off the water and we breathed sighs of relief. We could see a long white "rooster tail" against the sky, stretching out behind the aircraft, the pump was still throwing out a lot of water as the aircraft leveled out in its flight. We were convinced that without that operating pump we would not have succeeded in the salvage operation.

Both John and Jim had agreed that they would both radio Norman Wells advising that the Otter was on its way. The main purpose of the calls was to make sure that the ramp at the seaplane base, on the lake, was clear of equipment because the Otter would have to be driven up on to it without any delay, at the end of its landing run or it would sink. I think the lake was called Airplane Lake?

I heard later that the response was tremendous.

The ramp was all set up and soaped to guarantee good sliding up conditions on it. It was a fine example of northern co-operation and I still feel good, thinking about it.

I left in the helicopter right after the Otter disappeared from sight. We landed at Catalina and waited for a Northward Aviation aircraft for a flight, with our equipment, to Norman Wells. The Forestry's boat was secured and the authorities notified.

The Indians left, in the helicopter, for home in Fort Norman.

I arrived in Norman Wells and a group of fellows, who had, in one way or another made our mission a success, were waiting for me in the bar. I bought them all drinks but none for me, as my diary shows, I was dead tired and went directly to bed.

I was, as I proceeded to my room, practically dead on my feet for lack of sleep, but my mind was filled with thoughts of our narrow escape and pleasant ones regarding the help and thoughtfulness of so many.

It had been a little unnerving to hear that several people, including Water Resources, had been certain that the Otter and we would not survive on the raging river. They were sure we had been swept down and crushed against the cliff at the sharp bend in the river downstream from our position.

Our radio calls for help said we had survived and were responded to, magnificently.

We were so thankful for that and the radio operator in Coppermine, because response time was so crucial. We were, at that time, in deep trouble fighting Mother Nature.

The next couple of days were spent preparing the Otter for the ferry trip south. I was fortunate again when Jim Durchie and several others showed up and helped me block up the right float so I could get under it to make repairs. I was then in business again, patching over patches but a good bush repair. It was cold with a strong wind and I felt even colder when I was told that Arctic Red River, farther down stream, had a foot of snow and Inuvik, near the Arctic coast, was still ice bound.

That was June 8.

It was nearly suppertime on the second day and the patching was finished. After dinner I had some help in setting the aircraft back down on the ramp and turning it around to face the water. We put greased planks under the keels of the floats, ready for launching.

Andy Jacobson came to me at the hotel later. He had a problem and needed our help in a desperate way. He was ready to make a return trip up stream to Fort Norman in a northern type flat bottom riverboat, powered by an out board motor and a load of 10 gallon steel kegs of fuel.

That would not, under normal conditions, have been a problem. However, strong winds were continuing and had developed high swells on the river surface. He therefore had to reduce his load and wanted to know if we could take about a dozen or more kegs for him on our way south as we would be going right by Fort Norman. I didn't think that would be any problem at all but spoke to John Longden about it. We both agreed there was no reason why the Otter could not handle it and we were delighted to be able to help someone who had, earlier, jumped to help save us from almost certain disaster.

Next morning we launched the Otter, loaded our gear and the fuel kegs, refueled, pumped a little water out of the floats and took off for the south.

The aircraft performed very well and after a short flight, we landed on the Mackenzie River at Fort Norman. Andy had said that people would be waiting for us on the beach. We were to taxi close to shore where we would have a good sandy bottom clearance and dump the kegs into the river. We did that by circling two or three times. The villagers were into the water, even a priest, grabbing the kegs. One keg hit the water broadside in front of one man, covering him with a big splash. Great cheers went up from the crowd. I am sure the whole village was there.

The unloading was finished quickly; we waved good-bye with a tremendous response from the crowd and took off for Fort Smith where I had

another job waiting for me, a Cessna floatplane inverted in more fast water. John would continue on down to Edmonton.

There were two periods of time during that salvage operation, when I actually felt that we were going to lose the aircraft but we kept fighting it and those periods passed with us still floating.

There is a saying and a song, "What a difference a day makes." Our experience proved what a difference another day would have made in getting on the job at the onset. We would not have had an aircraft to work on.

In my younger days I spent a great deal of time with an Indian canoe, dragging it up a fast river just to shoot the rapids but I do not care to ever do it again with an aircraft, especially one the size of an Otter.

Unfortunately, as is so often the case, I have never been back to Fort Norman again, but I was in Norman Wells on a helicopter problem a few years later. It was a quick trip in and out, and Barney Cooper, whom I had known for some time, was the only one I saw that I had known previously.

However, I have good memories of both places and their people.

chapter three

School Children in Single Otter through ice

It was nearly Christmas time in 1972 when I was asked to investigate a problem involving a load of children in a Single Engine Otter ski plane that had gone through the ice of Ominica Bay in Williston Lake, which is to the north of Prince George B.C.

The aircraft, CF-GCV, flown by Captain Dave Whelan had taken off from McKenzie with 12 Native Indian school children, ages 6 to 12, who were going home to Ingenika for the Christmas holidays. The weather at the start of the flight was considered good with isolated snow showers, which is normal there for that time of year.

Dave explained that in the area of Ominica Bay visibility was about four miles but suddenly light snow conditions turned into a very heavy snow fall with visibility of one quarter mile. Rather than taking a risk with his precious load he decided to set the aircraft down on the ice covered lake and wait for a weather improvement which was the prudent thing to do under the circumstances. All was well until he was near the end of the landing and the ski plane had come to almost a full stop. The ice suddenly gave way and the aircraft began to sink into the water.

Dave made a hurried radio call to his operational

base and quickly removed the wet children from the machine as it sank. He demonstrated a terrific sense of survival in getting his passengers to shore where a fire was made to warm and at least partially dry everyone. Then he guided them on a two mile hike through the woods to a logging camp where, with the assistance of a lady who lived there, the children were given warm baths, a good meal and put to bed.

Our first inspection of Otter. Keith Carr checking ice. Helicopter behind Otter tail, rotors operating at the ready.

A beautiful ending to a most unfortunate problem. That type of reaction and level headedness personifies the qualities of a top flight bush pilot that Dave was.

Poor weather conditions continued for a few days. It was suggested by both Milt Ritchie and Ed MacPherson, of Northern Thunderbird Air that since the aircraft was locked into the ice it wasn't going anywhere. They thought it would be wise for us to delay our investigation a little until the broken ice immediately around the machine was safer for us to walk on. That made sense and I certainly appreciated that type of thinking because an accident is a major set back for a company and they are always most anxious to resolve it and get it behind them. Aside from that, I had had a couple of close calls with weak ice patches over deep water and I didn't need any convincing that we should wait a few days.

A couple of days later I received word that the weather had improved and the children had been airlifted to their homes in Ingenika where a big welcome awaited them. It was then the day before Christmas and their homecoming must have been the best gift their parents could have wished for.

It was decided that we should go to the accident site and survey the situation on Boxing Day {December 26} so off I went to Prince George where I was met by Chief Engineer, Keith Carr, a very experienced and knowledgable fellow whom I always enjoyed seeing.

Keith and I discussed the matter of going out to see the Otter the next morning. He explained that there was now a deep covering of snow on the ice and it was not considered safe to fly in there with a fixed wing ski plane, even a small one. We agreed to use a Northern Mountain helicopter.

We left next morning in a Bell 206 Helicopter. Weather plagued us most of the way and, in fact, forced us to land at Mackenzie for a while. The flight was continued, but low cloud conditions in the valleys and over the entire lake made flying difficult until an opening was found along the lake shore where we were able to go down, under the cloud cover. The base of the clouds varied from 200 to 300 feet above the lake. Our target, the Otter, was spotted quite some distance off shore and we gently sat down a short distance from it. The pilot was very cautious and stood ready, with power, to lift off again at the slightest sign of danger.

The ice on the lake appeared to be and felt safe enough to walk on but we had to keep a sharp eye out for areas of fresh ice on the overflow of water in the area of the hole the aircraft had made. The Otter, except for the tops of the wings and the empennage {tail}, was deeply submerged in the water and frozen into the ice. A complete sinking had been prevented by the wings spread out over the ice. There was a great deal of water inside the wings, much of it was already frozen.

Fortunately, the engine and its tubular mount were well below the surface of the water protected from the internal ice expansion damage that would occur if they were only partially submerged.

We cleaned the blanket of snow off all the ice around and near the aircraft for greater exposure to the freezing temperatures to increase it's thickness.

It was an awesome sight. I had never seen an aircraft so engulfed in ice as was that one and I never did again. It was impossible to imagine how anyone could duplicate the scene even if his life depended on it. The aircraft, had come to a sliding stop on the edge of a long crack in the ice and started sinking with it's nose pointed downward into 100 feet of dark water.

Luckily, not all the ice under the wings had broken up. Freezing temperatures had no doubt helped to hold the machine in it's precarious position and had prevented it from going to the lake bottom as the ice settled and broke with the continuous lowering of the water level.

When we were satisfied that there was nothing further we could accomplish until the ice was thick enough to safely work on, we left.

Keith and I discussed what would be needed for the salvage operation and a rough list was made up. He was a great help with it being one of the very few times where I would not have to do all the arranging for the manpower and equipment that was so vital in the guarantee of a successful salvage operation. It was certainly a nice change for me.

It was close to mid January when I received word that the ice was considered to be thick enough to safely proceed with a salvage operation.

I think I should explain, for those who may not be familiar with that northern area, that Williston

Lake is a man-made body of water. It is almost 200 miles long with a long arm extending eastward nearly 100 miles, and is at an altitude of 2200 feet above sea level. It has a beautiful setting in the Rocky Mountain Trench, which lies north of Prince George and extends in a slightly north eastern direction to 60 degrees north latitude, the Yukon border. It was developed, by building a dam on the Finlay River to provide a water reservoir for a hydro power plant. The dam at the southern end of the lake is approximately 80 miles, as the crow flies, north of Prince George.

That body of water is frozen over in the winter and during that period the water feeding rivers and streams are partially and in some cases, completely frozen. Therefore, the water level cannot be maintained as the hydro plant gobbles it up. It drops about twenty seven feet from the start of Winter to Springtime.

As the water level drops so does the ice or at least we sure hoped it did while we were on it. We did not like to think we could possibly be on the roof of a large cave of space with water at it's bottom. What if we were and the ice gave way? We had been warned that there were, at times, spaces as great as 15 feet between the bottom of the Ice and the surface of the lake water.

I left for Prince George where I was, again, met by Keith and who had everything ready to go. We drove via truck, to the Krause Logging camp that was to be our base instead of making a camp on the lake shore. Such a set up was plain luxury

Ice toadstool marking level of the water reservoir lake at freeze-up.

compared with some winter camping I had done. Everyone was anxious to get on with the job and my notes show that we worked until 9 p.m. that day, long after dark.

Keith and his crew were very capable hard workers.

Our trip to the logging camp was highlighted by a sight I had never seen before or since. We came across a large pack of wolves. There must have been fifty or more of them and I thought of what such a bunch would do to a herd of deer or moose.

The Otter was lying at an angle with its nose down, out of sight as were the greatest portions of both wings. Only one wing tip was visible. The largest parts showing were the very aft end of the fuselage and the complete tail section.

There was a large volume of ice in both wings from the root ends, out to the tips. In fact the aircraft had been steadily settling down through the ice, which was now up over the ailerons and flaps. Ice in the fuselage extended from the pilot's compartment, where it was right up to the roof, back to a point in line with the horizontal stabilizer (the tail end).

The lake had been formed in a very heavily forested area and much of the timber was left standing when the valleys filled with water. We saw one of those trees as we were going out to the Otter. There was, about 8 feet up from the ice we were standing on, a huge platform of ice about 2 feet thick and 4 feet in diameter, frozen to a tree trunk. It was like a monstrous ice toadstool.

That was a indication of where the level of the water had been when the ice formed at the beginning of winter. The power station had used an unimaginable amount of water since that time and of course the ice dropped as the water went down and left that piece on the tree.

We traveled back and forth to the aircraft on a skidoo. During those trips and while working out on the lake I often wondered if the ice was resting

(left);Retrieval started. Keith Carr (centre) building A-frame for lift. Two of Keith's men cutting through ice to reach wing attachment bolts to attach lifting sling. (right); Chain saw cutting ice around aircraft.

on the water or were we, at times, over a cavern with the water surface some distance below the ice.

We were out, in the early mornings, working at the aircraft by 6.30 a.m. with daylight at 8.30 a.m. The daytime temperatures were not extreme, about 12 degrees f. so we were not uncomfortable but that was not to last.

We needed two long sturdy logs for an "A frame" and we were trying to separate them from a frozen pile without any success. The lady at the camp was evidently watching us and the next thing we knew, she came out with a stick of dynamite. She placed it where it would do the most good and very quickly the logs were free. That Lady obviously didn't recognize the word defeat.

The logs were towed by skidoo, to the aircraft and the building of an "A" frame was started.

I should, for those of you not familiar with such equipment, explain that it consists of 2 logs that are fastened together at their top ends with cable. A shiv (pulley) is secured to that top assembly, through which a cable from a winch is threaded with its end attached to cables or a lifting sling secured to the aircraft. When the logs are raised up with their butt ends set in the ice, they resemble a huge letter "A" from which it gets its name. We then have a stationery lifting crane.

That assembly was drawn up into its upright position and held there by cables secured to the top end of the frame and run back to 45 gal. steel drums sunk below the ice as anchors. The "A"

frame could then be tilted up or down by long chain blocks [hand winches] that were set in as an integral part of each anchor cable. The cable that ran through the shiv was from the drum of the hand operated B-B winch that was secured to one leg of the "A" frame.

We were very much aware that the ice and water in the aircraft would greatly increase it's weight. We therefore had the lifting sling modified to include special steel fittings made in Vancouver for installation on the bolt that attaches the front spars of the wings to the fuselage.

I had made it a habit not to use the manufacturer's lifting points on an aircraft for such a heavy lift as that one, because they were not strong enough.

The overflow of water from the steady settling of the ice, had made the latter much thicker. We had to cut down through it to a depth of about 12 inches to reach the wing bolts.

The time consuming work of cutting the ice out from around the wings and fuselage was started using chain saws and long handled ice chisels. The cutting had to be done as close to the aircraft as possible and great care was required to avoid damaging the plane. Ice chisels can be difficult to control as they tend to ricochet off to one side as they are driven into the ice. The cutting was not completed in one day, by any means, and each night the cuts were again frozen quite solidly. A thicker section over the engine was more difficult to clear out.

A very delicate and awkward part of the work

involved the main cabin door. It had been left open after the children had been hurriedly exited through it and we found it wide open with its top end about 15 inches below the ice surface. That indicated that the aircraft had settled about 7 feet into the ice since the evacuation.

It presented quite a problem to cut the door free and close it before starting to lift the machine. If that had not been done it would very likely have been torn off and we would have been in a worse mess.

The scene was slowly set for the next phase of our plans and a major one for sure, lifting the aircraft. First we cut a small hole in the ice a short distance from our working area to make sure that the ice was actually resting on the water. We took another of many close looks at the security of the bottom ends of the A frame poles and just hoped they stayed exactly in place during the lift. Then we put tension on the winch cable and took another look around to see if any ice was going to interfere with a short lift.

The aircraft was raised until the bottoms of the wings were just clear of the ice with the engine and lower section of the fuselage still under the water. The tail came up a little and revealed that the tail wheel had been about 18 inches below the ice surface and had a 24 inch block of ice frozen to it and the fuselage bottom. The chain saws had done a lot of work. The forward parts of the wings were full of ice. We then covered them with blankets of insulation material and tarps.

Next, Herman Nelson heaters were set up with their ducts positioned to heat the wings and start the ice melting. The heat from another heater was directed into the cockpit and cabin. We were then well on our way and the A frame was operating beautifully. What more could we ask for?

The heaters were operated 24 hours a day with everyone taking turns during the nights to check and refuel them. Each heater consumed 1 drum [45 gallons] of fuel in 24 hours. Every day we had to go via skidoo and sleigh to get more fuel. When the nearest supplies dried up, Keith and I made one run of about 9 miles to get more. The most direct and tested route to shore was used, then we traveled along the shore as much as possible as a safety measure.

The temperature, for a few days, had dropped to well below the -0° F and then it warmed up to around +13° F during the day which was pleasant but the level of the lake ice started dropping. We had to be more alert for weak areas after some of us had broken through in several spots.

We continued lifting the machine a very little bit at a time each day because if the wings, for example, were too high up, any amount of wind would drastically reduce or cancel out the heating system.

The ice in the aircraft was finally cleared out and we could lift the machine higher in preparation for setting it forward, on solid ice.

We were nearing the end of the tough part of our project and with the engine and airframe clear of the ice it was thought that it should be left overnight that way. However, the engine and its associated units had been protected from freezing by their immersion in water. I was afraid there was too great a risk of damage to the water filled cylinders and engine mount with the low temperatures and strong winds.

It was dark, and too late to properly drain and service the engine to preserve and protect it. Keith was of the same opinion so the engine was lowered back down below the surface of the water for the night.

Next morning we were out on the job again before daylight. The temperature had dropped to -25° F during the night with a stiff wind. New, thick ice had formed over the engine and had to be cut

before we could start lifting.

The aircraft was lifted clear of the ice and water and swung forward over good solid ice. That was done by pulling the A frame up, which drew its top end back as close to a vertical position as we dared. The aircraft moved with it and luckily the main wheel skis were positioned over solid ice onto which the aircraft was lowered.

Our fear of possible freezing damage if the engine had been left hanging in the open, was well supported by a large piece of ice that had formed on a propeller blade near its tip end, which had been left sticking up through the water.

While we were maneuvering the aircraft, a serious problem suddenly developed and I rushed from an area behind the wings to help. When the

(left); Aircraft partially raised - insulation on wings and cabin, heaters at work 24 hours per day melting internal ice. Air temperature, -25°F. (right); Preparing aircraft for flight.

panic was over we all realized that I had run across a large piece of freshly frozen ice. The previous day it was open water left from the removal of the wings and fuselage.

Luckily, it hadn't broken but I had an awful feeling afterwards about what could have happened with my mind totally occupied with the aircraft's safety and not mine.

The heaters were now directed to the engine, cockpit, cabin and fuel tank areas. Sacks of mail had floated up to the cabin roof and had become frozen to it. When the ice in the cabin melted away from below the bags they had dropped down, taking the upholstery with them.

The fuel system was cleared of water and we went through the usual procedure of preparing a water soaked engine for running. When that was completed the engine performed very satisfactorily. The instruments and radios were opened up and serviced, without delay, for their water immersion. The method we used had proven to be very satisfactory in previous sinkings.

However, we found that some of the parts were corroded, some as bad as they would have been from a salt water immersion. We were quite sure that the water contained an acid formed by the rotting sunken vegetation. I had run into a similar situation in a northern lake filled with pine tree needles.

The ice was steadily settling in so many areas with much water overflow. A section of ice was carefully checked for security and an airstrip was marked out with small evergreen trees as a guide for the pilot in his take off run to fly to Prince George. The flight was made without incident.

Another successful salvage job was completed and I credit its success in no small way to Keith Carr and his crew.

chapter four

The Mayor & Me

In 1959 Denny McCartney Limited was still a
very young company, but it had established a reputation for salvaging aircraft that in the past had
been written off as scrap because they couldn't be
restored on the spot to ferry flight standards and it
was not cost effective to haul the wreck back to
civilization. This reputation got me a job with an
insurance company that wanted to limit their loss
on a claim. I hadn't entered the insurance adjuster
business at the time and this contract pushed the
decision off the procrastination pile.

I happened to be in Edmonton for a meeting with
Dick Hicks and Bill Myers, manager of British
Aviation Insurance Company. They had a Connelly
Dawson Air Service De Havilland Beaver down in
the Pelly River in the Yukon and they asked me to
go up to the accident and supervise the salvage
operation.

Little alarm bells rang in my head. I had heard
news of the crash and I knew that Gordon
Cameron, who also did salvage work, had already
been engaged to secure and protect the machine
from further damage. I felt uneasy about moving in
on another man's job. Bill said not to worry, he

would phone Cameron and make it clear my involvement was not a reflection on his ability in any way. Easy for him to say, but I was the guy who would have to live with the situation. Dick and Bill insisted and used their potential for future work to persuade me. Though I still wasn't happy about it, I went.

Everybody in aviation in the North knows each other and I didn't want to be at cross purposes with anyone. Mutual respect and cooperation is vital to survival in the North. And Gordon Cameron was not just any old bush boomer. He had first class aviation credentials. He was an engineer and a pilot. He had political clout. He was the Mayor of Whitehorse. I liked him and I wanted him as a friend.

He gave me a complete briefing on the condition of the Beaver and its specific location. He had already removed the struts and wires from the under carriage and lowered the fuselage onto padded wood beams set crosswise on the floats. He had removed the wings and stowed them on edge against the side of the aircraft. By doing this he had made sure the aircraft was secure from further damage as a result of a strong gust of wind tipping the whole lot into the river.

Dot, my wife, comptroller and home base coordinator of our fledgling company, had shipped my bush clothing and gear to me via CPA so I was able to charter a flight into the job site the next day.

I found that Gordon Cameron had done an even better job of securing the Beaver than he had

reported. The damage to the left wing and the fuselage skins were exactly as he described.

Back to Whitehorse for a pow wow with Gordon about what was needed to get the job done. For starters, a boat was needed to tow the plane up to the Ross River airport. The Department of Public Works had a 41 foot river boat in the area and offered it. The only charge would be for the fuel and the operator's time.

This type of cooperation from a Federal Government group may come as a shock to people who have only dealt with the Ottawa stone heads. Believe me, it was standard procedure for the people out on the front line. I always found them to be ready and willing to become part of the solution rather than part of the problem.

I asked the operators of the damaged Beaver to get the plane's wheel landing gear to Ross River. I ordered the necessary repair items from de Havilland in Edmonton and got prompt service.

I got busy trying to find Franky Slim, the operator of the Government river boat. It turned out he was somewhere in the bush but he wasn't answering radio calls so I chartered a plane and started a search from the air. We located him about 22 miles down stream enjoying a bit of recreational fishing.

Franky was not only ready and willing to help me, he was ready now. The pilot left me there. We camped for the night on the river bank; had a "fresh from the river" fish feed and Franky bent my ears with great campfire tales of his adventures with wolves, bull moose and bears.

At daybreak, I woke to the smell of strong coffee. Franky was up and ready to go and we were soon on the river and on our way to Ross River with the Beaver in tow.

It was slow going. Franky knew the river and he was careful. The Department people had said nobody told him what to do in his boat because nobody knew as much about the rivers as he did. They were sure he was the last of the Yukon river paddle wheeler navigators, so he deserved and got their respect.

Franky was a bonafide Yukoner. He was very friendly and loved sharing his knowledge of the river. As we moved slowly upstream with our tow, he showed me how to read the waters to locate invisible sand bars and shallow waters before we reached them. He had a wealth of river knowledge and he had a willing audience. I had been on the river in my own Indian dugout before I was a teenager. I knew I was in the company of a truly gifted river man.

We completed the journey to Ross River without

Beaver towed up Pelly River by Franky Slim, the last of the Yukon River Paddlewheeler navigators.

incident. Franky headed back to his fishing spot and I flew back to Whitehorse to pick up equipment and supplies. Gordon had everything ready to go.

I phoned Bill Myers and gave him a progress report. For some strange reason he was cranky about the time it was taking and complained about it. I don't know why because he wasn't paying me or anyone else by the hour. Perhaps head office was gnawing at him over something else. He had no personal experience with the north so he didn't know about sun spot and magnetic storm interference with radio and how hard it was to locate people in the bush. Bill's idea of roughing it was not having colored toilet paper.

Ron Connelly, who owned the Beaver, heard about Bill's complaints and called him to straighten things out. The matter was settled and Bill and I went on to enjoy many years of business relations.

Having Ron Connelly in my corner as an endorser has been almost a company asset. His rise to prominence in the aviation industry is a great British Columbia success story. Ron began flying at Sproat Lake on Vancouver Island where Slim Knight and Jack Moule had a flying school. I met him when we both worked for Associated Air Taxi in Vancouver. He later moved to the Yukon and established Connelly Dawson Air Service. Then he joined Les Kerr to form Conair Aviation, a corporation known world wide for expertise in airborne fire suppression and specialized equipment development.

A half ton truck was rented to transport Gordon Cameron and me with equipment and parts to Ross River. A boat took us across the Pelly to the moored Beaver. We set to work building a tripod over the aircraft to lift it for removal of the pontoons and installation of the wheel assembly. Gordon climbed to the top of the tripod to install a pulley with a winch cable and check the security of our rigging.

Here I missed a great photo opportunity. I could have and didn't take a picture of the Mayor of Whitehorse up a pole. I wonder if he would have paid me to burn the negative as he climbed the political ladder.

In jig time, the Beaver was moved on to the airstrip where the wings were reinstalled, fuel put into the tanks, all airframe work double checked, and the engine given a good run up.

We worked from daybreak to dark, sleeping in a nearby shack. Two workaholics on the job. Bill Myers should have been there. He'd have been walking on his tongue.

In three days we were ready to go. We were satisfied that the aircraft was fit for a ferry flight to Whitehorse.

The floats had to be taken across the river for transport by truck to Whitehorse. Franky had the only boat nearby and he was 20 miles away trying to kill a fish. So, old friend Bud Harbottle offered to tow them with his seaplane.

We were up at 4 a.m. on what we thought would be our final day on the job. Poor weather set in and scuttled our schedule. In the afternoon I decided I could not accomplish anything more so I loaded the disassembled floats into the truck and headed for Whitehorse. Bud agreed to stand by and help Gordon get ready to fly the Beaver to Whitehorse when the weather cleared.

He brought the Beaver into Whitehorse late the following day and Ron Connelly came down from Dawson City with the suggestion that he would fly the aircraft to Edmonton on condition that I went along with him. That suited me just fine.

A detailed inspection was done on the Beaver and as soon as the stormy weather let up a bit, we took off for Edmonton with an overnight in Fort St, John.

Gordy took off his aviation coveralls, put on his Mayors hat and went back to running Whitehorse. He did a great job of doing that too.

Ron and I had a pleasant, uneventful flight to Edmonton. There were no problems so we enjoyed a good game of "remember when".

The Beaver, on arrival in Edmonton, was turned over to Dick Hicks. I said my goodbyes to Ron Connelly and was lucky enough to get a quick flight to Vancouver.

All and all a good ending to an interesting experience.

chapter five

Upside Down in Tulsequah

Winter had arrived in northern British Columbia; the year was getting close to calling it quits. Mother Nature had, however, played games in spreading her white fluffy blanket over her possessions that had begun to bed down for a few months. The blanket had been spread in a spotty and uneven manner as Herman Peterson of Peterson Air Services found out to his regret.

Herman, a well respected and experienced northern pioneer bush pilot, made Atlin his base of operations. Part of his flight service included regular mail runs to Tulsequah, about 60 miles south and Telegraph Creek approximately 160 miles south east of Atlin.

Atlin was one of the bare spots in the snow blanket and Herman was still using his Cessna 180 on wheels. He loved the aircraft. It was brand new; purchased from Al Michaud of West Coast Air Services in Vancouver. He liked it so much he named it "Suzy", his wife's nickname. He chose "Suzy" for a service run to Tulsequah. When he got there he checked the airstrip and it appeared to have only a few inches of fresh snow on it. Down he came for his usual smooth landing, rolled a few feet and "whammo"...the wheels broke through a thick ice crust and jammed, throwing the tail over the nose and leaving Herman hanging upside down from his seat belt.

As a result, the phone rang at the home office of Denny McCartney Ltd. It was Bill Myers, who had gotten over the cranky spell he put me through on the Connelly Beaver salvage. Bill's insurance company, British Aviation Insurance Co., had the insurance on Herman's Cessna and he wanted me to investigate the accident and salvage the machine as soon as possible.

I called Canadian Pacific Airlines and booked for their 2 p.m. flight for Whitehorse. This was 1959

and the electronic navigation services were still primitive so I knew weather might delay the flight. But I didn't want Bill moaning about slow service so I was ready to go on the first flight out. It was canceled and we didn't get away until 11 a.m. the following morning.

After a pleasant trip with a friendly CPA crew I arrived in Whitehorse and checked in to the Whitehorse Inn...without my duffel bag containing work clothes and tools. Red faces at CPA and a promise the bag would be on the next flight and delivered wherever I wanted it. No big problem really; I had a full afternoon's work to do. I had to

left to right, Bill Nelson, Bill jr., unknown, Gordon Cameron, Herman Peterson.

track down Gordon Cameron, my work mate on the Connelly Beaver salvage and I had to reach Herman Peterson via a balky radio/telephone.

Gordon was off doing Mayor of the City work, so I decided to tour Main street. Gordon's secretary said it was a sure bet that if I stood anywhere on the street I would meet him within a half hour. In spite of the cold and swirling snow, Whitehorse was a beehive of activity. Mining company trucks and cars lined Main street and the stores were busy with pre-Christmas shoppers. Everyone in the Territory seemed to be in town. I really enjoyed watching the passing parade. And the secretary was right. Within twenty minutes Mayor Gordon Cameron came out of the newspaper office just as I was passing. He seemed as pleased to see me as I was to see him.

I asked him what he had been up to since we salvaged the Connelly Dawson Beaver and as we walked to his office he gave me an insight into the demands of political office.

Gordon had also received a call from Bill Myers and had been to the Tulsequah crash scene with Herman. They had built an A frame and hoisted the Cessna back on to its wheels, taken some photos and made a list of needed repair items. Mayor Cameron had put on his aviation hat and done his usual thorough job.

At this point, Bill Myers had me wearing my insurance adjuster hat and my next task was to meet with Herman Peterson and check his pilot's statement and the aircraft log books for required

entries. I couldn't raise him on the radio/phone so I settled for a shop talk dinner with the Mayor and a couple of his flying buddies then early to bed.

The next morning I rented a car and drove the 125 miles to Atlin. The roads were far better than expected.

Herman was home and surprised to see me. He said, "The insurance company said they were sending someone. I never expected it would be you, but I'm sure glad it is."

I said, " Well Herman, I was told to come up here and ask you if you truly knew how to fly and who said you could?" His reply was a rueful, "Good questions after what I did."

It was good to see Herman and his wife Doris again even though the meeting concerned an unhappy incident. But that's my business, dealing with unhappy incidents.

Herman gave me a comprehensive pilot's accident report and a check of the aircraft's log books showed everything to be in order. Unfortunately, Herman hadn't installed skis on any of his aircraft as yet, so he couldn't get me into the scene of the crash.

I returned to Whitehorse the following morning and felt good about being able to call Bill Myers of British Aviation Insurance Co., advising that all the policy conditions had been met.

My next task was to complete the survey by going to Tulsequah via a Pacific Western Airlines charter flown by Ray Simpco.

I picked up my lost luggage from CPA on my way

to meet Ray for the trip south in his ski equipped Beaver. We had good weather all the way. The scenery was spectacular. A most pleasant flight with a good pilot.

The Tulsequah airstrip still had Herman's wheel tracks on display. It was easy to see how the thick crust of icy snow had deceived him and sent the Cessna into a somersault.

Bill Nelson, caretaker for the closed Consolidated Mining & Smelting Co., who owned the airstrip, greeted us and offered to house and feed me while I assessed the crash and salvage requirements. That settled, Ray left for Whitehorse.

I got busy photographing and making detailed drawings and notes of the surprisingly extensive damage. It included such major items as the propeller, engine mount, the rear spar of the left wing, the vertical fin and rudder. My calculations verified that the costs of returning the Cessna to its previous condition were well within the insured value. Good news for Herman.

Bill Nelson, his wife and son, were the only inhabitants in the area. They made my overnight stay memorable. They not only provided complete hospitality, they assisted in removal of assemblies to be taken to Whitehorse for repairs and transported me to and from the crash.

The company house occupied by the Nelsons was, like all the other buildings, set up on tall timbers to keep them clear of spring flood waters of the Taku River. The river's banks were no match for the torrents caused by the annual melting of more than 40 feet of snow on the surrounding mountains.

This was wilderness British Columbia at its best and wild life abounded. Bill and Doris enjoyed having an audience for a few tales of their adventures. Bill told the story of how his dog had been lured to a sudden and horrible end.

One day a strange type of animal noise got Bill's attention and upon investigating he saw that a female wolf was enticing his large dog into the bushes and they were already a fair distance from the house. Bill knew what was going on and tried to get his dog's attention but the animal was deaf to anything but love.

As soon as the two entered the bush he heard the most terrifying cries of distress coming from his dog. They lasted only seconds and then there was silence...The wolf pack had been waiting for their temptress to bring them dinner.

The story reminded him that the same dog had endured a hungry bear experience. On this occasion he had heard the dog yelping as it approached the house and as he opened the door to check, the dog was at the top of the long stairway and practically flying toward the door. Right on his tail was a bear coming at the same speed.

Bill said, "I made a hasty retreat as both animals circled around the kitchen and living room. Doris was trying to get up on the ceiling; I was on top of the table shouting at the dog to get out of the house. After a couple of circuits the dog bolted out the door a few inches ahead of the snarling bear's snout. I jumped from the table, grabbed the rifle from its place by the door and got a killing shot into the bear before it was half way down the stairs. Life in the bush isn't dull."

I had, by noon the following day, completed the assessment portion of the work and was ready to go when Ray Simpco returned to get me.

Back in Whitehorse, I called the insurance company regarding the estimates and paved the way for the salvage operation that would take place as soon as the needed parts were obtained.

I sent the damaged propeller off to B.C. Propeller in Vancouver for repair and then took a call from Jack Mitchell, a Seattle insurance adjuster. He had a small claim that needed to be looked at for the record and wanted me to go north to Mayo, a mining town some 300 miles north of Whitehorse, and clear up the problem for him. I made arrangements to fly there in morning.

A hot shower beckoned and I was just contemplating a before dinner nap when the Mayor called and said, "Come on down McCartney and bring all your money with you and I'll buy you a drink."

During the "happy hour" someone needled the Mayor about his aviation work saying, "Gordie, I thought you did all the aircraft salvage work around here." He replied, "That's right I did until McCartney ran me out of business." That was Gordon Cameron — no malice or meanness.

As usual we talked a lot of shop and I got Gordon's commitment to join me in salvaging the Cessna.

The next day was busy. I got Mitchell's job in Mayo taken care of, got a crash report on the Cessna off to the Crash Investigation Branch of the department of Transport and caught the afternoon flight back to Vancouver.

The procurement of major replacement parts and assemblies was slow and before we knew it Christmas had arrived. I crated up many of the items, and on the second of January I was on my way back to Whitehorse. I had also bought some fresh fruit and vegetables, fresh meat and a few odd items as a treat for Bill Nelson and family. Whitehorse was still too far out in the boonies to receive fresh fruit service. A steady flow of staple groceries was shipped up there via coast boat and the White Pass & Yukon Railway from Skagway, Alaska. Tulsequah was even more out of the way and even the necessities were slow in arriving there.

Weather was poor in the mountain passes next day, blocking flights to Atlin. I used the time to complete some of the repair work started but not completed in Vancouver. I also got to know Roger Daigle, a young bush pilot from Quebec. Roger was looking for as much experience as he could gather in Western Canada aviation. He welcomed the opportunity to fly Herman Peterson's Cessna to Vancouver. It was great to have that little detail out of the way.

More snow was piling up and the weather remained marginal. Mayor Gordon Cameron and I were ready and at the first break we headed for

Atlin with our load of parts and gear with Ray Simpco and his trusty Beaver.

We transferred our load to one of Herman Peterson's now ski equipped planes. We made two tries to get to Tulsequah that day, but failed because of adverse weather conditions.

Next day saw a little improvement in the sky and we managed to reach our objective around noon. We worked until darkness fell about 4.30 p.m. We made good progress on the tail and wing repairs with help from Herman.

We worked hard from day break to dark for the next four days in sub zero moist air that was either filled with falling snow or threatening to snow. In one 6-hour period more than a foot fell. Somehow we stayed on schedule.

One day Bill Nelson shot a moose and butchered it where it dropped. He didn't take the carcass home. But he did remove the liver and Doris served it for breakfast the next morning. What a treat!

I got another lesson on wild life in the north. I suggested to Bill that the wolves would make short work of the moose overnight and he replied that they wouldn't touch it. He said, "They would investigate it and watch over it the first night but I better get it in the next day. If it is still there on the second night they'll clean it up."

Finally, all the fuselage and wing work was completed, we used a tripod and winch to remove the engine and replace the damaged mount. I took advantage of the opportunity to photograph the Mayor of Whitehorse up a pole.

We got the skis installed and after 2 hours of heating the engine with a plumber's blow pot, getting the ice off the wings and after a test flight that satisfied Gordon, we were ready to go.

The strip was covered with two feet of fresh snow on top of the ice crust that had been Herman's undoing. Bill Nelson took care of that with the company tractor. Just another of the many kindnesses the Nelson family managed to do for us. I thanked them for their hospitality, climbed in beside Gordon and we were off on a white knuckle ferry flight through questionable weather to Whitehorse.

My new friend from Quebec, Roger Daigle, had his flight plan for the ferry flight to Vancouver ready for filing, but storms that seemed to roll in one behind the other, kept us grounded. Even C.P.A. flights were way off schedule.

Our ferry permit the Department of Transport issued for the Cessna was restricted to visual rules only; no instrument flying and therefore no above the clouds flying. That was frustrating for Roger but was fine with me. Every "find it", "fix it" and "fly it" flight I did carried an element of risk so I wouldn't push my luck anyway when there was an option.

Work was piling up in Vancouver, so I gave Roger my Imperial Oil credit card to cover refueling costs when he finally got the ferry flight off and I caught a very rough, above and in clouds, C.P.A. flight to Vancouver.

Roger got into Vancouver International three

days later; pleased with himself and full of com-plements for both me and engineer, pilot, Mayor Gordon Cameron. He said the Cessna flew as though it was fresh from the factory.

He was pleased with himself because he had learned some new English words, made some new friends along the route and had proved to himself that he had first class flying skills. He was also pleased, and amazed that a Western Canadian, he had known for only a short time would trust him not only with the ferry job but even trusted him with a credit card.

We invited him to take a little holiday and spend it with us. He had a great time with the kids and proved to be quite an amateur magician. He opened up too and gave us an insight into why we have some of our communications problems with the folk in Quebec.

Roger said the experiences he had in the Yukon now amplified with experiences in Vancouver and his welcome into our home had opened his eyes.

He said his parish priest had always told his con-gregation and young people such as himself that English Canada was not friendly to Quebecers and they would have nothing but trouble if they tried to live outside their own culture. He said teachers, politicians and the Quebec media had brain-washed him from childhood to distrust Anglephones or "blokes".

The adventure into the west was undertaken just to fatten his resume so he could get more for his services in Quebec. When he left the McCartney household he had been through a remedial brain-washing and I am pleased to say that wherever he is he is not a separatist...at least not for the old bigoted reasons.

The main subject of this little story, the Cessna, was turned over to West Coast Air Services for complete restoration and permanent repairs then returned to a happy and wiser Herman Peterson in Atlin.

chapter six

The Frozen Yukon River gives up the Aero Commander

It was getting close to Christmas in 1960 when I received a phone call, late one evening, from Jack Mitchell in Seattle. He was handling a claim on a California registered Aero Commander Aircraft, the pilot of which had made a wheels up (belly landing) on the ice covered Yukon River. Jack had few details on the position and security of the aircraft but he did know that it was near Whitehorse, Yukon.

My instructions were to go up there, do a detailed inspection of the damage and make up one estimate on the approximate cost for permanent repairs and another on the costs of moving the aircraft to the airport and making temporary repairs for a ferry flight south.

I left Vancouver on an early flight next morning and on my arrival at Whitehorse it appeared that everyone seemed to know why I was there. The location of the Commander was common knowledge, so, with a few easy to follow directions, I arrived at a point from where I could see it on an island in the river, a short distance down stream from the shipyards, which had played a great part in the history of Whitehorse and the paddle wheeler river boat transportation of bygone days.

The paddle wheelers had transported prospectors and supplies from Whitehorse to Dawson City during the Gold Rush of 98 and beyond. Dawson City was the centre of the Klondike Gold Madness and still lives those lively times, especially in the tourist season.

Now, back to my story. I made my way to the edge of the ice and was then directly across from the island and the parked aircraft. I was in an area that was sometimes referred to as Moccasin Flats, meaning that it was Native Indian territory. On that subject, there was another spot a short distance away, named Whiskey Flats, where the American military personnel were apparently very productive during a few years of World War 2.

The river was completely frozen over. The stretch of ice, between me and the island, covered a small arm of the river that was split off from the main channel by the island.

It looked safe enough to walk on except along the shoreline and in some areas out farther, nearer the island. The ice, in those areas, looked too fresh and weak to walk on with any safety. The memory of an earlier narrow escape on questionable ice told me to be cautious. The fresh looking ice had apparently been formed from an overflow of warmer water discharged from a hydro power station a little farther upstream.

I was standing there wondering how I could get across to the island when a Native Indian fellow approached me. He seemed to sense what I was

there for and the problem I was wrestling with, because he immediately offered to lead me across. That sounded great to me but before we got out on the ice, his wife came out of their nearby home, grabbed him by the arm and took him back into the house.

I thought her forcefulness might have had something to do with pre-Christmas celebrations. He was very friendly and thought my problem was nothing, but he didn't have a chance to prove it or otherwise. She gave no explanation or apology for her action, but did it in a very determined manner. It was quite plain that he was not the Chief.

Now, I was back to square one. I thought of renting a pair of skis to distribute my weight or see what ideas my friend Curly Derosier had on the matter. Curly was a great outdoors man, in fact he was an Outfitter (big game guide) with a large hunting range in the Mackenzie Mountains and would surely know how to tackle my problem.

I decided to hunt Curly down and go from there. That, as it turned out, resulted in not only a good effort on Curly's part but developed into a pleasant afternoon with no solution on the matter.

Curly was willing to help and went down to the river with me. He didn't like the idea of walking out on the ice but he said there was a fellow I should meet, his brother in law Alex Van Bibber, who was a Government Water Surveyor. Curly was sure that Alex would have a solution, even if it meant skidding a boat across the ice and rolling into it if the ice started to fail. Well, that was one idea and it was worth considering.

Curly wasn't sure where he would find Alex. On our way back to town I was surprised at how many bars there were that Alex might be in. We never did find him and eventually ended up at Curly's house near the Taku Hotel, where I was staying. There were several visitors at his home and after a while I asked Curly's wife, Belle, where he was. She replied by saying he was napping. We laughed because evidently the short delays we had at several of the bars were now having an affect.

Belle, by the way, was also an Outfitter with her own hunting range. She said that the difference between her operation and that of Curly's was that she did the cooking for her hunting parties and

Curly hired a cook. While speaking of Curly I have a little story he told Dot and I. He at times, wrangled horses for exploration parties.

One evening while hobbling the horses for the night a university student came tearing out of the bush and on seeing Curly, fell down and fainted. When he had recovered he explained that he was out photographing the scenery when he spotted a bear on the far shore of a creek.

He moved down to the creek to get a picture of the animal that was then standing up on its hind legs and moving its head from side to side. The fellow should have got out of there right then. Bears are short sighted and it was trying to locate the human by sniffing the air.

Testing and marking out safe path across Yukon River.

He said the bear suddenly dropped down and came at him with a rush through the water. He continued by saying he turned and ran for the camp but tripped and fell. He buried his face in the brush and covered his head with his hands, frozen stiff with fright.

The bear sniffed him from end to end then got its nose under his stomach and turned him over face up to continue sniffing a little, then went away. The fellow said the bear's breath was so foul that he was almost sick at that point. Lucky for him he wasn't or the grizzly would have had a little desert. He waited for short bit, looked around and seeing no bear got up and ran until he saw Curly.

I still hadn't found a solution to my problem so next morning I went to the Water Survey Office and met Monty Alford who was in charge of that Department. Without any hesitation he offered to show me how to test the ice and in about a quarter of an hour we were at the edge of the ice. Monty had, with him, a round wooden pole about one and one half inches in diameter and about six or seven feet long. He raised the pole vertically to about two feet above the ice, then let it free fall through his hand to strike the ice as though he was attempting to pierce it. The pole bounced up without even cracking the ice. That indicated that the ice, in that spot, was safe to walk on.

That testing was repeated all the way across to the aircraft. The theory behind that method of testing was that the weight of the pole and momentum of the drop produces a concentrated impact over a small area, exceeding the weight placed on a man's foot, wich has a much larger area of disbursement.

I had just had another lesson in learning the tricks of the many skills that were not directly associated with general aviation but very much required in my work.

The knowledge I had obtained from Monty was used in several similar ice experiences at later dates. Life, in the very act of doing things, is a continual learning process, to be sure. Recommended reading is Yukon Water Doctor by Monty Alford.

I worked up a mental picture of the accident that indicated that the aircraft had approached the ice in an upstream direction for its wheels up landing. The surface of the frozen river was anything but smooth.

The lower part of the aircraft was extensively crushed and torn, with damage to both the frame support structure and the exterior metal skins.

The machine, during its landing slide, had swung around a little as it slid up onto the island with small trees. It came to a stop facing back in the opposite direction to its landing.

Upon completion of my survey and note making I removed the battery to prevent a possible electrical fire, and stored it in a shop to prevent damage from freezing.

There was only one way to move that aircraft from its resting spot to the airport. It would have to be raised and set up on its wheels, then towed up the river to a road.

Several questions immediately came to mind. When would that be and what would be used to tow it? Was the ice thick enough to support the weight of the aircraft (approximately 7500 lb.) concentrated on three wheels and if not, then hopefully it would be eventually but when? What could be used to grade off the rough ridges in the tow path? A road grader? How heavy would that be? That was enough thinking for the moment, with no immediate answers.

The thickness of the ice over the route to be used for towing was unknown but fortunately, the overflow from the power plant did not spread over onto the ice on the main channel of the river, as it did on that smaller branch of the river I had first seen. I borrowed an ice auger from Monty and cut a few holes over the tow route. It was, in my opinion, too thin and that was also the thinking of the Water Surveyors. The roughest parts of the ice contained pressure ridges. Those are formed by the upheaval of the ice under pressure from its continued expansion with low temperatures.

The ice would have to be much thicker for our useage.

Arrangements were made to have the thickness monitored until the required thickness was obtained, around three feet. When it reached that point I would be notified by phone.

Everyone around there seemed to feel that the aircraft would be free from harm by Mother Nature or anyone else for that matter. Vandalism wasn't a commonly used word then, especially up there.

There was nothing more to be done until the ice thickened. Therefore, I left for home. It was Christmas Eve.

The call from Whitehorse was received in the first week of February, advising that the ice was thick enough.

I had been preparing for the return trip by making up a load for my 25 foot flat deck trailer that included sheet metal, support structure for ribs etc.,tools and many other items on a list I had made up in Whitehorse. I was ready to go.

The Aero Commander is a high wing model having a very deep fuselage with the engines and propellers mounted in its high wings. I had not found any damage to them, thanks to the great ground clearances. My on scene inspection had indicated that I should be faced with repairs to the airframe only.

Little did I know what I was in for and how much those power units would add to the overall problem, all because of earlier poor or lack of maintenance required to maintain the airworthy standards and safety of the aircraft.

Preparations for such an undertaking were always a worry. Had I enough of this and that? Had I forgotten something?

Well, with the trailer loaded I hooked it up to the family's station wagon, which was not the preferred thing to do but I couldn't afford a truck for the job.

I left home about 6 p.m. for the north. That first night of driving six hours on snow and ice was an example of what I would have for the whole trip.

I arrived in Whitehorse at 1 a.m. Feb.13, having left Vancouver on the 10th. Driving time was 15 to 17 hours a day and a total of 1800 miles.

My diary shows that I was up and had breakfast by 6:30 next morning, then out on the river to check the aircraft. It was still dark of course but I guess I was just anxious.

Later, I borrowed an auger and checked the thickness of the ice while marking out a route over which the aircraft would be towed.

The choice in equipment, that could be used to grade the rough ice was narrowed down to a regular type road grader with large tires. It would also be used to tow the aircraft up the river.

Fortunately, the landing gear, mounted in the wings, had not been damaged and in a few hours the aircraft was raised and sitting firmly on its wheels. A tow bar was made up in a welding shop to attach to the nose wheel and we were ready to go.

The grader operator and other knowledgeable people agreed that the ice was thick enough to support the grader so out on the ice it went, heading toward the aircraft, smoothening the ice on its way down.

All went well and we soon had the aircraft going up river to the shipyards and the end of a road. An old paddle wheeler was beached there, an interesting sight.

It took the best part of a day, but I finally obtained permits from four separate offices to tow the aircraft up the road to the airport, a distance of about three miles, part of which was on the Alaska Highway. The authorities involved were the R.C.M.P., City of Whitehorse, Territorial Government and the Canadian Army. The latter was, at that time, responsible for maintaining the Alaska Highway. I received splendid co-operation from everyone and the machine was soon on the airport.

The forced landing damage was mainly in the crushed lower part of the fuselage or belly area, also some dents in the tail control surfaces and wing leading edges from contact with trees. It took about seven, 10 hour, days to complete the metal repairs working by myself. I used a local sheet metal shop to form up some pieces to replace broken sections of the ribs and other major structure. The new skin sections and support structure were secured into position with machine screws, plain metal screws and blind rivets.

During that period the temperature did not rise above minus 10 degrees Fahrenheit and to make matters worse there was a continuous strong wind with the hanger doors open at both ends of the building. I was working in a wind tunnel.

The airport fire marshal had approved of me using a gasoline fueled Herman Nelson heater, commonly used for pre-heating aircraft engines in cold weather as they produced a large volume of heat. However, the airport manager refused to let me use it, not even with the heater outside the building and the heated air piped into the working area. So I was most uncomfortable when it was not necessary. In fact, an R.C.M.P. officer and others including Keith Elliott of the Government Fisheries Department would come in to see how I was progressing and remark that they could not believe I would continue working in those conditions.

I was beginning to feel that I was over the "hump", when a mountain in the form of preaccident conditions, loomed up. I was never known to gold plate an aircraft remaintenance of any kind. However, I was always determined that it would be safe for flight in all respects.

The first, of many problems, was the elevator cables, which were so slack that I could hold a cable in my hand and bend it up into a right angle, and that was not due to fuselage distortion. When operating the control column from the pilot's seat one could feel and see the elevators flopping. There was no adjustment left in the turnbuckles so the cables had to be cut to get rid of the slack by shortening them and installing longer turnbuckles to reconnect the cables, retention and rig them.

The machine was finally ready to be moved outside for run up checks on the engines. Well, there were magneto problems on both engines. Two were sent to Calgary for overhaul. The carburetor for the right engine was not tight on its base and it needed a new gasket, some of the old one was missing.

That right engine was full of problems, it wouldn't run smoothly even with fresh spark plugs, oil dripped out of the exhaust stack and the manifold pressure was so low it was unsafe for flight. There

(left); Aero Cammander retrieved and sharing space with old originial Paddlewheelers. (right); Commander towed up highway to airport.

was not nearly enough power. I thought there must be a leak in the system but I couldn't find any.

I couldn't go any farther on the engine problems until the magnetos and other parts arrived from Calgary.

That slack time had just started when a fellow came into the hangar looking for the individual working on the Commander. That was, of course, me. His name was Don Pasco, a pilot with a Twin Beechcraft on the way to Alaska. It was interesting that he was from the southern part of the USA and quickly learned a great deal about sub zero weather.

He was flying for a drilling company and had parked the aircraft over night with no oil dilution (thinning the oil with gasoline just before shutting the engines down). The next morning he started running one of the engines without any preheating. It quickly came to grinding halt, solidly seized up, the oil was too thick to circulate.

I did a quick check for him so he could notify the head office of his employer. I also assisted him in preparing the engine for its removal and, later, the installation of the replacement engine. He returned the favour during the next couple of days although it wasn't planned that way.

The needed parts arrived and I soon had the Commander engines operating again.

Through a process of cross checking the manifold pressure gauges by hooking them up to opposite engines, plus other minor checks, I came to the astonishing conclusion that the basic settings of the propeller blades on the right engine were incorrect. It was difficult to convince myself that such a thing was possible because the aircraft had been operating, supposedly, satisfactorily in order for it to get as far as Whitehorse but there was no other explanation.

It was unbelievable that the aircraft was being operated in that condition. However, there were no indications that the propeller had struck anything in the accident. Also, all three blades are set independently in their own blade clamps and all the blades were out, in their basic settings, exactly the same amount. That satisfied me, as it did others, with whom I discussed the condition, that the settings had been unaltered in the accident. I had to pick some one else's brain to make sure I was thinking properly.

Therefore, by changing the settings on each blade one degree, I obtained an increase in the engine operating power reading. That procedure was performed six times until the required manifold pressure was obtained.

The basic settings had been out six degrees, disgusting to say the least, and much was said and thought about California maintenance

My diary shows that the temperatures were up and down, ranging with lows to minus 25 and minus 28 degrees Fahrenheit and to make matters worse there was a wind. I was so chilled through to my bones by the end of each day. However, I could then look forward to the comforts of a room at the Taku Hotel, not a tent as was the norm. A luxury that was not often available on my salvage jobs. I would run a warm bath and felt I was being scalded as I slipped into it.

I should have mentioned that, unbeknownst to me, a fellow across the airport had been listening to the engine performances. I had finished the last run when he came over and said, "I hear you got it." I didn't know what he was talking about quite frankly, and my mind was preoccupied with ill thoughts of the people who had been maintaining the aircraft, so I abruptly asked, "what did I get?" "The power," he said, "I have been listening and I could tell that you finally got it." That made me feel so much better, the disgusted feeling left me and I thanked him and explained why I might have seemed a bit rude.

It seemed that most people on the field knew of my problems, and while there was not much they could do to help, they were certainly willing when I asked for an opinion or a helping hand.

That is where Don Pasco stepped in and ran the engines for me each time I reset the blades. He also offered to do a test flight that was accomplished with satisfaction and the only negative comment was that the left brake was weaker than the right. I had made a mental note about that while taxiing the aircraft earlier but a visual check of the system didn't reveal any hydraulic leaks or traces of accident related damage. I wasn't looking for work as I would have, if I had been doing a standard maintenance inspection.

After all, I was not there to do one either. I was in for more surprises with that collection of junk.

My thoughts about poor or no maintenance was confirmed when the Imperial Oil Company pilots told me that Field Aviation Ltd. of Calgary, a very reputable and dependable maintenance company, had not been allowed to do any of the work that they considered important and necessary for the safety of the aircraft. I was also told that Field had considered the aircraft to be in very poor condition, so much so, that some said they would not fly to Edmonton in it, a distance of about 250 road miles due north.

In the meantime I was trying to figure out how I was going to be paid for all that extra non-accident related work. I had been told to do the necessary and thinking it would involve just an odd item, I carried on, but it snowballed on me with one thing after another. There didn't seem to be any end to it.

I received a phone call from my friend Bob McCullough of Field Aviation advising that I had better put a hold on the aircraft such as a mechanic's lien. My wife, Dorothy, had picked up some information that supported that approach, until the matter was settled. She was the bookkeeper in our little company and said she was going to add 10 percent to our total invoice to protect us. If everything was settled in a straight forward manner, we would reduce our charges by that amount.

I found out that a lawyer named Mr. Eric Nielsen was held in high regard by those at the airport and it was thought that I should go see him, which, fortunately, I did. He explained that there was no Mechanic's Lien legislation in Yukon as there was in British Columbia. I asked him if he could write a letter in such a manner that the owners of the aircraft and their insurers would think there was one in Yukon. He replied, "Yes, I think I can do that."

I must say that I did not receive an invoice for his help and have often thought of his kindness when I did not know which way to turn on that non-mechanical problem.

Eric Nielsen was, at that time, a member of Parliament for Yukon and practiced law in Whitehorse. He completed 30 years in the House of Commons with positions up to and including Deputy Prime Minister. He is also a veteran war time pilot, after which he was a bush pilot. His brother, by the way, is the Hollywood actor Leslie Nielsen.

It did not appear that the extra costs, in excess of those directly related to the accident, would be settled soon. I therefore secured the machine in a tie down area and arranged for a fellow to pull the propellers through once in a while. I also informed the R.C.M.P. and the Department of Transport of the situation.

The aircraft was then hog tied, so to speak.

I returned to Vancouver with the log books for the aircraft and other documents that would be needed for a ferry flight.

The tanglement that erupted between the Insurance Co., Wells Fargo Bank and the aircraft owners was so complicated that the aircraft sat in Whitehorse until October, 1961.

A total of over six months and I had not received payment for the extra work and expenses.

A pilot named Zogg was sent up from San Francisco to ferry the aircraft south, arriving in Vancouver early October and I agreed to accompany him to Whitehorse after being assured by the insurance adjuster, Jack Mitchell, that I would collect my extra costs shortly. He looked the aircraft over and was not happy at all about the engines seeping and dripping oil. I told him that it has been bothering me too but it was minor compared with other problems.

He took the aircraft up and flew it for about an hour with no complaints with its performance or the brakes.

He had said earlier that he had heard of a short cut south via the Rocky Mountain Trench. I said, "absolutely NO." "It is too dangerous a route to ferry that aircraft, we will follow the Alaska Highway or I won't go with you." I would not have either.

Winter was returning with very poor weather and snow in some places. There were no indications of any improvement in the next few days so he decided to give it up and go back home to his airline job. He didn't know anything about northern flying or he would not have thought that he could arrive there one day and leave the next with no weather interference, especially at that time of year. So it was a dry run and we returned via airline.

Pilot Zogg must have taken quite a story back with him because he asked many questions as we flew to Vancouver.

Later, discussions between Adjuster Mitchell and San Francisco improved.

The date was October 26/61 when pilot Slim Knight and I left for Whitehorse to ferry the Commander south. The day after our arrival it was snowing hard with a ceiling of 300 feet and fog in some areas, formed by an Arctic Cold Front over open waters of a few lakes.

We checked the aircraft over, and operated the engines. It was beginning to look like all the mechanical problems were behind me until we did some serious taxing. Well, it came as quite a shock to find that the left brake would not provide any braking power at all. I couldn't believe it was that bad but the fact was that the brake had now failed completely. I had not thought that the left one should be disassembled for inspection, after all, it had not been affected by the accident. Further more, Zogg had not complained about it following the flight test. Perhaps he was used to flying junk type aircraft.

Removal of the wheel revealed another HORROR SCENE of rotten maintenance. The brake pads were so thinly worn that one could argue which was thicker, when placed on a surface plate, the pads or a sheet of writing paper. The disk had been grinding into the casting, that housed the pads, for so long that all of it was destroyed.

That was just about the last straw but, sadly enough, it wasn't, there would be more waiting for me.

Parts were ordered from Field Aviation in Calgary and received the next day. Repairs were completed, with a good passing mark in a severe taxi test. Then I could not resist going to the airport manager's office and in plain English told him what I thought about the uncalled for punishment he had put me through.

Storms had been going through, one following the other with short intervals and there was nothing in the forecast that held any hope for better weather.

We took off behind one storm and ahead of another with a destination of Watson Lake, which is about 350 miles east of Whitehorse. Enroute we encountered snow storms and freezing rain. Weather grounded us the following day but there were no indications of a mechanical problem, which was a great relief, and we had a nice visit with Jeanne and Bud Harbottle, which was a plus. Bud was a war time pilot, a well known bush pilot, and above all, a good friend.

The aircraft had been operating satisfactorily, and I thought we would now be clear of mechanical problems.

What a surprise we had waiting for us.

The temperatures were now around minus 15 degrees Fahrenheit and the following day, after preheating the engines, we did the run ups and took off for Fort Nelson, British Columbia about 300 road miles east. We flew with the landing gear down and locked. I had no interest in gambling on the condition of that system.

We followed the highway with the thought that if it became absolutely necessary, we would use it as an emergency landing strip providing we were fortunate in being over a straight stretch of road at that time. If we were forced to go down where we could not use the wheels then we would do a wheels up belly landing. The aircraft was operating satisfactorily for the first hour but, sadly enough, that peacefulness was not to last.

We were about an hour out of Watson when I heard a change in the rhythm of the left engine. I was not wearing headphones as was Slim and he hadn't heard it. It was a habit of mine, on ferry flights, to listen for any such changes, new noises and remain alert for strange vibrations the rhythm change continued for an hour or better. The instrument readings had not changed so I didn't feel it was necessary to alarm Slim.

Well, we were east of Toad River when there was a terrific bang and shudder from the left engine. Slim tore off his head phones and looked at me like he had seen death itself.

I patted him on the shoulder and explained. "I have been listening to a change in the engine for quite some time and since we are in the mountains with a twisty road below us, just keep that so and so engine running as long as it produces power."

A sickly smile came over Slim's face and we continued on with much noise and roughness. Slim, was a cool and calm type, a war time bomber pilot, later, a bush and forest fire water bomber pilot.

I had never ever thought I would find myself feeling that I wouldn't care if an engine was further damaged while it was in my care, but now all I had in mind regarding that one, was our personal safety. We had no choice. Shutting it down and feathering the propeller to continue on one engine that I had no reason to trust, would have been, I thought, a suicidal manoeuver in that disaster plagued bucket.

Besides that, the landing gear, in its down position would cancel out a single engine performance. We had no choice but to continue on. I kept to myself the fact that I had considered the left engine to be more reliable than the right one and I was counting on it in an emergency. What should I expect now?

It is somewhat disconcerting to be sitting in the pilot and co-pilot seats of an Aero Commander with a rough engine and a vibrating propeller because they are right in line with the seats and close to the cockpit.

We continued on for about an hour in that fashion with vibration and noise. On our arrival in the Fort Nelson area we received a straight in approach for a landing. We both felt relieved to say the least. I recall saying to Slim, while we were taxing, "perhaps we should shut down that so and so engine before the propeller is in our laps." "Oh, good idea" he said with a big smile and we both relaxed a bit and took a deep breath of relief.

After parking the machine we checked into a hotel, then I went back to the airport and started on the left engine, removing spark plugs and inspecting the cylinders until dark. There was oil all over the place with heavy dripping out of the exhaust pipe. It was too dark to work any more so I returned to the hotel. The temperature was minus15 degrees Fahrenheit.

I was up early, had breakfast and out to the airport. It was still the same temperature as it was when I quit work the previous night.

Cleaned spark plugs were installed, the engine was preheated by using a Herman Nelson heater, borrowed from Pan Am Explorations, then it was started. The engine was still as rough as it had been so I ran it at low speed until the required operating temperatures were obtained.

Then it was shut off and I rushed out to check for a cold cylinder, that would indicate a dead one. That was done by placing my bare hands on them as quickly as I could before Jack Frost cooled them down and spoiled my readings.

I found two cold ones. Numbers 2 and 3 were dead (not operating).

That was the straw that broke the camel's back so to speak. I had had it with that aircraft and phoned adjuster Jack Mitchell, as early as it was, and told him I was leaving the aircraft right there and returning to Vancouver.

He knew me very well through other jobs I had done for him and I had kept him well informed regarding that assignment, so he was not upset about my decision. I did, however, tell him that a complete serviceable engine or at least a set of good cylinders and pistons should be installed for the completion of the ferry flight.

When I returned to the hotel Slim said he had felt sorry for me having to go out into that cold weather to check the engine.

Slim and I finished our trip to Vancouver via airline. The Commander was left in Fort Nelson, about 1200 road miles north of Vancouver.

Looking back, I found it so difficult and I still do, to believe that an aircraft could have been in such preaccident rotten condition and allowed to be flown and even worse, licensed to fly through some one signing it out for it's required maintenance inspections. It doesn't say much for the pilot who flew the aircraft. Perhaps he badly needed the job.

It was ironic that all the non-accident troubles were worse than any of the accident related damage. The story doesn't end at this point.

An individual in Seattle took over the problem of flying the machine to the U.S., in fact, I believe he bought it "as is where is." I tried to explain the engine problems to him but he knew it all, so it seemed. He wouldn't listen to me and in fact did not believe there was a serious problem at all. He did not want advice so I shut up and figured he was one who had to learn the hard way. I was later told that he had engine troubles and shut downs with a final complete failure en route to Seattle. He had done the minimum in Fort Nelson and paid for it.

The information I received later, was that the aircraft was eventually put into business in the Caribbean where it disappeared completely. There was no word on whether this was the result of a mechanical problem or a risky type get rich quick business. Who knows? I don't, but the latter venture was suggested.

That assignment to retrieve the Aero Commander had been full of challenges and surprises to say the least. I still hadn't been paid for the extra work and that dragged on until August of 1962 when I made the first of two trips to San Francisco to try to bring the matter to an end.

The first trip turned into something of a nightmare. It was absolutely unbelievable, but trouble was still waiting for me.

When Jack and I arrived in San Francisco there was a large lawyer convention well under way, with delegates from all parts of the U.S.A. including people such as Robert Kennedy.

One night Jack thought he would show me some of the city's night life. During the course of our sight seeing walk we stopped in at the Domino Club, a topless bar, for a drink. The entrance started with six steps up from the street to bat wing doors and a landing. A long stretch of steps continued upward, from there, to the club. The purpose of this description will be seen shortly.

When we had finished our drink and were preparing to leave, I, without looking behind me first, moved my chair backwards and heard a woman scream about somebody being fresh. She actually used another term. The fact of the matter was that the back of the chair had long spindle tops at it's corners, one of which had jabbed her in a sensitive spot as she was bending over, serving a table close behind us.

Needless to say I was as surprised as she appeared to be and apologized, hoping she would accept it as a genuine accident. I was pleased that she did. We then had another drink, gave her a nice tip and she was all smiles as we left.

That incident was the beginning of an entirely new and strange experience.

A problem erupted as we were leaving the club. Jack had gone down the stairs talking to another couple while I was talking to a fellow at the head of the stairs. During those few moments another man, also at the top of the carpeted stairs, dropped a cigarette on the first step down. Instead of stepping down to pick it up, he bent over in a forward fashion, while reaching down for it and took off head first in a swan dive down the long stretch of steps. He struck Jack who was on the landing and drove him through the bat wing doors, down the remaining half dozen steps and out on to the street.

Well, I lack the appropriate words to briefly sum up that performance. I thought I was indeed lucky as I could easily have been down there on the landing and driven out too.

Jack had a broken ankle, the high diver was uninjured, very ironic. I had to get Jack to a hospital or emergency first aid at least. I didn't know the city and Jack was in no shape to talk. He had been almost knocked out.

The club manager drove us, not to a hospital, but to the police station on Market Street. I had no idea where we were until he had us out of the car. That was a cruel and heavy handed action. The police desk sergeant was going to put us in a cell and was not interested in getting to the bottom of the problem or even asking questions.

I then demanded to know his name and number. I asked him to state the charge against us and not to use vagrancy as is so often done, because we were both respected business men and I was not an American. I also informed him that we had been innocent victims of an accident and that a business associate lawyer would be retained in the morning. Charges would be laid to include him, the sergeant, for unlawful detainment.

The officer went away for a few minutes and upon his return, asked me what I wanted to do. My reply was. "Call us a cab to go to the hospital and forget you ever saw us and that is good advice." He seemed relieved and called the cab immediately.

The time was 5:30 a.m. when I left the hospital, it had been quite a night on the town. Now to get some sleep, cancel our business appointment for

the day and locate the clown who had performed the aerial act.

Later in the day I was back to the hospital to finish checking Jack in and discuss our problem. I then went back to the club to obtain any information available and possible witnesses. Apparently, the man, I was looking for, was a visiting lawyer.

The club manager offered me an open house but I avoided him and his offer. His early morning assistance to the jail was too fresh in my mind and it was all I could do to keep from telling him off. The information I needed was far more important than venting my feelings and being ushered out.

I was making notes and about to leave when a gentleman, at the bar, came over and remarked that it seemed that I had a problem. It flashed through my mind that I didn't need any one to tell me the obvious but restrained myself and politely said, "Yes and I'm trying to figure out what to do next." He said he was a lawyer from New York attending the convention and, knew that I was a Canadian. His son had attended McGill University in Canada and while there, Canadians had treated his boy so well that he thought it was now his turn to do a Canadian a favour. I could hardly believe I was hearing correctly.

His advice was to have a writ served on the individual before the convention broke up, which would be in a couple of days.

He explained that by doing that, the fellow would be nailed down and forced to appear in San Francisco to face the problem, other wise he would

frozen yukon river gives up the aero commander   73

be in his own backyard at home, which would be much more of a disadvantage for us. Make that person face the issue in territory, strange to him.

The tables had turned and I was getting a break for a change. I thanked my advisor, obtained, from the club manager the name of our adversary, then left with a feeling that I was starting to win.

Next day I told Jack what had taken place and he agreed that we should act on the advice and gave me the name of the lawyer he wanted to use. In the late afternoon I went to the Fairmont Hotel, obtained from the convention desk a list of the delegates. The party I was interested in was a lawyer from the Mid West of the U.S. A few phone calls had provided me with information including his business location and who he was at home.

I located him that evening in his room where an after-meeting cocktail party was under way. As I entered he mistook me for being another lawyer until I mentioned the accident. I suggested that we go out into the hall and talk but he denied knowing what I was talking about and said no, we stay here, these are all my friends. However, when I congratulated him on his athletic dive with no injuries to himself and that he was still wearing the same suit that he had on at the night club, he thought we should go out into the hall

Out there, I proceeded to tell him what I knew about him, who he was, the office building with his name across it's front plus a few more details, where upon he said, "You have done your homework." "That is part of what I am paid to do." I

continued. "Your training as a lawyer provides you with a large shield to stand behind, admit nothing and deny everything but after the accident you showed your better side, you are human too. Your friends left but you, while not offering to help me, waited in the doorway until I had rescued my friend."

I denied knowing if he was at that time under the influence because I had not seen him drinking earlier.

He asked me what I wanted him to do. My reply was for him to meet me up at the hospital which he did. His first words beside Jack's bed were "WOW, my wife sure is mad at me."

Jack's lawyer set the wheels in motion for the issuance of a writ. I went to the convention centre with a Sheriff who stayed in the background while I had the desk page the lawyer to come to the lobby. I pointed him out to the Sheriff and the writ was served. Legal proceedings took place at a later date but I never did know how it all ended financially. Jack was no fool when it came to litigation and he had metal pins in his ankle permanently.

Next day, Jack with a leg cast, was put on a flight home to Seattle. There was nothing further I could accomplish in trying to collect any money so I started driving north to Seattle and Vancouver. The accident had made the trip south almost a dry run and increased my expenses.

Correspondence with San Francisco continued in regards to my account and about a month later I had to make another trip down there and wanted my wife Dot to go with me.

We finally received our money in U.S. funds plus interest, which took care of some of our travel costs. It took me three days to accomplish that.

One evening I took Dot to the Domino Club, an introduction to a topless bar. Well, what a surprise we had when a waitress came to our table and said to me. "Where did you get to, we haven't seen you for some time?" That made Dot sit up with a strange look on her face and I could see the wheels going around in her mind. It was the same girl who had had her privacy invaded by the back of a chair about a month earlier.

Explanation? None asked for and none made, I was innocent. The problem was, that the barmaid had too good a memory, that's all. Next morning we left for home.

That was the end of a long episode that had started in Dec. 1960 and it was now Oct. 1962. I had of course been very busy on other assignments, one of which was a trip to South America to bring a de Havilland DHC3 Otter to Canada.

I received a request early in 1965 to attend a court case as a witness in a dispute involving the owners of the Commander, Wells Fargo Bank and a finance company regarding the preaccident value of the aircraft. I was asked to testify as to the mechanical condition of the machine as I had found it.

This was a pleasant change because this time the problem wasn't mine. The trial was held in Sacramento, California where I spent quite a few hours on the witness stand.

The opposing lawyer, as is their normal procedure, attempted to discredit me regarding my knowledge and experience of northern areas in winter and my aircraft mechanical ability.

As he must have soon realized, he was wasting his time.

An attempt was made to blame the Canadian Government Accident Investigators for having caused internal damage to the engines when they test ran them at the accident site.

It was claimed that with the weather being very cold, the investigators did not properly prepare the engines before they started operating them. I countered that accusation by saying those men were from Edmonton, Alberta and had maintained and operated aircraft for years under severe northern winter conditions prior to and since becoming investigators. That type of experience and ability was a requirement in applying for their present occupations.

I further impressed upon the court that it was not at all reasonable to suggest that those well trained and prudent technicians would operate the engines in any way different to their proven successful procedures. There were no further questions on that topic.

The programme continued with a series of questions containing terminology that was not familiar to me. Example: "What is peak ice?" I answered by saying I didn't know. however, I did not help them by asking if they meant pressure ridges.

Another question "Did I think the engines could possibly have been damaged internally because they weren't acclimatized?" I answered that by saying "I did not know that engines could become acclimatized. I knew humans could be but I didn't know it could happen to machinery or metal."

I was sure he meant that the engines had not been winterized as is done in cold areas but I did not ask him if that was what he meant.

The lawyer then said: "You do not know the answers to these questions and yet you call yourself a Northerner?" I replied by saying. "I did not at any time say I was a Northerner, however, my home is north of Sacramento."

The questions and my replies were received by the jury with fits of laughter. I was honestly not trying to be smart or clever but they were to a great degree annoying me with their display of ignorance in their attempt to show me up.

The questions continued with phrases and terminology that to my way of thinking, did not make sense. They were fishing and hoping I would be caught somehow.

I thought it had gone on far enough so I asked the Judge if I could speak to him and he replied: "certainly." I said. "Your Honor, I have tried to answer the questions as correctly and honestly as possible but I have not understood the terminology as related to the subject matter. It would be a great help to me if you would please provide me with a dictionary on American Slang then I might

be better able to understand the questions."

That really broke up the jury and the whole court. It took a few minutes for His Honor to restore order. I didn't get the dictionary but that line of questioning stopped.

It was getting late and I had been on the witness stand all afternoon. An attempt was made to give the pilot of the aircraft high marks for the landing he made.

I was asked, "Do you not think that the pilot did an excellent job, in the emergency, in setting the aircraft down on the ice so well?"

My reply was: "The talk I heard on my arrival up there was that it was a Canadian bush pilot in the co-pilot seat who made the decision and forced the captain to land on the ice. He was said to have started the setting up of the aircraft for a belly landing by reducing the power to start with and nosing the aircraft down toward the ice."

"I also heard a story that the pilot (the Captain) had thought of using a main street in Whitehorse for the landing but apparently the co-pilot objected to that thinking."

"It was late in the afternoon and close to Christmas. The aircraft, no doubt, would have scattered a few last minute shopping old ladies and others in such an attempt plus damage to buildings. Under those circumstances, he would have been thinking only of himself, if indeed, he was thinking at all."

"There is still the question of the accident as being fuel related and in addition to that, he was operating an aircraft so badly in need of maintenance."

I continued by saying. "Many people up there thought that any one with ideas like that should be tied up to a tree on the bank of the Yukon River as an example of a danger to the public."

That set the jury going again.

During the examination, I had been permitted to refer to my diary to answer the technical type questions that I related to as the result of poor or no maintenance. Those notes were accepted as prime evidence and very supportive of my condemnation of the preaccident condition of the aircraft.

As I left the court the opposing lawyer spoke to me. I remarked that he had not had very knowledgeable assistants. He replied by admitting he didn't win all his cases. He then said "You are from Vancouver, British Columbia are you not? My parents came from Nanaimo, British Columbia." It truly is a small world.

The lawyer I was assisting said, outside the court, "I might as well have gone to bed early last night instead of spending several hours preparing you for court."

I immediately thought I had messed up and spoiled every thing so I asked him if I had. He replied by saying "Absolutely not. You were wonderful on the stand."

Jack Mitchell, the adjuster, said. "Until you got on the stand the jury was sleeping. Then you turned the whole thing into a Barnum and Bailey Circus show."

That brought the Aero Commander episode to an end. It was a long dragged out affair that had started from, what I had considered to be, an uncomplicated salvage job.

chapter seven

Wilderness Airlines

Cessna 180 on a Glacier

On a sunny fall day in 1968 Dan Schutze was returning home when the engine on his Cessna quit and he was forced to land on one of the many glaciers in the high mountains above Bella Coola, BC.

We received notice of the problem and Dan, a practical fellow by nature, was able to give us a good description of the damage that seemed to be centered around the front struts and bottoms of the floats.

Thankfully, Karl Frisk, my favorite airframe technician, was available. West Coast Air Services had the parts and materials needed for temporary repairs. An air charter to Bella Coola would complete the good news package but no such luck; poor weather ruled that out. So I loaded everything into the family station wagon for a grinding journey into the West Coast wild country.

Karl and I left early the next morning and drove to Takla Lake in the Chilcotin Country, driving on horribly rough roads. Somewhere between Takla and Nimpo Lake a big rock and a deep rut teamed up to rake off the muffler and tail pipe. We got to

Nimpo Lake at 9 p.m. and were relieved to find Dan Schutze waiting to fly us from there to Bella Coola and possibly on to the crash site. Poor weather washed out the crash visit part of his plan. So he made arrangements with Dick Burton of Trans West Helicopters to ferry us to the accident the following morning.

The Cessna was on its nose, with the tail high in the air. Dan was fortunate to walk away; put a mark on the wall for seat belts. We were lucky too; the fuselage, perched on the ice like a small grain elevator, made a terrific target for a high wind. We could have been faced with a twisted mess.

Dan couldn't have had much choice for his landing but the choice he made was exquisite. The aircraft was on a solid area free of crevasses. Had he

landed a little farther back toward the main part of the glacier, it could have been fatal. That portion of the glacier was covered with crevasses and ice bridges with crevasses under them. Those bridges are very difficult to spot and can strike terror into one who has to navigate across such a stretch of hazards on foot let alone a skidding aircraft.

A quick inspection confirmed that only the front struts were broken. A tripod was needed to lift the machine up so we could ease it into a level position without putting any stress on the pontoons or the undamaged struts and fittings.

Dick zipped away and soon returned with three sturdy poles for our tripod slung below the helicopter. It wasn't long until the aircraft was back to a normal horizontal position. A careful inspection

(left); End of Landing on a field of glacier crevasses. (right); Denny McCartney and sad aircraft

of the undercarriage verified that we had everything on hand to make that part of the aircraft airworthy.

Next came an inspection of the engine. A quick check of the fuel system located the broken line that had brought the plane down. - A radio call to Bella Coola and a phone call from there to Ralph Coates of West Coast had a replacement part on its way for next day delivery in Bella Coola. Great service and communications.

Full attention was now given to replacing the damaged struts. Dick Burton said he would pick us up before sunset then left on other business.

Sunny weather with no wind made work easier. We weren't long in getting the new struts installed. Every thing was going along first class. I always had a feeling of relief when such an important phase of a salvage job was completed. That gave us valuable extra time to get on with patching the float bottoms. The makeshift tripod made this job easier. By lifting the front of the aircraft we could reach the damaged sections without strain.

What a difference working with someone like Karl makes. We could each work on different locations independently and accomplish a great deal even though we were using hand drills.

Dick had dropped by once to check on us. His thoughts were that any thing could happen up there or maybe more damage would be discovered and we might need some parts or material. We appreciated his concern and his back up. Delays in getting the aircraft ready for a ferry flight could develop into a nightmare with a change in the weather at that altitude, especially with high winds. So the answer is to get in, get the machine ready and get out quickly.

(left); Aircraft leveled up with tripod, Karl Frisk hard at work. (right); Temporary repairs completed and Dan Schultz is crossing crevasses on his way to take off.

Dick picked us up just before the sun slipped below the horizon and back to Belle Coola we went for a great meal and an evening of socializing with a group of true blue aviation pioneers. Next day was pretty well taken up with float repairs. Karl put the "delivered as promised" fuel system parts in place and the engine performed 100 percent.

We had estimated that the aircraft would be ready for flight by about 5 p.m. and it was. Dan checked the engine out by putting it through a complete run-up test. Having satisfied himself on its performance, he then carefully walked the area over which he would have to taxi the aircraft for a take off run on the snow field beyond all the crevasses.

Being an experienced, prudent pilot, he was a little nervous and said it was a real white knuckle adventure. Karl, Dick and I shared his concern. Normally I would have gone with him but weight was important; the lighter the better. It was not known how much smooth area there would be for a take off run and the high altitude was a negative.

The floats were a plus. They provided a great deal more surface in width and length in bridging the crevasses than skis would.

Taxiing to the right take off area was a source of high anxiety for all of us. The floats would have to be kept at right angles to the crevasses, which were, as they are developed, all lying in the same direction, parallel to one another. We stood there and watched as Dan slowly made his way to the snow field. The surface of the glacier was far from pool table level and we crossed our fingers as he nursed the machine along. He must have had an occasional butterfly in his stomach; I know I did.

When he reached the snow we actually cheered. Slowly he edged the nose around into the wind, then he was off. He had done a great job. What a relief.

We packed up and, with Dick, returned to Bella Coola and a victory dinner. A member of Dan's family was not happy about him having flown off the glacier and seemed to feel I was responsible for him doing it. It was true that without the work Karl and I had done on the machine, it would have been impossible to fly it but the decision was all Dan's. I made no comment. Dan was very capable and knew what he could do.

In the morning Karl left with Dan for a flight to Vancouver, where the aircraft would be repaired. I went back to Nimpo Lake via a Cessna 185. There, I was asked to take a load of moose meat on board the family station wagon and transport it to a frozen food locker in Williams Lake for Bob Stuart, a friend of a friend. Lucky Bob; it was a prime moose. It was 10 p.m. on my arrival in Williams Lake. The next day I got a very early start for home, arriving there about 2 p.m.

Cessna seaplane registration CF-UQL, saved from an icy grave on a glacier by its skillful pilot, is still in service to this day.

chapter eight

A Cessna 180 in Hippie Village

Human nature, at times, is a complicated mystery but one, I stumbled on, didn't need any translation or imagination. It was a basic performance of "Nature In The Raw."

A Hippie Commune gave me a good look into a different world, totally foreign to the square one most of us know. It was quite a vision of another way of living. The year was 1973 and many of the cohabitants were Americans who had opted out from the U.S.A. and it's requirements for the Viet Nam conflict.

A Cessna 182 aircraft, CF-IAG flown by David Smith, was on its back in a field about 7 miles north east of Rock Creek on highway #3, east of Osoyoos B.C.

A Pacific Western Airlines flight to Castlegar and a meeting with the owners of the Cessna, Adastra Aviation Ltd., started the adventure. John Laing of Adastra accompanied me on a flight to Rock Creek from there, to the accident site by road.

The aircraft was located on the lower end of a sloping hay field that was more like a swamp in places. Smith said he had an in-flight loss of engine power, which forced him to attempt a landing in the field. The nose and its wheel sank deeply into the bog area and the aircraft went over onto its back. The field, according to a group of hippies was part of an old homestead they had bought. It was cultivated and growing a crop that didn't look like grain or hay.

They were, as you will see, rebellious in their anti social outlook on life but used their wits in leaning on society for their monetary needs without contributing anything. None that I met were lacking in intelligence.

They weren't a bit backward in making it clear to me that they intended on turning our situation into a profit-making venture for their benefit. I, on the other hand, wasn't out to try taking advantage of them and I would need their help.

During our conversation, they repeatedly stressed the problems the accident had caused them: inconvenience, damage to their crop of hay, environmental damage to the earth from acid dripping out of the battery and oil from the engine.

The leader of that group, which I soon learned was one of three such encampments, was quite well educated and his Father was in the insurance business in Vancouver. He was, to some degree, quite aware of the possibilities of going after an insurance company. I must say that he was well mannered.

The aircraft had to be put back up on its wheels and two of us could not do it alone. The Forest Service was very willing to help us but their road vehicle, the only piece of equipment available, could not be used in the swampy field. All their

other machinery was out fighting forest fires.

We were at a dead end with no choice but to ask the commune leader for assistance. He told us that a fellow in another camp had a tractor and perhaps he would help us for a price.

A tractor is for farming although they did not look like industrious farmers. But it wasn't long before we had reason to believe that it was quite possible they were. The field next to the aircraft, according to John, looked like it could be producing marijuana. That was my guess, but I had never seen such a field before. John thought some of the group appeared to be a bit nervous, perhaps from thinking that the police might come up to investigate the accident and confirm our suspicions.

We were given directions on where and how to locate the tractor man but that was no good, for one thing we weren't sure we would be able to identify him much less find our way around the commune he was supposed to be in. Also, we could have been barred and ignored in our search. So I talked the leader into acting as our guide and introducing us to the tractor owner.

That was, as I soon found, the smartest thing I could have done. It was still quite early in the morning when we headed down to the next hippie encampment named Toad Hill. We entered a building with a very large room and what a sight it was. It would have out exposed any Hollywood Night Club Burlesque show imaginable.

My mind boggled. I asked myself what would happen if the police raided the joint. I started to turn around to leave but our guide shook his head saying no. We were in the bedroom for dozens of guys and gals sleeping on the floor. They were all in the process of getting up and in various stages of dress, from naked, on up or was it down, I was not sure which.

A room full of flower girls who seemed to care nothing about us being there. It was hard to believe what I saw and there was no attempt on their part to cover up as we made our way through the room. Nature in the raw.

The tractor man wasn't there. We had to go to a second and third camp in our search.

The same thing all over again, with lots of good looking girls but no trace of the man we were looking for but we were directed to look for him in the barn. Again, no one objected to us being in there. Perhaps there was no age limit.

Many questions about their habitat came to mind but I thought it best not to be too nosy. However, I did ask our guide how they kept track of their women. His answer was quick and simple. "No problem, everyone switches around often."

We entered the barn and searched it for the tractor man with no luck.

It was taken for granted that he would be tending to the farm chores and indeed he was busy but not in the kind of work I imagined farmers were usually involved in every morning.

Suddenly, all three of us looked upward and said, in one voice. "The hay loft." There he was with girls a plenty. He didn't seem perturbed by our presence and the girls didn't bury themselves in the hay, out of sight. Perhaps it would be too itchy.

At any rate, he agreed to help us and we tried to get through to him that we needed him and his tractor up at the aircraft right away. I had the feeling that his mind was blocked off for some reason or should I say reasons.

We returned to the aircraft. An hour went by with no sign of the tractor so back down to that "Hippie Heaven." We found our tractor man. He had a contented looking smile on his face, alert and ready to move.

I was tempted to kid him a bit about his activities. However, I thought better of that because it might delay getting our job done. We might have been locked out of the area too. So, no jokes.

We were not long, with help from several hippies, in setting the aircraft back up on its wheels and moving it to what the leader said would be a safe place at his camp. I agreed to pay the tractor man $30.00 for his great effort. That was quite a bit of money that time but I had no choice and he knew it.

Next came their demand, in the form of compensation, for a seemingly endless list of items.

The leader, with whom we had first made contact, estimated that a ton of hay (a lot of it was actually swamp grass) had been thoroughly tramped down. They claimed to have made a great sacrifice in allowing us to dig a hole in the field to accommodate the nose wheel and its support structure in the turn over. Had we not done that, it would have been severely damaged.

Digging the hole was sacrilege to their ecology. The soil, onto which the battery acid and engine oil had dripped, would be contaminated forever, they claimed. Allowing us to deeply bury rags soiled from oil and acid clean up another sacrifice.

The Forestry had warned me that we would have trouble with that group. A casual question about what was growing in the next field might have slowed them down a bit but we could not afford to bring that up. We needed their co-operation for the safety of the aircraft, which they had not touched.

The discussions and haggling over a dollar figure went on. They demanded a high figure and I worked on trying to have them be reasonable. I was in a tight spot, a very unusual one, and I did not question the ownership of the property because the aircraft was going to have to be left on it until transported out.

The settlement had to be willingly accepted by them or I could see trouble later on. Eventually we agreed on a sum of $100.00, which took care of their labour, property loss and effort on their part, as they called it.

What we had actually bought was safety for the aircraft as part of the deal included them keeping a close watch on the machine while it was in their custody, so to speak. I had a better feeling of sincerity about that group and their leader we had contacted at the onset than the hippies at the other communes farther down the hill.

We were finished for the moment and left them thinking I would be returning for the aircraft shortly but I hadn't planned that part yet.

We returned to Castlegar where I caught a flight to Vancouver. It had been, in many respects, a very successful trip when I considered how a large group like that might have acted negatively. The aircraft could have been vandalized, if nothing else.

I had heard many things said about hippies, but that direct brief association was an eye opener and made it difficult to believe people would live like that. Perhaps I was too naïve. I must say that they were polite and courteous to us.

The aircraft could have been made flyable, but it was out of the question to use that field to fly out from and there were no suitable areas nearby.

Al Beaulieu in Vancouver used my trailer and hauled the machine to B.C. Central Air Services in Kamloops for permanent repairs.

Come to think of it, I never did ask that Romeo for a report on his activities up there, other than taking care of the aircraft.

I think it appropriate to say that as a result of my investigation into the reason for a landing at that village I was totally satisfied that the pilot had no choice. He had not planned such a visit.

That was the finish of a grand working assignment and floor show provided and paid for the generous Underwriters of the British Aviation Insurance Company.

chapter nine

Single Otter through ice in Northwest Territories

A single engine de Havilland Otter with registration CF-ITS had gone through the ice on a lake positioned about half way between Uranium City, and Great Slave Lake.

I received a call from Phil Clayton in Edmonton who explained that the aircraft was in a very precarious position with only the wings, which were flat on the ice, preventing it from sinking completely. Phil reminded me that spring was on its way and if Mother Nature speeded up the process we would be in big trouble.

It was the end of the first week of May. And as a general rule, lakes in the northern areas are free of ice, or at least open enough for float planes to use, by May 24. I lost no time in getting to Uranium City in northern Saskatchewan, the base out of which the Otter operated. There, I obtained more details on the ice conditions and disposition of the aircraft from Ms. Jean Buck, a very pleasant and capable lady in charge of the Gateway Aviation office. Jean then sent a radio message to their men at the accident site advising them that I, the one who had salvaged another of their Otters from the Redstone River the previous year, was in her office and would be up there shortly.

I felt a little uneasy with that announcement because it sounded too much like I was the answer to their problem but I realized that Jean had not said it in that context. She was simply identifying me.

Maintenance personnel, on site, reported that a long stretch of ice would have to be taken out to float the aircraft to shore because the ice was too weak to support an "A" frame or other structure to lift the aircraft. That meant the ice would have to be blasted. Fortunately the services of a powder man (an explosive expert) from the uranium mine were available.

A Single Otter aircraft was loaded with a barrel of fuel, oil and equipment including 14 boxes of 40 percent dynamite and a box of 500 electric caps.

I was concerned about the caps in the event we were to have an in flight problem and a possible forced landing. The explosive chap said that the safest way to handle them was for him to sit on them and if there was a problem he would pass them up to me to throw them out the window. That sounded reasonable to both the pilot and myself but we would have to manoeuver the aircraft, in such an event, so the box would not strike any part of the plane.

Our destination was in that area of the North West Territories north of Saskatchewan and south of Great Slave Lake containing a mass of lakes large and small.

The flight was completed without incident and

we landed on a lake with lots of open water, close to the one we were destined for. A helicopter from an exploration camp, on the shore of the lake to which we were heading, transported us and the cargo to the camp.

The Otter we were to rescue, was quite some distance off shore. The ice had started melting around some of the shore line leaving in some places, fairly wide strips of open water.

Ron Polaski, an engineer and pilot who was in charge of several men from the Aircraft Charter Company's base of operation in Uranium City, took me out to the distressed aircraft via helicopter. The Otter had sunk through the ice with the fuselage (body) in the water including the engine and the wings were flat on the surface of the ice.

There were no signs of serious airframe damage except the left wing tip which was bent upward a small degree. Steel fuel drums had been placed alongside the fuselage to prevent it from sinking if the ice, supporting the wings, gave way.

The pilot explained that he had made a good landing and at the end of the landing run had come to a complete stop when suddenly the left wheel broke through the ice. He shut off the engine and scrambled out of the aircraft in complete disbelief of what had happened.

The aircraft had continued to settle into the water as the ice failed, until the wings were flat on the ice surface. It was the broad expanse of the wings resting on unbroken ice that prevented the complete aircraft from going to the bottom of the lake.

I think it should be pointed out at this juncture that pilots who fly fixed wing aircraft in areas subjected to the freezing over of rivers and lakes are often confronted with having to decide whether or not the ice is safe for a landing. Quite often there is no one on the ground to provide any information. If there is radio communication from a ground station the information he receives might not apply to a large area that he may have to use for a landing. There could be weak spots. He is, so to speak, damned if he decides not to make a landing and can be damned if he proceeds with a landing and has an accident.

The client or customer wants the service completed and the operator of the aircraft wants the revenue for a completed trip. Added to this and

perhaps more important to the pilot is how his decision will affect his reputation especially if he is a relatively new pilot with a low number of flying hours.

It appears that the failure of the ice under the wheel was the result of an unusual circumstance involving wildlife. The pilot reported that he had had enough time to check the ice around the sunken wheel before it gave way completely. He said there was a distinct dark colouring and traces of manure.

It was concluded that a caribou, at an earlier date, had stopped to relieve itself and left a patch of droppings for nature to take care of them. The sun rays are drawn to dark colouring and apparently this was no exception to the fact and led to the weakening of the ice under the droppings at a much faster rate than in the surrounding areas.

(left); Otter through fast rotting ice   (right); Rare photo of candle ice that forms in advanced stages of rotting ice.

It was a bit of bad luck that the aircraft came to a stop with the wheel directly on that spot. The accident that followed was a most unfortunate one over which the pilot had no control of the circumstances leading up to it.

Regarding the effect that dark colouring has in attracting the rays of the sun, it might be of interest to mention that knowledge was occasionally put to good practical use. There were times when exploration companies wanted to speed up Nature's spring melting of ice on a lake to make it accessible for seaplanes sooner than it would normally be. This was done during what I called "The In-between Season", it was neither winter nor summer. The process called for the spreading of soot over the ice to speed up the melting.

The ice, in our situation was in an advanced stage of deterioration commonly known as candle ice. Ice rot starts at it's bottom surface and works upward, leaving a candle like formation. At the time of my inspection, these candle shaped sections were from 18 to 24 inches long. The upper or top part of the ice, that we were standing on, was only three or four inches thick and not in very good condition.

We agreed that the ice was in too dangerous a condition to lift the aircraft up onto its surface and further, it would be a matter of only a few days before the ice would fail completely and the aircraft could go to the bottom of the lake. We had to get the aircraft to shore. A canal would have to be made between the aircraft and shore by blasting

out ice and then we could walk along it's edge to guide and push the aircraft along while holding onto the wing tips. The fuel drums under the wings were replaced with helicopter pontoons, that we had brought with us, to provide greater flotation and lift the wings free of the ice.

We started near the shore and blew out the first section of ice. Our powder man was most willing to show some of us how to set the dynamite. Shallow depressions were cut out in the ice surface

Dynamite set in blasting lines.

equal in length to that of a stick of dynamite and a little deeper than the thickness of a stick. Then one and a half sticks of dynamite and a cap were wired and set into each depression. There were three rows of these, one for each edge and one down the centre.

The last thing to be done was to make one axe cut in the bottom of each depression to let water in to cover the charge. A small amount of water covering the dynamite charge prevents all the explosive force from going skyward. It directs a portion of the blast sideways and downward whereas without any water coverage all the force goes upward.

I considered the channel, we were blasting out, to be too wide. It would be too dangerous for men to walk along the edge of the ice holding onto the wing tips to guide the machine to shore as it was almost equal to the wing span. The upper part of the ice was weak and dangerous to walk on. Several of us broke through but escaped with only a wet foot. The blasting, of course, shattered some of the ice we would be walking on.

My suggestions that we should reduce the channel width in the remaining detonations fell on deaf ears of Gateway's crew chief. However, a little later on, one of his men would prove my point.

Next morning we were up by 3 a.m. and working by 4 a.m. The second section of ice was blown out at 5:30 am. The helicopter, with it's large pontoons, was used to taxi behind the broken ice, pushing it into the open shoreline waters clear of our operation. We had also used it, at times, to transport us and the equipment on and off the ice until we found a narrow stretch of shore water, over which we felled trees to form a bridge.

A couple of us started blasting a narrower channel from the aircraft end of the project and as close to the machine as was safe. It had frozen hard during the night, leaving new ice almost thick enough to walk on. Later we had a heavy snowfall and strong winds. We did our final blasting with 3 boxes of dynamite, which also shook up the new ice in the previous day's blast areas. We quit early because of a strong wind that could have started the weak ice rippling and breaking up with us on it. It had been a wild day out there on questionable ice.

The next day we hand cut and chopped the last 40 feet of ice to the aircraft and all the ice around it. The Otter was then floated down the channel, to the shore where it was winched up onto solid ground. The tail rotor of the helicopter had struck a tree, putting it out of service. I must say that the pilot, who flew for Elsin, worked with us as hard as any one. He was a big help.

While we were moving the Otter toward shore and in that stretch of the channel that I had argued was too wide for safety, a man, reaching out to the left wing tip, fell into the water.

There was a great scramble to get him out and up to the camp before he was frozen solid. He had proven my point and it could have been fatal – so unnecessary.

The engine, at the time of the sinking, was not operating. It had had time enough to cool down below a critical temperature before it became submerged. Experience from previous similar cold water submersions led me to believe that the present engine had not been damaged.

We would, to return the engine to an operational status, use previously successful procedures including drying out the ignition system, changing oil and flushing out the fuel system.

The engine performed 100 percent. Luckily, the instruments and radios had not been submerged.

The only structural damage of any consequence was in the left wing tip area where the front spar was bent upward about 18 inches. That was the result of its contact with the ice as the left wheel settled into the water.

Inspection of the aileron\flap installation and its controls did not reveal any abnormalities and the rear spar had not been disturbed. That was a big plus.

The deformed area of the front spar was very closely inspected. No cracks or visual evidence of over stressed metal could be found. I concluded that the deformity would not be a problem for the ferry flight other than the application of a little aileron would be needed to compensate for a small amount of added drag and loss of lift.

I had learned, from de Havilland, in conjunction with an earlier job, on Max Ward's Otter, that there is a very small wing load at the tip. Useful information in making a decision but not to be used in a thoughtless manner.

I proved the safety of the wing by going out on to

(left); Floating Otter out in a 2,000 foot blasted out channel. (right); Otter lifting off our rough land air strip.

the tip and using my weight to rock it up and down which in turn, also rocked the whole aircraft vigorously. Some might say it seemed like an attempt to break the tip off. Well, if it was weak enough, then better there than in the air. Ron who was to fly the aircraft, did the same thing and after another inspection, seemed to feel better about it and agreed that it was safe for a flight. If a temporary repair had been needed, additional tools, metal repair materials and other miscellaneous items would have had to have been flown into us with considerable delay. So we were lucky in not having to make a temporary repair. But, I might add, it would have been done if there had been even the slightest doubt about the wing being safe.

We had not discussed how the aircraft was to be flown out from there. Our prime objective up until then had been to get it safely on shore. If floats (pontoons) were to be used, a set would have had to be flown in as well as timbers or steel tubing for an 'A' frame that would have been needed to lift the machine. The local trees were too small and scrubby for the job.

It could also have been a few days of waiting for the ice to go out enough to provide safe open water for an aircraft to land with that freight. Then we could have still been hampered by ice flows, like small icebergs. Converting the aircraft into a seaplane could have extended the salvage operation at least another week providing we didn't get a series of cold nights that would slow down the ice thawing process.

It was suggested that an airstrip be made along the shore line which was, in fact quite level. A fellow by the name of Ron O Brien was enthusiastic about it. That was indeed, the way to go. Ron Palaski who would be flying the aircraft, didn't reply to that idea immediately but next morning he suggested that an air strip should be built.

We cut down a line of stunted northern spruce trees level with the ground consisting of sand and dirt. Luckily there were no large rocks to move. I signed the aircraft log book certifying it as being fit for a ferry flight to Edmonton for permanent repairs as was my usual practice.

Ron Polaski did a full and thorough engine preflight warm up. The engine performed beautifully and following that he positioned the aircraft at the end of the strip. Then with brakes on he advanced the throttle to take off rpm, released the brakes and made an Aircraft Carrier type take off in a short run. That was May 12.

It was another 2 days before I could get out to Uranium City via a de Havilland Beaver seaplane. I generally flew out on the ferry flights but this time the lowest take off weight possible was most important so I stayed behind.

Strong winds, in the meantime, had broken up the ice and there was lots of open water with floating islands of ice that could complicate a seaplane operation. We had finished the salvage operation with very little time to spare, a bit too close for comfort. It was getting close to that magic date May 24 and springtime. The timing between getting the aircraft safely on shore before the ice totally failed, reminded me of the close call we had with one of Gateway's Otters on th Red Stone River less than a year earlier.

One evening prior to our departure from the lake we talked about our various jobs and experiences. Our Powder Man, regretfully I don't recall his name, had a most interesting story to tell.

Our conversation had, to some degree, centered on aircraft repairs and other similar projects. He joined in on the discussions saying that his birth place was Poland and he was in the Polish army at the beginning of World War II. He hated Germans and Russians. One lot had driven him in one direction and the other had chased him back the opposite way. He escaped from the country, joined the British 8th. Army and fought in North Africa. His classification was that of an explosive expert. His main job was to defuse enemy bombs and other explosives to examine them for their secrets, then blow them up.

After the war and to that day he worked as an explosive specialist for a mining company. He paused for a moment and then looked at us. He was almost in tears. "You know fellas," and he paused, "I have never repaired or built anything in my life. I have blown everything up." We were all subdued by that statement and tried to make him feel better but I am afraid we were not very successful.

I got a flight out to Lac La Biche Saturday May 15, then down to Edmonton where I met up with Phil Clayton and John Gladstone, the Insurance Adjuster and Underwriter in that order and for whom I had just completed the salvage job.

They told me that the aircraft had made a safe and uneventful flight to Edmonton. Another job completed with a pleasant ending.

I arrived in Vancouver that night and on Monday both Phil and Dick Hicks in Edmonton had another job to be done and I left home again on Tuesday on another challenge. Or adventure??

At a later date I had just finished breakfast in the McKenzie Hotel in Inuvik, N.W.T. when someone called me by name. I was embarrassed at not knowing his name. He said that we had met while removing an Otter from the ice north of Saskatchewan.

I instantly recalled the job and we talked about it for a few minutes. Then I mentioned that we had almost lost a man because too much ice had been blown out and a fellow fell into the lake. He loudly replied with a laugh "YES, THAT WAS ME." It's a small world indeed.

chapter ten

Single Otter on frozen Yehenika Lake

I haven't checked it out, but it seems that I got more crash calls on Friday than any other day. One Friday morning, April 21, 1967, I got word that a wheel/ski equipped single Otter with registration CF-ROW had been damaged in a landing accident on ice and snow covered Yehenika Lake approximately 250 miles north of Terrace, B.C., near the Stikine River. I caught a flight out in the afternoon and was in Terrace before nightfall with sleeping bag and winter clothing. Winter had left Vancouver but it surely was dragging its feet in departing the northern regions.

Garry Reame of Transprovincial Air Carriers was on the same flight and he drove me to the hotel. After dinner Doug Chappel and Peter Dychakowski, also of T.P.A. met with me to discuss the damage I'd be dealing with. They had been into the accident site to pick up the pilot and had taken time to look the aircraft over and they had a good briefing from the pilot.

Peter was the Chief Engineer for T.P.A. and he had a well-deserved reputation as an efficient technician. He was a "let's get it done" kind of guy so it wasn't surprising that he had brought back the broken landing gear leg and bent wheel/ski. He had already ordered a new leg and he had the shop working on repairs to the wheel/ski. Both were vital to getting the aircraft ready for a ferry flight and time was precious; a quick spring thaw could hit and the ice could rot on the lake before we were ready. Then we would have another serious problem.

The following morning, Roy Jobling, Government Accident Investigator, arrived in Terrace enroute to inspect the crashed Otter. I shared flight costs with Roy to go in and do my required inspection for the insurance coverage.

The damage was extensive; two bent propeller blades, the outer five feet of the right wing bent up and both spars broken, the inboard section of the rear spar broken near the fuselage and the cabin roof was buckled. Less serious, non-crucial damage was visible on various parts of the aircraft. We would be very busy for a few days for sure.

Weather conditions worsened with strong winds and snow very nearly preventing us from our return flight take off. Luckily, we landed in Terrace before dark but prospects for getting back to the crash scene on Sunday or Monday were not good.

Peter had found a loaner landing gear leg and his shop crew had repaired the wheel/ski unit. We had everything ready to back

and do the repairs except for the replacement propeller we had ordered from Vancouver. Weather was holding up incoming flights. After a morning of thumb twiddling, we finally found out it had been lost in transit. We decided to go without it and get on with repairing the wings and fuselage.

A single Otter was loaded with all our camping (survival?) gear, repair materials and tools. The weather eased a little and we decided we could make it to the crash site. Peter and I would have been happier with a bit more improvement but crossed our fingers and went along with Doug. Off to Yehenika Lake...without the propeller.

A low cloud condition prevailed for the duration of the flight but it remained high enough so that our pilot didn't have to fly around trees. We got to Yehenika Lake by late afternoon. A nice landing

Meal time. Left to Right: Peter Dychakowski, Ron Wells, and Doug Chappel.

was made on the lake in five feet of snow and we had to use snowshoes while transferring our load of goods into the cabin of the damaged aircraft that would be our home for a few days.

Camp was set up quickly. We put our bedrolls down in the cargo section of the aircraft and placed the cooking toys under the shelter of the undamaged wing. That certainly beat putting up a tent among the spruce trees.

Work began on the Otter as soon as our transport was safely in the air and on the way back to Terrace.

The first project was installation of the landing gear leg and ski which went very well and the aircraft was then sitting reasonably level. We finished the task before night fall and we were able to serve ourselves a hot dinner and enjoy it while there was daylight. Early to bed.

Structural repairs to the vital areas of the fuselage were first on the list after breakfast. These were now routine jobs for me and our team got them taken care of without difficulty.

The propeller problem was a different story. Changing blades in a constant speed propeller out in the bush was one thing; but straightening blades out in the bush is another matter all together. A real challenge. Fortunately, one of the blades was not damaged, providing a guide for straightening the other two.

Peter suggested we have a go at straightening the bent blades. A new experience for both of us. I had spent time in propeller shops and had witnessed some straightening of bends that came within the limits of cold straightening.

A propeller repair specialist, known to most of us as Clarky, was always ready to explain and show us what could be done. I dipped into my memory bank and came up with Clarky's method for dealing with our problem.

Looking back, I realize a valuable body of knowledge most of us in the business acquired was accumulated in sessions with generous maintenance engineers such as Clarky, Harold Rogers and Gordy Peters. Their tips relieved us of the stress of learning these techniques by trial and error.

I had checked the prop blades for stretch lines in the curves of the deformities that would cancel out the straightening idea; there were none. The bends were of a gentle nature and extended backwards only a short distance. I decided it could be safely done and the necessary tools had been included in our load.

Clarky's method of taking a gentle kink out of a prop blade was really quite simple; having the eye that told you it was right made the difference.

The technique was to treat the blade like a bow, attaching one end of a cable to the base and the other to the tip, leaving enough slack to insert a small hydraulic jack between the cable and the blade. The jack is then tightened against the outer arc of the bend. As the pressure of the jack is increased, the tip of the blade is pulled back into line. By moving the jack inch by inch along the arc and taking the bend out in small increments the blade is brought back to its original configuration without subjecting the metal to excesses that would reduce its stress qualities. In the bush, without shop mounted test equipment this has to be done by eye.

Peter and I took on the blade job while Doug tackled a section of the damaged fuselage. When one of us needed extra hands the others dropped their task and helped. This type of teamwork made the repairs go faster.

Going between each job to help wasn't easy because the heavy wet snow made it impossible to move about without snowshoes. Picture yourself playing tennis wearing hip waders and you will have some idea of the effort required.

My experience repairing Max Ward's Otter on Baffin Island came in handy when we started to restore the wing. We followed the same process with the main spar.

We worked from daybreak to dark every day, still haunted by the fact that spring could replace winter in minutes at that latitude, putting us in a real pickle; a repaired aircraft on skis and no snow.

With a couple of hours to spare we finished all the repairs on the third day. We shoveled a lot of snow, got down to the skis and cleared a space to move the aircraft around a bit. The engine was run up and the propeller operated. It was rough at low revs but smoothed out with an increase in power.

(left); Propeller blades a bit bent   (right); Our northern propeller shop straightening bent blades. Very smooth in flight.

I was not sure that the bush repaired prop would be reliable, so Doug and I decided a quick test flight was in order to evaluate the prop's performance at cruising speed. Full power was needed to move the aircraft as the skis ploughed up through the snow. At low revs the vibration made the instruments impossible to read; at higher revs centrifugal force pulled the repaired blade tips straight as they bit the air and the instruments ceased being a blur.

Doug made his usual nice landing, pronounced the Otter ready to go and we loaded all our equipment and took of for Terrace. Not on a straight line; storms and rough air made a direct flight impossible. As a result we saw a lot more country but we landed before dark.

That evening was enjoyed in the company of old friend Ron Wells. He showed me slides he had taken of the Arctic. They were great, evidence that he had the eye of a fine artist as well as a fine pilot.

Several of the pictures brought back memories of the two of us bringing out a Cessna 185 in November 1964. What a trip that was.

The weather was terrible; swirling snow, wind gusts and low cloud. We tried one mountain pass and couldn't get through. Didn't upset Ron. He said, "I know another one." So back we went, turned down the Porcupine River to another dead end of solid cloud. Ron wasn't a bit excited as he turned the aircraft around, slowly relit his cigar and said in his calm, unruffled manner,

"I know another one." I was hoping he wouldn't run out of escape routes. I wasn't asking but I was counting. He wheeled into the Iskut River. The air was bumpier than a corduroy road and I thought my stomach was going to object to the punishment at any moment but there were no clouds and we were out of the trap. My knuckles go white just thinking about it. Our little ride from Yehenika Lake was a buggy ride in the park in comparison.

Next morning started with an early swim in the hot mineral waters followed by a big leisurely breakfast. After making several phone calls dealing with other problems and snarling at the people who still hadn't found our missing replacement prop, Doug, Garry Ream and I, boarded the Otter and started our ferry flight to Vancouver.

The weather was very bad. Snow storms and head winds caused us to back track and circle several times. With daylight fading we had to settle with overnighting in Williams Lake in the Caribou.

The following morning we were off to Vancouver. Great weather all the way and no aircraft problems.

It was the end of April and I got word that spring had hit Yehenika Lake. Our hard work had saved us from a nightmare.

There is a feel good ending to this salvage. Clarky called from the prop shop to tell me he was having trouble deciding which two of the three blades we had straightened. I think he was telling a friendly white lie.

chapter eleven

Territorial Airways Limited

a unique Beaver retrieval

Winter had a firm grip on the northern areas of the country when John Rolls took off from Ross River in a wheel ski equipped de Havilland Beaver Aircraft, CF-FHZ. He was on a charter flight, north to the MacMillan Pass area in the Mackenzie Mountains of the North West Territories.

Mac Pass, as it was commonly called, is approximately 300 air miles north east of Whitehorse, Yukon with Ross River at about mid way.

Unfortunately, John, with a load of fuel and two passengers, had been caught in a sudden change of wind speed and direction as he prepared to land on the Mac Pass airstrip.

Apparently, the landing finished up in a ground loop, which is an uncontrollable change in direction with the aircraft going sideways. That manoeuver often causes damage to the landing gear and at least one wing.

I was appointed by John Gladstone of the British Aviation Insurance Co. to proceed as quickly as possible to the accident site, to investigate the problem as an insurance adjuster and an aircraft salvager.

I have always had a great deal of respect for those people who worked in the aviation charter business in our northern areas, especially during the winter periods. Those who took the big step in setting up an air charter business displayed the courage and determination needed to face the sacrifices and obstacles that so often followed.

The ground work of those ventures varied considerably from one to another and that of Terr-Air was a typical struggle with some originality. Both John and his brother Phil, were not short of energy and ambition. But apparently money, as it has been in so many instances, was another matter.

It appears that at least a portion of the money needed to buy the first aircraft was obtained from the Canadian Government. That source of income was not new, but their approach to obtaining it certainly was, I thought, a very unique one.

I do not know how long it took them to earn the needed funds, but they did it by cutting wood for the Federal Government Department of Indian Affairs. The wood was then distributed to the local Native Indians for their winter heating needs.

That fundraising project was not only original but interesting in other aspects.

The Pacific Western Airlines flight to Whitehorse was plagued with poor weather at Fort St. John and Fort Nelson causing delays and arriving at Whitehorse well after dark.

Following a phone call to John Rolls I spent a nice evening with Bud and Jeanne Harbottle whom I spoke of in an earlier venture. I also met Al Warner again and his wife Iris. That was great because Al and I had been together in the Fleet Air Arm of the Royal Navy during the war years. Al had also been on escort duty on the Murmansk,

(left); Grading a ramp up to a USA army junked sleigh   (right); Beaver loaded for trip down the Canol Road to Ross River.

Russia supply run. He returned home a little earlier than me and upon arriving in Vancouver he took a dozen red roses to Dorothy, then, my Fiancee and later my wife. He presented them as coming from me, a fine gesture that describes Al very well.

I waited all day, hoping for better weather for a flight to Mac Pass.

Al Frowler and Bob Cook, two well respected inspectors from the Edmonton based Ministry of Transport Accident Investigation Division, learned that I was in town on the Terr-Air problem. Those fellows had the log books for the damaged aircraft and knew that I would need to inspect them for my investigation purposes.

They tracked me down so I could do just that. They had been to Ross River but, because of poor weather, had not been able to proceed any further. Now they had a more pressing and serious problem to attend to some distance away, along the Alaska Highway. Their thoughtfulness and willingness to help me with my investigation for the Insurance Company was typical of them and very much appreciated I can tell you. It was an absolute necessity for me to inspect the books on those occasions but sadly enough there was the odd inspector in the system who made it difficult if he got his hands on the logs first as was too often the case.

A very pleasant evening was spent with them, as I recall.

It was clear that Mother Nature intended to make it more awkward by sending a fast moving colder system at us. That night it was -55 degrees Fahrenheit in Dawson City which is approximately 175 kilometers, in a straight line, to the north.

The following day the weather conditions had improved enough to permit a flight into the accident scene via Yukon Air. We picked up John Rolls in Ross River en route to the Hudson Bay Mining air strip in Mac Pass which is at an altitude of approximately 4500 feet above sea level. On our arrival the temperature was about minus 30 degrees Fahrenheit with a stiff breeze.

The mining people were so helpful especially Don Huppe of Canadian Mine Services, who had been a passenger in the accident. We used their truck for protection from the wind while I made written notes and changed camera film.

My investigation included statements from passengers, one of whom was Don Huppe. They spoke well of John's efforts in fighting a sudden increase in the poor weather conditions as he approached the air strip for a touch down. Increasing snow and poor light set up a white out type situation and one of the wheel/skiis caught a mound of snow, that he had not seen, and which whipped the aircraft around in a circle during the landing run. As I had suspected, the right hand landing gear leg was damaged and both the right wing and rear section of the fuselage would need extensive repairs.

When the inspection of the damage had been completed we returned to Ross River and the home of John and his wife Margie. John's brother Phil came over and our conversation settled on the situation of the Beaver and how best to retrieve it. The two most common methods used, in out of the way locations, is either make temporary repairs and fly out or lift the machine out with a helicopter.

The helicopter method was not considered, firstly, because there was not a large enough one in the Whitehorse area and secondly, the winds in the mountains would make it too dangerous to give it a second thought.

The accident site was not totally cut off from civilization as it was in so many cases. There was a road to Ross River although, at that time, deep snow made it impassable, by truck, for its approximately 140 miles. The road access canceled out the thought of making the damaged machine ready for a flight. We agreed that the most practical procedure would be to disassemble the aircraft, load it on a sleigh and tow it to Ross River where it would then be loaded on a truck and taken to Vancouver for repairs.

Now came the big question. Where could we find a large enough sleigh and maybe more important, what would we tow it with?

John and Phil knew that part of the country very well and while they did not think the exploration people at Mac Pass had a large enough sleigh, they were sure one could be found at an old military equipment dump a little farther up the Canol (Canadian Oil) Road. If not, we could build a stone boat type of sled.

We would approach the exploration people about the possibility of renting a cat to do the towing and return it in the Spring by truck.

I should explain, for those of you who are not familiar with that part of Yukon and the North West Territories, that the Canol Road was built during WWII. It was constructed and paid for by the U.S. Military after that country entered the war. Its purpose was to run a pipe line from the oil fields of Norman Wells, situated on the MacKenzie River in the North West Territories, 1500 kilometers south to Whitehorse, Yukon to a refinery, they built. The Americans wanted to have fuel available for their equipment in the defense of Alaska. Japan had already made a landing on the end of the Aleutian Islands.

At a much later date it has been revealed that there was, apparently, much contention in the American Government circles over the wisdom and value of building the pipeline. It was started in 1942 and completed in 1943. The line produced at capacity from April 1944 to March 1945 and was officially abandoned as war surplus in June of that year.

Huge amounts of road and pipe line construction equipment including trucks of all kinds and an assortment of heavy equipment were brought in for the job and when the war ended it was not taken out. It was left in large depots like huge junk yards at many locations along the road. Those eye sores are still there at the time of this writing.

No one was supposed to touch those vehicles

but there were stories about how one or more transportation companies got their start with some of the trucks. True? I don't know.

John and Phil did not need any help from me in trying to locate or scrounge a sleigh but had they not been available and able, I would surely have had to do it. In the meantime, I had received word from Phil Clayton, an adjuster in Edmonton, that I was needed on several other problems. They could be fitted in very well in the few days it would take John and Phil to find a sleigh and set it up.

An interesting event, at least it was for me coming from Vancouver, took place while Margie was cooking dinner. She called out, to John, saying the flame in the burner of the stove was going down and was almost out. John jumped up and took a kettle of hot water out the kitchen door which he left wide open as he poured the water on the propane tank pipe, leading into the house, to thaw it out. The low temperature had started to convert the propane gas back into it's normal liquid form, as it is in the tank.

While he was doing that, the kitchen, from the door to its very end was engulfed in solid fog with everything within it, completely invisible. The outside temperature was minus 60 degrees Fahenheit.

As soon as John had warmed up the pipe the propane reverted back to a gaseous state and Margie was back in business, preparing dinner. A very productive and enjoyable evening came to an end all too soon and off to bed we went.

The next morning was another new adventure for me with the minus 60 degrees Fahenheit cold. I helped John in the getting his truck started.

We were heating the engine from underneath with a tiger torch which is a propane torch with a very wide flame spreader tip. The engine turned completely white. What a sight for me, coming from Vancouver, where it was a rarity for the thermometer to drop to any where near 0 degrees. We were on our fourth battery before we had a good sign of a start. The next problem was with the engine coolant system because the anti freeze would not circulate. It had jelled and lost it fluidity.

It took time but eventually we won and had the engine running. During that period, I met John's and Phil's father Jack who had worked as an aircraft engineer for Pacific Western Airlines at an earlier date. He had a hobby of panning for gold. I had several visits to that area in the years that followed and always enjoyed listening to Jack explain his advanced procedures on gold panning. John's mother was always a joy to see and talk to and on later trips I stayed at their hotel in Ross River.

I recall that Rene Leduc, an aircraft charter pilot and Don Huppe picked me up for a flight to Whitehorse. Don introduced me to Russ McIntosh of Hudson Bay Mining Co. I then had the opportunity to ask about the availability of a Caterpillar Tractor as we were certainly going to need one. Both Don and Russ were anxious to help so a phone call to John assured him of the availability of a cat when it was needed to pull a sleigh to the air strip, if one was found.

I caught a C.P.A. flight to Edmonton, arriving there after 12 p.m. because of weather delays. There was Phil Clayton, an adjuster who worked with Dick Hicks, waiting for me to take me to his home. That was always a nice way to end a trip. We sat in his living room for an hour or more having a drink and talking. Finally his wife, Agnes, came staggering into the room in her night attire and suggested we go to bed and call it a night. We did just that.

Next morning Agnes set up a nice breakfast and off we went to meet with John Gladstone, manager of the western office for the British Aviation Insurance Company. They had some problems between there and Vancouver that I was to attend to. The afternoon was spent with Dick Hicks re a couple of troublesome files.

I left Edmonton for Calgary, Kelowna and Vancouver.

I no sooner arrived home than I had a trip up the coast where a sea plane was upside down and badly damaged. We turned it right side up, serviced electrical and instrument systems for the salt water soaking and operated the engine. The wings were removed and machine was loaded onto the deck of a West Coast Ferry for transport to Vancouver.

Time seemed to fly by so quickly. Shortly after getting back to Vancouver, from that latest problem, I had a call from John Rolls. They had located and moved a large sleigh to the airstrip and were busy putting a deck on it.

I left for Whitehorse and on arrival contacted Don Huppe. It was now -29 degrees F. but at Mayo, approximately 250 miles as the crow flies, directly north, it was -64 degrees F. and there was reason to believe that that low temperature could move to Ross River where it was then -54 degrees F.

Arrangements were made for the use of a charter aircraft into which we loaded rope and packing material such as a lot of mattresses to protect the wings etc. from damage on the sleigh and later, a truck. A few barrels of Fuel were also taken for the cat. Perhaps a more important package was a box of chocolates for John's wife Margie.

Don Huppe went with me on the flight to Mac Pass with a brief stop in Ross River.

As soon as the aircraft was unloaded it was again filled with the mine operators' equipment for the return trip to Whitehorse. That was done as a favour to Don, a small one compared to his generosity in my direction. We had a nice evening at the camp.

It was now January 29 and the mining operation was slated to close down, for the rest of the winter at the end of the month.

I should mention, as a point of interest, that there were a large number of wolves in that area. They were classed as timber wolves, huge animals with legs like small fence posts. They offered us no problem contrary to what many people, who read this, may imagine or think. They were always an interesting animal to see.

The sleigh that John had located and brought down from some distance up the Canol Road was a very large, heavy one, a beauty for our job. The decking that we needed, was well under way when I returned. The sleigh had originally been the property of the American Army and abandoned in one of the junk yards I mentioned earlier.

We set up camp in a shack at the edge of the airstrip which was much better than tenting. The temperature was not too bad at a steady -30 degrees F. even though we were at 4000 feet above sea level but here was the clincher. We had a wind of about 25 to 30 M.P.H. that made it a lot colder for us. In those days the wind chill factor was not used to establish a lower temperature reading. It was as cold as we felt. However, in the calculations, used today, it was about -66 degrees Fahrenheit.

We located some old construction lumber from a demolished shed and used it for a shield from the wind while disassembling the aircraft. I found an 8 foot x 4 foot sheet of plywood with 2" x 4" framing wood nailed to its four edges. It was perfect for a wind shield and I was able to move it into position, on my own by lifting one edge. The wind did the rest of the lifting and held the assembly at 45 degrees while I moved it to the aircraft.

The fur on our parkas, around our faces, was very frosty looking and I had frost on my eye lashes.

We did not wear wool head gear with openings for eyes and mouth such as one sees in a movie. However, we watched each other for signs of noses and ear lobes turning white. That would indicate frost bite.

I well remember that once I had cooled down during the mornings I did not go into the shack for coffee because I would have to go through the cooling down process all over again. We did not stop for lunch either. I had very good Arctic clothes too, padded over pants and a Woods eider down filled parka with a heavy wool sweater and shirt and I could still feel the wind chill through all that a little bit.

John, Phil and a fellow named Jerry continued with the decking of the sleigh which was done up at the mine, with electric power. I worked on the disassembly of the aircraft which was slow while keeping my back to the wind.

We were over the hump on the decking and disassembly work when John had to return to Ross River to move some men out of a bush camp.

Finally the sleigh was pulled down to the airstrip and the wings were removed from the aircraft. All that was needed then was to get the aircraft up on to the sleigh. That was done by building a snow ramp with the cat and packing it down. Then the aircraft was pulled and maneuvered up on the to sleigh with cat power. The wings were set in place then Phil and I got on with securing and packing the complete load to prevent chaffing damage. All was set to move as soon as John returned.

Late that afternoon Don Huppe and Jerry took

the cat down the road for about 5 or 6 miles, clearing out a series of glaciers and slides. That section was the worst part of the whole road and their thoughtfulness gave the journey to Ross River a good start. It was very late when they returned.

John arrived back next day with more fuel plus groceries and camping equipment. We had made a deal with the owners of the cat to use it to tow the loaded sleigh to Ross River. We would pay for the fuel and operators time then the owners would have the machine in Ross River where it could be given maintenance for the next season's operation. That was indeed an excellent arrangement for us.

It was then February 1. The mining camp closed down and the sleigh ride south to Ross River began for John, Phil and Jerry. I had been notified of two other complicated problems in the Whitehorse area and with a request, from the same insurance company that covered John's loss, that I get to them as soon as possible.

It was and still is very important to attend to the needs of an aircraft owner, following an accident, and put the wheels in motion for his recovery from the loss, with the least loss of time.

Three very reliable fellows would be moving the aircraft to Ross River and a fourth body, me, was not needed so I left for Whitehorse. Quite frankly, I would have liked to have gone with them in spite of the hardships they endured.

I think it was the first night on the trail that a wolverine got at the food that had been stowed on the top of the cat roof, hopefully, out of reach of predators. What was not eaten was left with the foul scent excreted by the animal, commonly call the Skunk Bear.

Everyone went hungry for while and in the interim the fuel injector shaft, of the cat's engine, broke. Luckily, and not surprising, their ingenuity took over and it was repaired by binding and washering it up so that the trip could be continued but at a slower pace, about 5 m.p.h.

A moose put in an appearance on the road and was promptly shot for much needed food.

At an earlier date, Phil Rolls had had to leave his broken down truck alongside the road. This was added to the tow train.

The story behind the abandoned truck went like this: Phil had gone up the Canol Road to gather up and haul some pack horses back to Ross River. After he had found the horses he had a break down in the drive system of the truck. There was nothing he could do but walk to Ross River with the horses.

It was late in the season and one or two of the animals were in poor condition so he fed them and waited with them for a few days hoping they would recover. However, one did not respond enough to walk out so he had to shoot it. I do not recall how long it took him, in his walk to Ross River but he finally made it over the one hundred plus miles. That must have been a rough journey without camping gear. There were, no doubt, some interesting side notes in the trip but I have no knowledge of them.

John had thought they would finish the trip by Wednesday but when Friday rolled around with no sign of them we became very concerned. Margie said all radio signals were out even if they tried to call. I was completely satisfied that John and Phil could safely remove the aircraft from the sleigh and load it on a truck for the trip to Vancouver without my help. However, John Gladstone insisted that I go back and finish my job, as he put it, because he would hold me responsible for any problem that might arise.

I took a U Drive to Ross River, arriving at the hotel quite late.

Next morning I called Don Huppe who agreed that the cat train, failing to show, was getting serious and I suggested that if they were not in Ross River the next morning an aircraft should be used to locate them. He agreed. We watched the hill pretty well all next day and they finally arrived just before dark. The aircraft had survived the trip without so much as an extra scratch and the boys had plenty to talk about which would be a story in itself.

The following morning we got on with transferring the aircraft from the sleigh to the truck, bringing the rough phase of the salvage operation to a successful finish with the credit for that going, in no small way, to John and Phil.

I would be very remiss if I didn't include Don Huppe too. I returned to Whitehorse on ice covered roads all the way.

Don Huppe was waiting for me at the airport with a Yukon broach I had, earlier, arranged to buy at Murdoch's Gem Shop for my wife Dot who was always waiting for me to come back from some place. Don was a fine example of those Good Northerners.

I left for Vancouver with another successful job done and as a favour to John, I would, although not at all necessary, look in occasionally at the repairs as they were being done by West Coast Air Services Ltd.

chapter twelve

The Drowned Widgeon

The Grumman Widgeon is an aircraft well named. Like its feathered namesake it is ideally suited for its purpose. It is built to withstand the tough going faced in north country aviation.

This particular Widgeon proved it had all the performance qualities promised by the manufacturer.

According to the crash report, the pilot, caught in a sudden summer squall, tried to get the aircraft down on remote and dangerous McConnell Lake. Apparently Mother Nature grabbed control just before touchdown and slammed the aircraft onto the surface. It began to sink immediately, giving the pilot and his two passengers about three minutes to get clear before it went under. Everyone escaped injury and they got safely to dry land.

The famous Ben Ginter, road builder, industrialist and entrepreneur owned the plane and being a 'right now' kind of guy was keen to get it back in action.

I was called and immediately flew to Prince George to meet with Mr. Ginter and Finlay Young the insurance broker. I looked forward to the experience. Ben Ginter had a reputation as a true 'up by his own bootstraps' achiever. He had parlayed a grade three education, a team of mules plus a natural talent for organizing opportunities, into outstanding success stories.

I wasn't disappointed. He was a big bear of a man with a quick smile and the capacity to listen carefully and ask the right questions. Our meeting was short and all the points were covered. Ben accepted my credentials as an insurance adjuster and salvager and told me to get going on the job.

I went directly from the meeting to Fort St. James and chartered a Northern Mountain Air seaplane to take me into McConnell Lake to check out the scene of the crash; do an investigative survey for the insurance company; and lay out a retrieval plan. Time was important. We had turned the corner into August and we had only a few weeks before the weather man would be forecasting snow.

McConnell Lake is beautiful. About one and a half miles long, it cuts an icy blue slash in a trench running from the northwest to the southeast. At 4200 feet above sea level there was a chill in the air that the August sun couldn't warm.

We tied up to the shore near a sturdy cabin and received a warm welcome from big Olaf Hagberg. He looked like someone who had been cast by a Hollywood film director to portray a north woods outdoors man.

Over a cup of his coffee, that would take the edge off an axe, he gave us the approximate location of the sunken Widgeon. It was quite a distance from the south end of the lake and in deep water.

Olaf offered the use of his row boat to locate the aircraft. What a row boat. It was a one of a kind invention produced from the "make use of what's available" school of ingenuity. He said he had knocked it together by making a few alterations to a pontoon from a German Junkers machine that had crashed near the lake some years ago. It was a high class, high performance, row boat.

Strong winds kept us off the lake until mid afternoon. As soon as it was safe we rowed out to the

The table has turned and we are beginning to win.

search area and started the slow process of crossing back and forth dragging a large three pronged hook along the lake bottom, hoping that we would be lucky and quickly snag the hooks on the some part of the aircraft. Electronic location devices were not yet available in the northern bush.

Fortunately, the lake bottom wasn't strewn with sunken logs or boulders so when we finally felt the hooks catch something solid we knew we had our lost bird. We pulled the rope until we were directly over the wreck and attached a buoy as a marker.

Next came the plan to raise the machine and get it close to the only useable slope available on the south shore.

I did a sketch of a large log raft with a centre opening for a hand crank winch and asked Olaf if he could find enough dry, high buoyancy logs to build such a raft. He was delighted to take on the project, said he would recruit a couple of fellow prospectors and it would be ready in a week. Having used his row boat, I knew I had a winner. What a relief! I could now put the hardware together to grapple with the lifting job.

I headed back to Prince George to bring Ben Ginter and Finlay Young up to date and assemble the needed equipment.

Everything I needed was available so I avoided hauling stuff in from Vancouver.

Two skin divers were required to fill out the salvage team and luckily two of the best were waiting for a contract. Russ Logan and John Chatco had a well deserved reputation for creative use of their diving skills and they polished that reputation in dealing with the problems presented by the drowned Widgeon

With arrangements made I headed for Vancouver to sort out how we were going to fit the family vacation into the Widgeon project.

When I arrived home the anxiety needle was in the red zone. My wife Dot and the two youngsters, Maureen 12 and Murray 10, were worried. They thought the Widgeon was going to create a repeat of last year's holiday cancellation. I had good news. This time the crash was going to support the vacation - I had reserved a trailer camp spot at Francois Lake. I could spend part of the week it would take Olaf to build the raft with the family and then go north to the crash site to get the work done while Dot and the kids enjoyed the swimming, fishing, riding and hiking at Francois Lake. Spirits bounced and we were soon packed and ready for the highway.

A short stop in Prince George gave me time to set up a rendevous with divers Russ Logan and John Chatco at Vanderhoof and confirm delivery of equipment and supplies. Two days later, after getting the family holiday launched, we got together and checked in at Stuart Lake seaplane base where we loaded our gear into a Thunderbird Air Grumman Goose and were off to McConnell Lake.

While others set up the camp two of us took the row boat out on the lake to check our marker buoy. Disappointment! The buoy had moved. It had come loose from the aircraft and drifted. We began dragging again and at 10.30 p.m., well after dark, we were forced to abandon the hunt for the day.

I was cold sleeping that night and at 5 a.m. I woke to see fresh snow on the surrounding hills. Mid August and Old Man Winter was giving us a warning. It prompted a resolve to get going at top speed.

The raft was a joy to behold. Olaf Hagberg and his pal Tom Howell of Fort St. James had done a super job. It had all the bells and whistles including cleats and safety features.

We finally located the aircraft 135 feet below the surface, tilted at a 45 degree angle with the left wing buried in the mud up to the engine on that side. I knew the mud would fight to hold the wing and I thanked the Grumman engineers for designing a very strong airframe that would make the lift ring, located at the top of the cabin, reliable under extreme stress.

The raft was anchored securely over the aircraft and the divers fastened the winch cable to the lift ring about 10 a.m. Wind and rain made working conditions miserable. By 1.45 p.m. we raised the aircraft 12 feet. The mud had put up a battle.

Suddenly disaster hit.

The winch crank handle and its shaft had moved outward, thus disengaging its spur gear from the cable drum and somehow the latch or dog that drops into the drum gear teeth and prevents the drum from unwinding was now disengaged. The drum was spinning backwards and the aircraft

was plummeting back into the mud at greater speed than when it had gone in with air filled wings and cabin.

The winch man was reaching for the latch and I shouted, "Leave it - don't touch it. Keep your fingers away from the gears, let the machine drop to the bottom." Happily, he froze with his hand in mid air and didn't lose any fingers. At that moment the latch dropped into place and the drum was stopped. The aircraft didn't. It pulled the raft about two feet under water before the dive was halted.

The raft bobbed back to the surface but we knew something had suffered under the strain. All that happened in a few seconds.

The cable was brought up and we could see that it had broken at the clamps that formed a loop in which a shackle was placed and in turn, was secured to the lifting ring.

We didn't waste time on rehash. Everyone was thankful that there were no injuries.

My attention was totally focused on how to get going again. There wasn't a spare shackle so we needed a substitute. One of the prospectors helping us remembered a couple of abandoned mines down the valley and suggested we might find a cable shackle on the equipment left there. That sounded like the answer.

The two offered to lead me to the mines and help in the shackle search. I jumped at the offer. I didn't know at the time that I would be subjected to a test of endurance well beyond the wildest imagination.

We set off immediately at quite a pace. Most of us have seen mountain goats in wild life films as they travel over rough terrain. Well that describes my two guides. They were really mountain goats disguised as people. Those two went at a steady clip,- up hill, down hill and through creeks, never changing speed. As you might have guessed, I was always a little to the rear. I had thought, up until then, that I was in pretty fit condition but my previous activities hadn't included competing with mountain goats.

We did not stop for rests and they seemed to assume that I was an outdoor type like them. Well, I did spend a lot of time out in remote areas but I wasn't as fit as they were.

I found out later that what I didn't know, and they did, was that the first mine was about 10 miles away and we would have no daylight to spare. They had a method in their madness in not telling about the distances until we arrived there. At any rate that was the life they were used to and I had to adapt to it for the occasion.

We found the shackles we needed at the second mine and back we went at the same pace up hill and down with no stops. We arrived back at our camp about 6.30 p.m. much to the surprise of the rest of the crew. They had been told, by our raft builder, how far we would have to hike.

It was figured out that we had done about 4 miles per hour. When you consider that 5 miles per hour is considered a fast walk on level ground you'll get some idea of the test those two rascals put me to. In polite north woods terms, my backside was dragging. That night my air mattress

(left); The worst stage of the retrieval is over.   (right); We were indeed so happy to use this rowboat. It was made from the pontoon of a German Junkers aircraft. The fuselage bore the name Prince George.

went flat. I didn't notice and I slept soundly on the rocks.

Next morning it was frosty and there was ice in the cooking pans, and some of them were in the tent. We were on the raft by 5.30 a.m. and the divers were in the water again. They had the rough end of the job but not a complaint was heard. The pressure at 135 feet down blew up two water tight battery power lamps, leaving them in the dark. It must have been quite a job securing the cable to the aircraft by feel only. The water temperature, at that depth, was below freezing level, which didn't help.

They had the cable connected again before the sun got too high in the sky. The wing and the nose were well into the mud again and we had the same hard fight getting them free.

This time the winch worked smoothly and after a while we noticed that the raft was moving toward the south end of the lake. We then knew that the aircraft was clear of the mud. The divers, working directly with the mud around the imbedded wing, speeded the process. They were in the water almost all day and did an heroic job.

It was rough going all day. Tension was high. Yesterday's mishap put everyone on edge. It made us sharp and efficient. By 10 p.m. we were nearing the south shore. The aircraft was still below the surface but we now could put floatation bags containing nitrogen into the fuselage and let the semi buoyant aircraft move clear of the raft.

I showed the divers how to drop the landing gear manually – easier for me to show than for them to do it in the murky water. That done we were ready to haul the machine onto the beach, the next day's job.

Now, instead of pulling the aircraft straight in we were going to have to go laterally up a steep, muddy incline.

The winch was lashed to a sturdy tree a short distance from the shore and a braided nylon rope was used instead of cable. The rope tied in bridle form to the undercarriage reduced the danger of damaging the legs of the landing gear.

The wheels dug deeper into the mud than expected and tension on the rope became a concern. I reached out to touch and test that tension at the very moment the bridle broke. It came at me like a snake, wrapping itself around my left arm with a sharp snap. I thought my arm had been yanked out its socket.

The crew's reaction was to come to my aid but I shouted, "Take up the slack on the snubbing rope. Don't let the son of a b---- slide into deep water." To me, they seemed to be moving in slow motion but in reality they were as quick as cats and instantly had a potential disaster under control.

Second time smart. I replaced the broken bridle with a double one and we had the aircraft up on the beach by late evening.

As for my arm, I had good news. Marv Hess dropped down in his Grumman Goose to check on our progress and he had a doctor as a passenger. The doctor checked my shoulder and said the joint had not been damaged and although painful it would be okay. He was right on both counts. It hurt like the dickens but the ache was out of it in a couple of days.

Marv's timing was perfect. The divers had done their much appreciated work and were ready to return to civilization. The doctor's visit was a bonus.

I was more relieved than I could find words to say, seeing the Widgeon perched and secure on the beach. Slept like a dry baby.

Early next morning we did a cleanup work and everything possible to secure and preserve the integrity of the aircraft. The frame was not damaged as badly as we expected and I didn't want to lose any ground to the elements. - I had a good news for Ben Ginter. The Widgeon could be prepared for a ferry flight out and recertified.

We radioed for an aircraft to pick us up.

While waiting for our ride I walked over to the old Junkers crash site and wondered what magic Olaf the raft builder would work with some of the other parts. His row boat was a prize and I'm sure he would come up with other creative uses for the debris.

As for the marvelous raft. Olaf said it would be positioned near the cabin and used as a dock for aircraft and boats. It was built to last.

Ben Ginter was more than pleased with the good news I had about his Widgeon. But his eyes really lit up when I produced his rock samples. I wonder if it turned into a successful mining venture. Things like that happened for Ben Ginter.

I filed my report with insurance broker Finlay Young and received a response compatible with the money saved for his company as a result of the salvage.

Another hectic success story entered in the company's log book.

I returned to Francois Lake to find the family having a great time. Maureen and Murray were both brim full of exciting stories including one special high adventure that they recall vividly to this day. They had the thrill of holding hard to their saddles when their horses were spooked by a bear.

Mention of the name Widgeon brings a fond memories smile to a McCartney face.

chapter thirteen

Helio Courier left to Freeze

The last half of August 1967 and the calendar was clear, no prangs in the moose pasture to tend to and silence from the bank. We were looking forward to a genuine "everybody together for a summer holiday" when Bill Myers of the British Aviation Insurance Company called to say he had a Helio Courier down in Henik Lake about 250 miles northwest of Churchill, Manitoba...Crash went the family holiday. Thanks to Dot, understanding wife, comptroller and mother, the kids were not too disappointed. She was better at salvaging those situations than I was at rescuing bent aircraft. I booked a flight to Churchill via Winnipeg.

Several of the people on staff at the airport in Churchill were old friends from my days as chief engineer for Northland Airlines in Manitoba. They had been following my salvage activities in the aviation magazines. That opened the local gates for me to get good information on sources for needed supplies and equipment. The fellows at Lamb Air were at the top of the list and proved to be most helpful.

Churchill was at peak season. The huge grain ships were being loaded night and day and the grain elevators were being refilled from the trains bringing in this year's crop as fast as space was available. It was nonstop activity; three loading docks each completed loading a ship every three days.

The hotels, bars and restaurants were humming. The bulk of the workers were itinerants from Saskatchewan and southern Manitoba. I found this strange because Churchill is really a combination of Indian and Eskimo villages. Perhaps I was seeing evidence that the "hunters" didn't want to be paid by the hour.

The work frenzy was really weather driven. Summer was over at this latitude and soon, ice would close the port. That same threat effected me.

I was anxious to get out to the crash scene on Henik Lake. Lamb Air didn't have an unbooked aircraft but they introduced me to the manager of an exploration company that was leasing a Cessna 180 from them. They were working in the Henik Lake area and were pleased to put me on the Cessna for a flight into the Helio accident.

The flight was interesting and educational. The tundra was virtually bare. There was absolutely nothing that could be used to supplement a salvage job.

There was little that could be done to the damaged aircraft other than secure it with rope I had taken in for that purpose. It was sitting solidly on the lake bottom with the floats full of water. Luckily it had come to a stop almost at the shore line. It was safer in it's present position than it would be if it was pulled up on shore and left until the damaged float struts could be replaced to secure the aircraft on it's floats.

I made some descriptive notes and took photos of the damage from which approximate cost estimates for temporary ferry repairs and permanent repairs would be made up.

The tundra of course did not have anything on it except fractured rock, which meant that special portable equipment would be needed to lift the aircraft. The only growth consisted of caribou moss and very low small bushes spotted here and there. The large structures of rock had big cracks and fractures through them.

Inquiries around Churchill only served to confirm that the needed equipment would have to be shipped in. The exploration chief, from his own experience, suggested that it would be wise to ship everything from Vancouver to avoid disappointments with lack of deliveries and delays. How right he was!

Back in Vancouver, I brought Bill Meyers up to date and gave him confirmation to accept the accident claim. He instructed me to retrieve the aircraft and I immediately assembled all the toys needed to get the Helio into ferry flight shape. They were shipped air cargo to Winnipeg then by rail express to Churchill.

Next, a call to Harry Cowan, an ex Royal Navy Fleet Air Arm colleague, in Edmonton. He had designed an "A" frame made in threaded sections of heavy wall steel tubing; light, easily packaged for shipping and ideal for my purpose. He had it crated and on its way to Churchill that day.

The Supplier of spare parts for Helio was also located in Edmonton. I ordered the replacement aileron, flap and propeller to be expressed to Churchill. They didn't ship the same day. More about that later.

I had learned, through some one else's unfortunate experience in a very remote northern location, not to proceed ahead of my supplies. However, winter was closing in up north and I forced myself to break a good rule and I would suffer as a result.

In September I left for Churchill with the last leg of the flight on Transair Airlines.

We had a one-hour stop at Thompson, Manitoba and while walking around the aircraft parking area I spotted two PBY-5A aircraft CF-CRR and GLX. I had been in charge of maintenance for them and a number of other machines, in Netley, Manitoba that were operated by Northland Airlines in Winnipeg, a few years earlier. We had done major inspections and overhauls on them at that time and I was interested in looking them over.

While I was walking around the machines, a fellow named Al Stokely came up to me with a very friendly greeting and said that the results of my high standards of maintenance were still evident and have proven to be a wonderful thing for the airline. He continued by saying that the two machines had been worked very hard with very lit-

tle maintenance needed other than the normal inspections. The conversions to the aircraft had provided them with water dropping capabilities for forest fires and each had been making as many as 110 drops on fires in one day.

I got a lift from the compliments but the real satisfaction came from the implication that the company had benefitted from my days as their engineer and had stopped being so bottom line oriented that they were fudging on maintenance.

The flight continued on to Churchill where I met Connie Lamb and Don Boone, Lamb Air pilots. Connie said we shouldn't be working at Henik Lake much later than September 1 because we could get weathered in and we wouldn't get the aircraft out. The weather at that time was so pleasant that his remarks seemed exaggerated but he should know, he lived there.

Next morning I had breakfast with Barney Cooper, who was flying the Helio when engine trouble forced him on to Henik Lake. He had signed on to help me get the aircraft back to ferry flight condition. We did a little planning and then got busy moving all the supplies down to the seaplane base. We were all ready when heavy fog rolled over Hudson Bay. All flights were canceled. Stopped in our tracks. Connie Lamb was right.

Everywhere I traveled, especially in the northern areas, I was most interested in seeing everything and learning what I could of the different places and the people. I had heard about a rocket launching site not far out of town and since we were grounded, so to speak, we decided to go look at it. We were taken on a tour by a technician in the employ of Pan Am, operators of the site at that time.

The reason for the site being at that particular location was because it was closer to the Van Allen Belt than any other place on earth. The Belt ranges from 2000 to 12000 miles above the earth. It catches the ionized particle thrown out from the sun and we see the results as Northern Lights.

Recordings of the conditions in that part of the stratosphere were made from a transmitter mounted on a Brandt Rocket that was launched from the ground and penetrated the Van Allen Belt. The site was used by many countries of the world to collect data. I should mention that the recording was done on a board that was completely covered with small holes into which electric wire were inserted for specific data recordings. It resembled an old style punch board. - The rockets, by the way, were manufactured in Winnipeg, Manitoba.

Our guide was directly associated with the rocket site at Cape Canaveral in Florida.

While we were in the weather phase of the tour I asked our guide if he knew someone named Ayling. He stopped dead in his tracks and said "how do you know him?" I told him we were related and knew he had made quite a name for himself as a weather specialist up in Alert, the most northern point in Canada.

A Vancouver meteorologist, had told me that Ayling had developed a very effective and accurate system of his own in forecasting weather at Alert. I had lost track of him and was pleased to find someone who knew of him.

The guide told me that Ayling was at that time Chief Quality Control Officer at the moon rocket base in Cape Kennedy. Curiosity prompted me to ask what the title meant. Our guide quickly responded by saying that Ayling had the authority to cancel a launching at any stage of a moon shot preparation if he considered it necessary.

Wow! That is power. How did this Canadian get so important a job at such a large and specialized American installation. I asked our guide the question. The guide said, "It is really quite simple. Whatever Mr. Ayling does, he does well." Now that had to be the ultimate compliment one professional could ever pay another.

More than idle nosiness motivated me – Ayling is my high IQ step brother. The update gave me ammo for my next name dropping opportunity. Maybe some listener would think genius ran in the family.

Next day we had 1800 pounds of gear ready at the seaplane base including the two of us. The pilot of an Otter wanted full tanks of fuel so he couldn't take all our stuff. Don Boone took the rest of it in a Cessna 180. Poor weather had come in at Eskimo Point about 125 air miles east of Henik Lake and it was a threat to our plans.

We landed near the wrecked aircraft but the water was too shallow for us to nose the pontoons up onto the beach. So our load had to be taken off down the lake a ways then packed up to our work site. Don brought a third man in from the exploration camp on Cullotin Lake to help us.

We chose a spot near where we would be working and set up the tents then placed everything in such a fashion that we would be able to find items if it snowed. When that was finished we assembled my navy buddy's slick new "A" frame with a pulley or shiv at its top then raised it into its operational position. It was held there by a thick weave nylon rope secured to it's top with the other end of the rope wrapped around a huge rock that had a large crack through it's centre. It wasn't as safe looking as I would have liked but there was no other choice. I had chosen to use the rope as it would not tend to slip on the rock as I thought steel cable would. - I was wrong.

The winch cable was run through the shiv and hooked up to the lifting sling we had rigged on the aircraft and we started lifting.

The first part of the lift brought the tops of the pontoons above the water, just where we wanted them. We then pumped the water out of their undamaged compartments. However, when we attempted to lift the aircraft clear of the water to remove the damaged floats, the nylon rope wouldn't stop stretching and we gained nothing.

Usually, on such expeditions, I did not have a portable radio because we were generally too far from a station and batteries didn't last long unless we had a gasoline driven generator to keep them charged.

Experience showed that even when we did have all those goodies we were blocked off by a range of mountains or some other impediment. Well, this time we did have a radio - and it worked.

A call to the exploration camp for some steel cable got a positive reaction and soon it was flown in to us and we were back in business.

The exploration camp had arranged for us to check with them via radio at a designated time each day. That was the first and only time I ever enjoyed that luxury. In the meantime we hadn't wasted any time as preparations were made for the removal of the pontoons as soon as they were clear of the water.

Mother Nature seldom failed to remind me that she was near by. Not that she was always willing to help as she sometimes did by giving us good weather but she just had to, it seemed, remind us that she was power to reckon with. Believe me, she always got my attention.

This time the Old Girl wreaked vengeance by sending in clouds of small black flies and as if that wasn't enough, she reinforced them with masses of sand flies. The black devils were the worst. They came in swarms so thick they resembled a cloud and of course they were ravenous with bites leaving welts where they had crawled down inside our shirts. Everyone was having trouble keeping them out of their nose, eyes and ears.

We would get some relief when there was a breeze but when that dropped off the flies were back and made up for lost time. Barney Cooper, who was a third generation resident of the North West Territories in the Yellowknife area, said that he had never before, seen such hordes as that. We had no effective defense.

We had the best insect repellent of that time, called "Off" but the flies just ignored it. I suppose they were after their last supper before winter cut them down. Don Boone came by to check on us and of all things, he had some head gear mosquito netting that we didn't refuse to accept. What a relief. I felt like some kind of tourist by wearing it but the results canceled out those thoughts.

Two days later a change in the weather brought strong, cold winds from the north west. The bugs were gone; there was ice on the water in the tent and on the tops of the barrels outside.

This added speed to our efforts. We boomed the aircraft into the shoreline fighting the wind and swirling snow flurries. The rigging was changed on the aircraft and we lifted it so the damaged pontoons and support structure could be removed.

We got on with the float repairs, removal and cleaning up of instruments. What a scramble, draining and cleaning the engine with ice in many parts. It was then that we found a problem that supported the pilot's report that engine trouble had led to the accident. Number 4 cylinder exhaust valve was broken. There was damage to the belly of the fuselage and to the aileron plus the flap on one wing.

It was a bit unnerving to see the machine hanging in the air because everything depended on the fractured rock anchor.

Night came with our wounded Helio still suspended in the "A" frame. I was awake most of the time looking at the aircraft swinging in the wind. We had it tied to restrict movement but the wind was gusting hard enough to swing the aircraft against the ties. Another sleepless night for Denny.

I had company across the lake; the wolf pack was howling to greet the coming winter. As often as I hear it, the hair on the back of my neck still wants to stand up. It crossed my mind that I could and should be somewhere else.

My companions slept through the hard driving rain that hit about midnight. My tent leaked.

Finally morning; a hot breakfast and coffee. We soon had the float repairs completed and attached to the replacement struts. Then the assembly was skidded into the water under the suspended Helio for installation. All of us breathed a sigh of relief when the aircraft was again perched on its pontoons and securely anchored against the wind.

Well, for a change, everything was going along quite well that day until we suddenly found a badly cracked right rear strut attach fitting on the fuselage. I had missed it on my initial damage inspection. Question: What do we do now? Answer? - At that moment I had no idea. The fracture was a hair line type crack but it couldn't be ignored and definitely would not be safe for a flight.

All of us were soaking wet from a steady downpour and Barney was trying to dry clothes at least a little. Some were still wet from the previous day. I put my attention to the fitting problem and finally decided that if we had a fairly long bolt about 1 inch in diameter a "Rube Golberg" type repair might be made. It would mean drilling a hole through the fuselage fitting through which we would pass the bolt to be jerry rigged to the float strut.

The seemingly impossible part of the problem was: "Where would I find a bolt that size"? Not in my box of miscellaneous bits and pieces. My mind rambled on. What about one somewhere on the aircraft? But, bolts that size were used at major installations such as the engine and the wings. Design engineers called for bolts of various sizes depending on the required sheer and tensile strengths for a safe joint. No designs called for large bolts if they were not necessary.

One part of me said it didn't make sense to even think about finding a 1 inch bolt that wasn't needed where it was already in use. Another part told me that there was one, just go find it. Those two thoughts were 180 degrees apart and the latter one seemed an impossibility but my impulses forced me to think positive about it.

It was as though some one was pushing and telling me that there was a bolt I needed, find it. I'd had that very same feeling with a Beaver Aircraft problem in Headless Valley a few years earlier with a successful ending.

With chest waders I walked around the aircraft and looked at every part of the airframe without a glimmer of success. Barney called occasionally to see if I was ready to give up because he was positive that I would not find a bolt that size, that was not needed where it was already positioned.

I was ready to consider taking a rear spar attach bolt and replace it with a shimmed up smaller bolt because the front spar was the load carrier and the rear one had minor loads by comparison. I continued wading around in the water and steady rain searching, it seemed, for the impossible.

Suddenly BINGO! My eyes came to rest on the water rudder assemblies. There was my bolt attaching a rudder to the pontoon. I had been searching and looking too high. Only one water rudder would be needed for a ferry flight out so off came one in a hurry.

Barney, as I recall, set up quite a scene--dancing and yelling "you deserve a medal, "repeating it several times. As for me, I didn't know who I should thank for my stubbornness but I also felt a little dumb about not finding the bolt sooner.

We made quick use of the bolt and soon the aircraft was setting securely on it's pontoons. The weather hadn't improved, in fact, it worsened with snow added to the rain.

While we were rushing around, Don Boone of Lamb Airways arrived at our camp with his Cessna 180, he had problems. He needed a patch on one of his float bottoms and an inspection of the aircraft.

There was no doubt about it and even though we were racing against time, a return favour for him was long overdue so we jumped to it. We patched the float and I did an engine inspection and a basic airframe check. I assured him that the aircraft was safe in all respects. I was pleased to be able do him a favour in return for his many concerns for us.

We turned our attention to the Helio's engine and replaced the number 4 cylinder with a spare unit we had brought in on spec. Then we went through the usual procedure of preparing it for running up.

It was Thursday, September 7 and the exploration camp on Cullaton Lake would be moving out on Sunday. We should be ready to go also but some parts. The aileron, flap and propeller had not arrived in Churchill.

Next morning we had a successful engine run up but the bent propeller made for very rough vibrations. I wasn't happy but it was something that had to be done because even at low speed we could get the remaining water out and thoroughly lubricate the engine internally with several changes of oil to preserve it.

Finally, there was nothing more that needed to be, or could be done, for a ferry flight until those needed assemblies arrived. I couldn't for the life of me, understand why those units, on order for so long, had not come in.

We had been getting up at 6:30 A.M. and to bed at 11 P.M. with 15 minute meal times. Now we had nothing to do but wait for the parts.

Radio communications with Churchill were now poor and not dependable much of which was due to electrical disturbances from outer space such as the Northern Lights. As long as the exploration camp was at Cullaton Lake we had radio and personal contacts to a degree but when they left we would be totally on our own with poor or no radio to the outside.

A tough decision was coming at me fast. A little easier if it was not winter time and we were in an area farther south with trees, we would still be in an awkward spot but it was winter time and we were in the Tundra.

Low temperatures that were due any day now would freeze the lake and prevent the use of a seaplane and it could be two or three weeks or more before the ice would be safe for a ski plane. In the meantime we would probably be out of food and heating oil in that bare country. We decided it would be foolish to stay and wait for parts.

What to do with the Helio? We fully realized the possibility of us not being able to return and finish the job because of severe weather conditions. It was most important to position and secure the aircraft for a possible winter stay. We found a small back wash type of shallow water area with a soft mud bottom, positioned between two small embankments.

The aircraft was moved into it and all the float compartments were partly filled with water until the pontoons were sitting firmly on the lake bottom. The floats would, in time, be frozen solidly into position. That, would prevent the aircraft

122   picking up the pieces

from being turned over by strong winds. There was not enough water in the floats to cause damage from ice expansion. External locks on the all the flight control surfaces were installed to prevent wind damage.

Having prepared for the worst we now hoped for the best. We hoped the needed parts would be in Churchill or at worst, in Winnipeg and a shift to good weather would see us return to finish the job.

That night the whole sky was ablaze with Northern Lights. Next morning we put our stove, heater, fuel, canned food and other items in the Courier. Don Boone then flew us and the rest of our gear over to Cullaton Lake in the Cessna 180 I had certified for him. A DC3 would be in next day for the flight to Churchill. I slept on the floor of the cook house. It was harder than a banker's heart but I was warm and dryer than I had been for some time and I slept the sleep of the just.

Next day the flies were back in even greater numbers. The ptarmigan, when we could see them, were replacing summer feathers with winter white.

We helped the cook and others clean up the camp and prepare for departure. On our arrival at Churchill I met Don Houton of Selco Explorations and he said he had wondered when we would meet again and wanted to help us when we returned to finish the job.

Much to our disappointment the parts needed had not arrived in Churchill. This necessitated a rush trip to Winnipeg.

The flight in the DC3 was uneventful but I did a lot of mental floor pacing thinking about the missing parts and where they were. As soon as we landed I headed for Transair Air Freight. I found the problem.

Air Canada (then TCA)had delivered the supplies from Edmonton but the dolts at Transair had refused to tranship them to Churchill via air. They had sent them over to the Canadian National Railroad. I could have been put in jail for my thoughts.

The incident was another verification for the opinion shared by most of us who worked in the wilderness; there were very few jerks in the aviation business but when you found one it was usually in a city.

I rushed down to the Railway where I checked boxcars until I found my crates which were in such a position that they could very easily have been crushed en route. I moved them closer to the door and placed them on top of heavy boxes.

There was nothing more to be done and the train was leaving shortly for Churchill so I thought I'd go down to the seaplane base at Selkirk and see what was going on. That visit as it turned out, did a great deal to get my mind off trouble for a while and made me feel mentally better about aviation.

I mentioned earlier that I had been in that area for a short time reorganizing the maintenance programme of an airline. While I was walking down to the seaplane docks I heard my name being called repeatedly by someone running towards me from the river embankment.

He kept yelling "Denny, you're back, you're back." His name was Lyal Johnson and he had been a great help to me in the shop office and stores at Netley. I was new in the area at that time but he made it much easier for me by knowing who to contact when the necessity arose and he did it with a smile and pleasantness.

He was almost out of breath when he reached me and still saying "You're back."

I was taken by surprise and didn't twig to his actual meaning and words for a few seconds when suddenly it dawned on me that he thought I had come back to work at the airline. Then I had to say, "No Lyal, I'm not back to work here, I'm on my way to a problem in Churchill." He expressed immediate disappointment and said "Every one will be sorry to hear that."

Lyal continued by saying, "The talk around the shop is that you were coming back." He went on to say that "no one would mind that kick in the behind first thing every morning to get us going. We learned, from you, a better way to work."

That was a great morale builder and to hear one of the old crew say something, like that, was like a tonic. "The kick in the behind", as Lyal put it, was just imagined and based on my insistence that everyone had to be on time in the mornings and ready to start work at 8 a.m. and quit at 4:30 p.m. - Over and out.

Our conversation will remain ever fresh in my memory and I put it on my mental replay when ever I'm tempted to peak into my pity pot.

Next day I went north again. It was very cool in Thompson and snowing in Churchill where Barney met me and as it was too late in the day to travel further, we crated all my heavy tools and equipment for rail shipment to Vancouver and went to bed early.

The train arrived about 9:30 in the morning and we went directly to the car containing our parts then rushed out to Landing Lake where we loaded our gear into an Otter that was already well loaded and with me crammed in the back with the load we took off.

Strong winds were not in our favour for the first half hour and the aircraft seemed to stagger with no gain in altitude. We then had head winds of 50 to 60 mph. Low cloud moved in and when we had reached our half way point we were getting low on fuel so we turned back with a stop for fuel on Diamond Lake. We arrived back in Churchill near dark and unloaded the aircraft.

During the flight the rotten weather had caused us to lose our bearings twice. We were desperate to get in and finish our job and our pilot made a 100 percent effort to get us in but Mother Nature had different ideas. I thought, at the time, I would not want a repeat trip like that one and it gave me a fresh appreciation of the situations charter pilots find themselves in at times. It snowed heavily all night and was very cold.

Next morning we had low temperatures and

blowing snow with winds at 60/70 mph. I stopped in at Lamb Air to see what they thought about our position re finishing the job.

They had more than enough of their own problems with one machine on the rocks at Eskimo Point, located farther up the coast from Churchill, another with engine trouble and one somewhere in the area of Anodye. Typical troubles experienced, at times, by air charter companies throughout our country but so much at one time is horrible.

The date was Saturday September 23 and we were stuck until Tuesday or Wednesday when a Lamb Air machine would be up from Thompson.

Don Hooten called me late Saturday night wanting me to get his aircraft off the rocks up the coast. I explained that the best way to do that would be to take thick plywood up in a Nodwell (Tundra vehicle) and slide the aircraft to the water. However, Barney and I still couldn't get on with our problem so we were up at 5:30 A.M. and went out in a Track Master to help Don who had picked up two more fellows to help with the job.

We worked most of the day during low tide moving the aircraft over and through rocks to an area where it would float freely at high tide. We left Don there with one man in a nearby shack to wait for high water and we returned to Churchill.

I tracked Connie Lamb down and found out that the waters in the area of our disabled aircraft were frozen but not thick enough to land on and would not be for at least 2 or 3 weeks or more. Now we were really stuck. Good flying weather was coming in but ice, or not enough of it, was stopping us.

It was now Tuesday September 26. Apparently it was expected that the weather would get milder before the final freeze up and that would slow down the thickening of the ice that we needed so badly. We had to make a decision--wait or give up until Spring - We gave up.

Lamb Air were kind enough to offer to store the parts for us. That took a worry off our minds. I must say that the Lamb Air people were extremely helpful and courteous. That smoothed out much of the stress that reared it's ugly head every so often.

I recall what I thought was an interesting scenario that took place the previous night, totally unrelated to aviation.

Churchill, is widely known for it's polar bear population especially at certain times of the year. It appears that during the night a resident heard unusual distressful yelping coming from his dog in the back yard and on taking a look, saw a polar bear at the dog's kennel doing his best to prepare a meal. The fellow went out with a .22 caliber rifle, right up behind the bear and shot it in the ear, luckily, for him, he made an instant kill or the bear's menu would have been quickly changed.

Art Look, the Government Wildlife Officer, whom I had met one of my walk-abouts, said the "hunter" may have ben upset because the R.C.M.P. had confiscated the dead bear but wait until he finds out that he will be facing a fairly heavy fine for the shooting.

An awful chance was taken in going right up

behind the bear. They are like seagulls, always hungry. Some people claimed that the bear could possibly have been scared off by making a loud noise from a safe distance such as beating on a dish pan.

At any rate the dog's owner was lucky he didn't just wound the bear. Every year the town loses a few voters who go for a one way walk while under the influence of an adult beverage. Another slant on the old story about being loaded for bear.

I left for Vancouver and was home that evening.

It was the first and only time I had to leave an aircraft like that and I felt bad to have to do it. Dot asked me if I had taken on a polar bear personality and seemed pleased that the following day, Thursday, September 28 brought a call to attend to a prang somewhere north west of Prince George, B.C. and I left home again, this time taking my grudge against Mother Nature and the jerks at Transair with me.

The Helio Courier, by the way, was removed from it's winter storage by Barney Cooper, the following Spring.

chapter fourteen

MK5
Anson

A Major
Winter Repair
in the High Arctic

Dot said, "Its your favorite caller on the phone."
And it was. Jack Mitchell, Seattle manager for Leo
Leclerc Ltd., Montreal, had a job in the high Arctic
for me.

The pilot of a PWA Avro Anson, registration CF-
PAC had overshot in an attempted landing at a
D.E.W. Line airstrip and the aircraft had come to
rest in a small valley just below the end of the runway. Jack wanted me to obtain details on the state
of the aircraft and the prospect of doing temporary
repairs so that it could be flown out. He wanted
photos and a detailed estimate of the cost of the
salvage operation and the subsequent permanent
repairs.

Check the map on this one. Richardson Island is
north of the Canadian Arctic Coast and west of
Cambridge Bay, which is on the southeast corner
of Victoria Island.

It was the location of one of the many Distant
Early Warning Line (D.E.W. Line) stations built and
manned by the U.S. Government to monitor
Russian aviation activities in the north.

It was the end of February, springtime in
Vancouver but deep, serious wintertime on

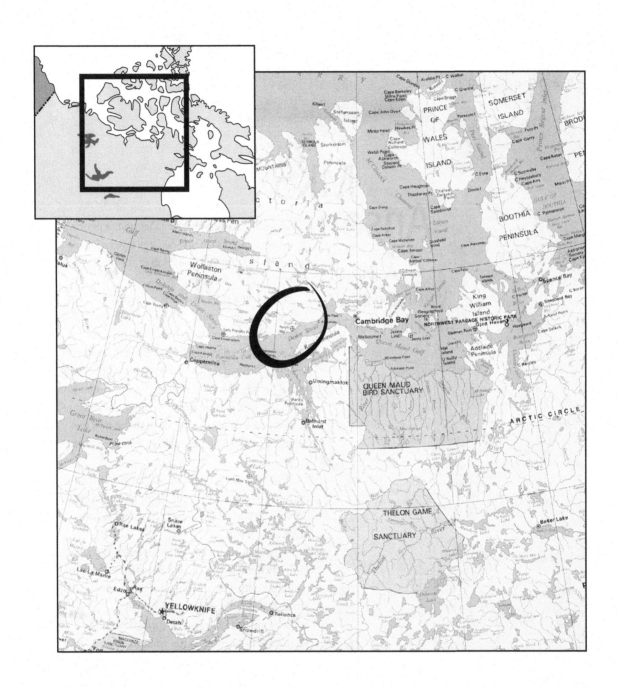

Mother Nature had put the Anson to bed for the winter.

Richardson Island. I packed accordingly and set out for the accident site via Edmonton and Cambridge Bay where I checked in with the D.E.W. Line authorities and turned in my clearance papers. No problems and no hassle.

The flight in to the crash site was a pleasant one in an Anson. Snow covered everything with wind packed drifts that swirled and twisted in a never ending series of unduplicated patterns. Beautiful but not too hospitable.

Wilf, the friendly maintenance supervisor, who turned out to be very resourceful and helpful, met us. He introduced us to the station manager, who was fully briefed on the purpose of my visit. He was a co-operative host.

A little daylight remained so Wilf agreed to take me down to the crash for a quick look. Luckily, there was little snow on or around the damaged areas. The aircraft was resting on its belly in a fairly level spot. I had a look at the bent propellers and the damaged right wing - enough to get the plans going for tomorrow's work.

Back to the dining room with Wilf. I really looked forward to it. The Americans don't penny-pinch when it comes to looking after their personnel on foreign duty.

I wasn't disappointed. The chef turned out a meal that would have received rave notices in Chicago. And Wilf and I had an entertaining companion, Father Metie, a Catholic priest based in

Cambridge Bay who looked after the church's flock over thousands of square miles. He had hilarious stories to tell about his missionary work and a few hair raisers about exposure to high arctic storms.

Finally, later than I had planned, bedtime. The three of us were assigned to a large room lined with double-decker bunks. I made mental notes for tomorrow's task

I knew that Wilf was going to be very helpful in speeding things up and calculated I would have things wrapped up by noon. Those good thoughts acted like a sleeping pill. Later in the night I was suddenly awakened by a loud voice. Apparently I had nodded off while the priest was reading in his bunk and missed Wilf's request that the light be turned off because it was keeping him awake. The good father wasn't prompt enough for Wilf and the loud roar I heard was Wilf saying, "Put out your light. You don't have to be up early for work but I do. Put it out or I'll knock it out."

The next morning at breakfast, I told Wilf he'd be saying 'Hail Marys' for a year if he stepped out of line now. Wilf grinned and said, "Not to worry. He's a good guy, He has just got used to living on Eskimo time."

A hearty breakfast and off to the job. A thorough inspection of the damaged areas was efficiently accomplished. The intense cold was an incentive to do it quickly and right the first time. Detailed notes were made and nothing was passed over.

The worst damage was to the rear spar in the outer section of the right wing.. The belly was only slightly damaged. This was due to the fact that the main landing wheels, in the up or stowed position, extend below the fuselage and the tail wheel is mounted in a fixed down position. The aircraft, on a hard level surface, could actually be taxied even though the wheels were up, without causing damage. In this case the wheels held the belly clear of the terrain.

Because repair pieces were to be made in Vancouver, careful sketches and accurate measurements were a must. And photos were taken from every possible angle.

Cameras and cold weather are not good friends. To keep mine from freezing up I carry it inside my parka when not in use, being careful to shield it from direct body heat.

That could cause moisture to form, which would freeze the works immediately I tried to snap a picture.

Next came arrangements for a portable generator and a heater needed when we started the repair work. That being done, I was away on an afternoon flight for home. I used the time to prepare estimates of the approximate costs.

I got great pictures that proved useful in doing the repair pieces and gave Jack Mitchell, the insurance broker, just what he needed to make his adjuster decisions. He called within a few days giving instructions that I effect temporary repairs to the aircraft for a ferry flight back to Vancouver.

The Anson was no stranger to me. I had maintained them for both Central B.C. and Pacific

Western Airlines. But I had not done any major work on one outside the shop. Now I was committed to doing just that and it was a long, long way from a shop.

Every detail had to be checked and double checked. I had to make sure that I knew all the technical requirements and I had to be sure that we had the right tools and equipment. The parts and materials had to be exactly what was needed. I had no wish to find myself sitting through a long embarrassing wait for some essential that I had forgotten or didn't know about.

Karl Frisk, who had worked with me on several such projects was not free to go that time.

Fortunately, Hugh Gilmore, a very capable engineer, who thrived on hard work, was available and willing to get things ready and to accompany me.

His solid back up took the anxiety out of our preparations. Soon the repair parts and the tools were on their way north. This time we didn't have the added task of sending in food, tents and other camping goodies. We would sleep and eat at the D.E.W. Line station.

Off again from sunny, springtime Vancouver to the chill of Arctic winter in Cambridge Bay where we were held up for a few days by bad weather. Then to Pin D D.E.W. Line Station on April Fools Day.

We arrived in the late afternoon at the end of February 1959 to a totally different scene. Strong winds had covered the machine except for part of the top of the fuselage and the tail fin and rudder. It was shovel time. After dinner we got two hours of snow removal work in and it hardly showed. We

(left); **We dug down eight feet to the wheels. Damage to wooden wing. Snow in cabin entered through the key hole of the door.** (right); **Wind driven snow formed a Plaster of Paris type mould under cowling. DEW line maintenance man Wilf on left with Hugh Gilmor.**

did clear the area around the cabin door and upon opening it we encountered a display of Mother Nature's artistry.

Just inside the cabin was a pile of snow in a perfect cone shape with its pointed top in direct line with the keyhole in the door. It was about two feet high and the snow was as fine as talcum powder. Even so, the wind must have been very strong to drive the snow through such a small opening. We soon found out just how strong that wind could blow in the very dangerous experiences that lay ahead.

The next day Hugh, an Eskimo named Andy and I shovelled snow for 8 hours. We went down 8 feet to the level where the belly rested. I hadn't counted on that. I hadn't counted on losing the work time and I surely hadn't counted on the exercise. It was a massive excavation and shovelling became part of every day. Nose to nose with Reality.

Our next task was to raise the aircraft high enough to drop the main wheels to the down and locked position. There was no lifting equipment available so small hydraulic jacks on wooden blocks were used to lift the machine a short distance at a time. When we got to the right height a 45 gallon steel drum and blocks were placed under the bottoms of each engine to form the main support while we lowered the landing gear.

A pair of long radius rods extended back from the lower end of each landing gear leg to fittings on the bottom of the fuselage acting as a brace to keep the main wheels from being driven back-

wards. The two on the left wheel assembly were damaged.

I crawled under to install the replacements. The attachment point was midway between the nose and tail. I was well into the job, concentrating so hard that I didn't notice a slight shift in the machine's position. Hugh had seen it and apparently was yelling his head off trying to get my attention. The wind was howling at gale force and drowned him out. Finally I noticed his hand signals and realized I was in a very dangerous situation.

The wind had driven the aircraft sideways. The steel drums were tilted at an angle. The only thing that kept them from going all the way was a stub wall type snowdrift that we had seen no reason to remove. A guardian angel? Maybe.

I still wasn't out of trouble. Snow drifts have been known to crumble and drift.

Lying on my back with my head toward the tail I checked my options. The snowdrifts down both sides and across the tail left no space for me to escape by a short route. That meant crawling on my back, feet first all the way until I was clear beyond the nose of the aircraft. During that short time that seemed so long, I watched for signs of more movement. The wind had been noisy but suddenly, in the emergency, it sounded worse and there seemed to be an increase in the volume of blowing snow. I realized that my imagination was working over time and I had better get it under control.

Hugh was as relieved as I was when I was finally out. It was unbelievable that the tilted steel drums and blocks had not collapsed and strong winds were still striking the aircraft on the right side. Any further movement, even an inch, was all that would have been needed to drop the machine completely on me.

Wisely, Hugh didn't try crawling under to warn me. He showed good judgement .

As soon as the blocking under the engines had been reset, all appeared safe enough for me to go back under and finish the landing gear repairs. Everything went well on the second try and soon the aircraft was sitting up on its wheels. What a relief!

We even stopped to take a deep breath and remind ourselves that we had plenty of proof that things could be a lot worse even with the low temperature and strong winds.

Our next main concern was the wing damage. After a lot of snow shovelling and vital help from Wilf, a plastic tent was built over the damaged section to give as much protection as we could muster from the gusting 40 M.P.H winds and 20 below temperature. Repairs to the spar were started.

The Anson wooden spar is one piece that extends from wing tip to wing tip. Temporary repair work must not extend into the undamaged area any further than absolutely necessary.

We used pieces of angle iron welded together to form a frame work bridging the spar damage.. A birch plywood web, cut to the required size in Vancouver, was bolted to the frame, completing a sturdy assembly.

It wasn't all work; there was some socializing. One day a family of three Eskimos, on their way to see Andy and his family, stopped to see what we were doing. The mother wore a beautiful mink parka, caribou skin pants and seal skin mukluks - their version of rubber boots. The father wore a caribou parka, polar bear pants with his mukluks Even in the north, it is the woman who makes the fashion statement. The son was dressed in a mix of native and imported clothing that indicated he had been away to school.

All three carried a piece of caribou carcass. The main part of the carcass was left on the snow at a safe distance from their anchored down dog team. The parents couldn't speak our language but their son could do some translating so we were able to satisfy their curiosity and we enjoyed the visit.

Repairs continued at a steady rate with interruptions to shovel snow. We treated these as planning opportunities to deal with the next phase of our work. We discussed everything but one key problem that faced us; how we were going to get the repaired aircraft back onto the airstrip. We were confident that a solution was available but we didn't want it to cloud the issue of repairs. Little did we know that a stranger, an angel in disguise, would solve our problem.

A few days into the job, while we were having lunch at the station dining room, a Mr. Kelly, who introduced himself as the sector supervisor from Cam Main, approached me. He said he had looked at our situation from the air as he approached Pin D for a landing that morning. We had watched him come in. He said, "You have a big problem. How are you going to move the aircraft up to the strip?"

I said, "I don't know. We are dealing with the repairs first. We can't afford to let that one occupy our minds even though it is a major concern."

Mr. Kelly went on to say, "I have run a check on you and your company and found that it consists of only you and your wife. Is that right?" I, to say the least, was caught off guard, not knowing what he was building up to but I managed to verify that he was right.

He then looked me straight in the eye and said. "I think that anyone with enough guts to come up here and take on a job like that, deserves to be helped." He then explained that the Station had a D-8 cat that wasn't used much and could do with some use. He said, "I have told the station Manager that the cat and the operator are to be made available to you whenever it is needed and at no cost to you. The usage is to be treated as an exercise and the needed fuel is to come from the leaking steel drums.

He was doing me a favour but he was also doing something about the Site's fuel storage problem at the same time. Forty-five gallon steel drums of fuel had been brought in by ship and stacked on

(left); Eskimo visitors with emergency rations (right); On the airstrip and getting ready for trip to Vancouver. Pilot Jim McInnes standing and Hugh Gilmor above.

their sides like cordwood. Time and handling resulted in some of them leaking.

I was so surprised with Mr. Kelly's generosity that, thinking back, I must have seemed a little slow in thanking him and saying, "You have just solved our most major problem."

It is difficult for me to explain just how I felt about Mr. Kelly's offer. The Station Manager had authorized our use of the heater and generator and it was also possible that he had known we would need that cat too. Mr. Kelly made me feel like we had been rescued because, in our position, with an eight foot wall of hard snow in front of the aircraft and more of the same all the way up to the airstrip, we would have been in a very awkward situation

I had found, early in my experiences with aircraft salvage, that one should concentrate on one problem at a time and take it to a specific level before letting the mind move to another. Distraction usually causes delay.

Strangely, somehow a solution, not always mine, was found for those seemingly impossible situations. Mr. Kelly appeared out of the blue with, to us, a heaven sent answer to our moving problem. Unfortunately, I never did see Mr. Kelly again but I think of him often. Wilf was very pleased because he knew we were in trouble without the cat and he didn't have the authority to let us use it.

The repairs were continued with renewed vigour. Then we were hit with 5 days of blowing snow. On the first night of the storm I heard the wind pick up and begin to howl and thought for sure the plastic covering over the wing would be torn out. I toyed with ideas about going down to the valley to check it but changed my mind because I might lose my bearings in the blizzard. The rest of the night was a sleepless, worrying about what havoc that wind was visiting on our project. With daylight and a hot breakfast in our bellies we bundled up and fought our way in the gale down to the aircraft to find the plastic holding well and successfully deflecting the drifting snow.

I had heard it said that it does not snow in some parts of the Arctic; the snow is blown in from other areas. True? I don't know. However, I was ready to believe it because the blizzard continued with a steady flow of dense snow that extended up about 100 feet above ground level, rising and dropping with the contour of the terrain. It was interesting to watch and perhaps even more so from a Vancouverite's point of view.

That five day snowstorm seemed more like 50. It seemed like it would never end. Finally, we woke to a morning of absolute silence. The storm was over. We had worked through it but it had added a lot of shovelling hours to the contract.

The silence and calm covered the scene at the aircraft. We were enjoying the change when all of a sudden there was a flurry of action from one of the drifts. A large black body burst free and launched itself into the air with a loud series of screams. The raven, a true resident of the north, treated us to his post storm celebration.

Apparently, ravens, during storm conditions, burrow into a snow bank for shelter. When the storm passes they use their large beaks to cut their way out. They are one bird, if not the only bird in the Arctic, that does not migrate south for the winter.

Two other citizens of the north had an adventure during the storm. Our Eskimo helper Andy's two young sons were away on a fishing and trapping trip when it hit. Andy said he wasn't worried because they would build an igloo for shelter. Well, when the storm was over they showed up. As Andy said, they had settled down in an igloo and feasted on the raw fish they had caught earlier.

Every so often we had a visit from an Eskimo lady who arrived with her sled and dog team. She was always smiling and friendly while looking around to see what we were doing. At the end of one visit her dogs became tangled up in their traces and she was having quite a time getting them back in their running order. I wanted to give her some help but as soon as I approached the hackles on the backs of the dogs went straight up.

All of us took time from our tussle with a fractured but static bit of transport to watch her deal with the twelve parts of her transport that seemed determined to go in twenty different directions at the same time. We got a wonderful lesson in patience and temper control. She was quick, methodical and efficient and unbelievably strong.

The lady was dressed in the most beautiful furs that she had sewn together herself and we learned that she used her skills to make dolls dressed in furs of the region. She sold them and traded them. I bought several and I have never seen anything to match them.

Calm but cold weather made it easier for us to get at the work and we didn't have to break to shovel so we were soon finished with repairs to the wing and the fuselage. We now turned to the engines and the propellers.

When we removed the engine cowlings the engines were completely encased in solid, white, perfect mouldings. The wind had driven the fine snow into the open front of the engines and now they were set in what looked like plastic casts. It was a very unique sight.

It didn't take long to clean up the engines and replace the propellers. We were the beneficiaries of mechanical characteristic.

When the pilot used a long approach to the airstrip under low power in extremely low air temperatures and then decided to abort he created a situation beyond his control. During the approach the engine temperature dropped below operating requirements. That prevented them from responding when the pilot advanced the throttles to go around again. The engines died. So we were not faced with the mess caused by racing engines twisting spinning propellers into the frozen ground. Inspection of the crankshafts confirmed they had not been damaged.

Here I would like you to meet Herman Nelson another part of our crew. Herman Nelson is the name given to a fuel fired unit that produces very large volumes of heat that is blown out through large ducts by an electrically driven fan. Thanks to Herman Nelson we quickly heated up the engines. Started them and they operated normally. We were nearing the end of our job much sooner than if we had been faced with using the slow old plumber's blow pots .

That night I sent a wire to my wife, Dorothy, advising her that we needed a pilot and to see If Jim McInnis was able to come up. We received a quick affirmative reply.

Next morning was move the aircraft time and the first need was a pair of skis to put under the wheels. So a steel forty-five gallon drum was cut in two lengthwise. A half drum was placed under each main wheel and secured in place.

Now it was up to Wilf. He picked out the best route up to the airstrip and brought the cat down that route, clearing the snowdrifts away as he came. A fail-safe towline was fastened between the aircraft and the cat and it skied up out of the valley like an Olympian. The gas drum skis performed as though they were factory specified. Wilf did a superb job of making the trip smooth and easy.

I was tickled to see Jim McInnis. He was just the pilot I wanted to nurse our Anson back to Vancouver. Jim was a busy guy at this time, flying part time for Western Airmotive and at the same time on the spare board for Canadian Pacific Airlines. He was just getting his career going. It wasn't long before he had his Captain's rating with Canadian Pacific. He was one of the genuine nice

guys who earned the nickname, "Smiling Jim" among the cabin attendants. He retired from flying Boeing 747s in 1994 after a long career of accident free flying. He thinks the little adventure I got him into with the Anson was one of the highlights in his logbook.

While we were busy refuelling the aircraft and doing a final pre flight check, the two Eskimo boys, Andy's sons, took a fancy to Jim and stayed close by him. I'm sure there was more to admire about him than the large stock of candy he carried.

Our stay at Pin D finally came to an end. It was April 19 and the daylight hours were stretching out rapidly but it was still cold. We left there in mid afternoon under orders from the Station Manager not to use our radio for transmission. He said he would notify the D.E.W. Sites along our route and that would serve as our flight plan.

We were to listen to our radio and if we went off course we would be told to bear left or right as needed for correction. That procedure was not at all satisfactory but those were his instructions and it was his turf. I think he must have been using us in some sort of training or evaluation exercise.

We were on our way for some time in complete radio silence; no instructions; not a word. We were getting a little concerned because there were no land marks or any other kind of map reference markers. We didn't know whether we over snow covered land or snow covered sea. Added to that, the Magnetic North Pole was only a short distance to the North East of us. That did nothing but confuse our compass. So we only had a directional gyro for navigation purposes over the 50 miles that separated each D.E.W. site.

A decision was made to break silence and ask for a course check.

What a surprise! No answer from any of the sites we had been over or the ones we hoped to be approaching. They were silent. We got our response from a Russian who told us we were right on course. So much for what ever scheme our Station Master had in mind.

We thought our problems were now behind us but they were not.

We landed at Pin Main on Cape Parry, a peninsula a little north of Inuvik and Jim had no sooner brought the Anson to a stop when a group of security types came running at us waving rifles. They were quick to tell us we had landed without permission.

I was darned well annoyed at having foreigners pointing rifles at me on Canadian territory so I pushed a rifle aside while I told them so.

They were told to contact Pin D and the manager cleared the matter up.. Obviously, he hadn't done the job he said he was going to do or there wouldn't have been any trouble. Maybe he had reasons but it still puzzles me.

Mention of the rifles brings up a little story about a problem with D.E.W. Line administration.

As a result of some incident in the early days of the D.E.W. Line construction the Royal Canadian Mounted Police insisted that all the arms on the D.E.W. Line had to be sealed by the RCMP. Any broken seals had to supported by a full report.

One of the reasons for this procedure was to prevent off duty personnel and others from being tempted to shoot all the wild game near their site as had happened along the Alaska / Yukon border.

We overnighted at Pin Main. The Anson was refuelled and put in the hangar for the night where we did a visual inspection on it.

Next morning it was standing in a puddle of water. The warmth of the hangar had melted all the hidden ice in it.

We were soon off to Inuvik then up the McKenzie River to Fort Norman. We requested landing instruction but received none. There were two landing strips. One had a crew and vehicles on it. The other had no obstructions. It was icy looking but we had no choice. Shortly after the wheels made contact the aircraft swung to the left and we went sliding sideways for a short distance. I had visions of the landing gear collapsing but Jim handled it very well and we came to a safe stop.

Men came over in a truck from the other strip to tell us we had landed on the wrong strip. They had no excuse from not getting off that strip when they saw us approach and circle. They didn't have an excuse for not having the icy strip marked as unserviceable. However, no harm was done and the matter was dropped.

We overnighted in Fort Norman.

At dinner Jim asked for a glass of fresh milk. Both the waitress and I were surprised at the request. I reminded Jim that we were still in the Arctic where there were no dairy herds and Musk Oxen were not milked.

We completed our trip to Vancouver the next day, with refuelling stops at Fort Nelson and Prince George. The Anson was taken to Western Airmotive Ltd. for permanent repairs and Karl Frisk took charge of the work in his usual proficient way.

Hugh Gilmore was a top engineer and had done a tremendous job under extreme weather conditions and with a good sense of humour. He made an indispensable contribution to the project

Jim McInnis finalized the whole operation with an excellent display of pilot visual flying across the frozen Arctic, unassisted by ground navigational aids or high tech radio as we have today.

chapter fifteen

Cessna Retrieval

A Nervous and Dangerous Ending

The contents of this story are, to say the very least, most unusual. We all know that we have to take the bad with the good in this life. I must say that I have been most fortunate in having experienced a great deal more good than bad. The aircraft industry provided an excellent atmosphere for meeting so many real and genuine people of whom I have many fond memories. However, of course there is always an odd exception as this tale will tell.

It was a Saturday afternoon at our family camp on Cultus Lake, about sixty miles east of Vancouver, when I received a phone call from Dick Hicks in Edmonton. Everyone else in the company I worked for, had clear weekends, but me?--well that was another story.

Dick had been appointed to investigate an accident involving a Cessna 180 seaplane that was upside down in Great Bear Lake in the North West Territories. The actual location, Cameron Bay, was within about 1 degree of latitude, south of the Arctic Circle that cuts across the northern part of the lake. Dick wanted me to leave for Edmonton on the first flight possible that same day and he knew

I would. I was to assist him in retrieving the aircraft from the lake. I left for Vancouver about 6:30 p.m., packed tools and misc. equipment kept at the ready for a quick departure and was at the Vancouver airport by 9 p.m. Dick and his wife Nora met me at Edmonton International Airport and took me to their home for the night. That was first class and sure beat going to a hotel. My big rush was over for the moment.

In the morning we were up by 5 a.m. then right after breakfast left for the Edmonton Industrial airport and caught a flight going to Sawmill Bay on the southern end of Great Bear Lake. The aircraft was filled with American sport fisherman going north to compete with the large northern lake trout. We flew from there to Cameron Bay via a Norseman seaplane. Our equipment including a hand operated winch would arrive a little later, on another airplane. We checked into Branson's Lodge, the owners of the sunken Cessna.

We lost no time in getting out on the lake to asses our problem and plan the salvage operation. The aircraft was well off shore floating safely in an inverted position in deep water and anchored as the owners had been instructed to do, via phone.

It was always a worry upon receiving an assignment involving a seaplane positioned as this one was, fearing that it might drift into shallow waters. It could be destroyed on rocks or other hazards by any amount of wind. This was of course a great concern when British Columbia coastal waters were the local with the constant wave action. Our

equipment arrived in the late evening so we were ready to start work in the morning.

A team of two Federal Investigators from the Department of Accident Investigation in Edmonton had arrived in the meantime. They were Jim Dick and Jack Hendricks. We had a pleasant dinner in the dining room of the lodge with some of the guests who were quite interested in our work.

It was to be the first and last time Branson would permit Dick or me to enter the dining room and associate with his guests.

We started work next morning by selecting a position on shore from where we would operate to remove the aircraft from the water. Past experiences on similar type retrieval jobs led me to believe that we should not have any unexpected problems on that one. Added to that, I had three friendly and willing fellows with me who were no strangers to hard work and technical set backs in the north country. However, in the overall picture of my time up there, Branson would make it most unpleasant and finalize it with an action totally in violation to the unwritten laws of the North Country.

It is preferable, in the turning over of an aircraft as was about to take place, to have the lake bottom slope upward toward the shoreline. It is also a big advantage to have high ground on which to set up and anchor the winch. We were fortunate in locating that combination near the boat docks. The higher the winch is above the water level the more advantage one has in pulling the rear of the aircraft upward for the turn over.

The seaplane was slowly moved toward shore, nose first, until the cabin roof touched the mud bottom. Then a rope bridal was attached to the aft end of both pontoons and secured to the winch cable.

The propeller was a two bladed unit which was in our favour. A three bladed one would have complicated matters somewhat. The propeller had come to a stop with the blades in a vertical position undamaged and our objective was to prevent it from being bent from contact with the lake bottom as the machine was turned over. The forces applied to the bending of a propeller could easily be transferred to the engine crankshaft flange to which it is bolted. The propeller therefore had to be turned until the blades were horizontal.

Turning it was not as easily done it may seem because the cylinders of the engine were full of water and resisted piston movements on their compression strokes. Experience had proven that in reversing the piston movements by turning the propeller in the opposite direction to its normal rotation i.e. backwards, the compression strokes and their blocking actions were eliminated. That was accomplished by me standing on the trailing edge (rear edge) of a blade and forcing it into the horizontal position. A bush propeller shop technique!

The aircraft was now ready to be turned over. Then with Jim and Dick operating the winch, Jack and I with additional ropes secured to the rear of the pontoons, kept the aircraft in a vertical position as it was pulled upward. The propeller spinner and hub dug into the mud almost immediately. It was on its nose for only a few moments until the noses of both pontoons were on the lake bottom supporting the full weight of the aircraft in it's vertical nose down position. That is always quite a sight. A little more pull from the winch brought the aircraft down on to the water and into its normal upright position. It was interesting to see how nicely and slowly the pontoons settled into the water. No big splash. The other three fellows had done a super job through out while all I did was give signals.

I recall Jim Dick being so complimentary on the method and smoothness of the turn over. Jim, prior to becoming an accident investigator for the Department of Transport, had been an Aircraft Maintenance Engineer for quite a few years and I believe part of that time was with Pacific Western Airlines. He was a very experienced and practical individual whom I and everyone else respected very much.

He remarked that during the operation so many people, lodge guests included, had made suggestions on what should be done next but he said "you carried on with your own procedures to a smooth and successful finish." His remarks made me feel so good and I have never forgotten them. I should say that I did listen to the other ideas that might apply under other circumstances. However, the conditions and even the aircraft were almost a dead ringer for several other successful jobs I had previously done and which provided me with a mental blue print for that one. I was just using proven procedures and experiences.

The plane was turned around and pulled nose first up onto the shore. When the government boys had completed their investigation they left on another assignment. The work for Dick Hicks and I now began. The instruments were removed, cleaned and treated with a water inhibitor/lubricant. We would use a minimum of a couple of instruments for the flight south, one of course would be the oil pressure gauge which, on that aircraft was a sealed unit. We went through the usual procedure of cleaning and drying out the engine. Drying was accomplished by exposing it to the wind and the sun.

The oil was drained, and I might add, into a bucket not the lake as were the fuel tanks. Then with the ignition system dried out, fresh oil in the engine and fuel in one tank only, the engine was run up for a brief minute. Then the oil and some remaining water that had been trapped in the engine was drained out with the usual gray colouring. That was repeated twice more with increased time runs until we were satisfied with the operation of both the engine and the propeller. We could do nothing to improve the condition of the wings. They were both twisted and bent from the cart wheeling across the lake surface following an attempted landing. They were beyond the possibility of being temporarily repaired (patched up)

and for me to come to that conclusion they had to be very badly damaged, believe me.

That evening Dick and I were in for a very unpleasant surprise. It was the beginning of much more unpleasantness to come before that assignment was finalized.

When dinner time arrived, Branson told Dick and I that we could not have our meals in the dining room. We were to eat in the kitchen away from the lodge's guests. Dick, who as a Major in the reserve army following his wartime overseas service, was accustomed to eating in the Officers' mess. He nearly turned purple and was at the blow up stage. It was the abrupt, discourteous manner used to inform us that was so offensive. It was, after all, Branson's lodge and it was clear that we were not considered guests. It was not that our clothes were soiled or that we had not cleaned up for dinner. It seemed to be Branson's way of showing us who he was and what he thought we were. Neither of us said anything to him. It would have given him great satisfaction had we done so and would have brought us down to his level.

Quite frankly we had absolutely no objections to dining with the kitchen staff and the other employees because they were so pleasant and had offered to help us in any way they could. It was Branson's bully and demeaning attitude that got to us. He had been snarky with us all day and we couldn't for the life of us figure out why. Perhaps something was bothering him and we were good targets. It was the most unpleasant atmosphere and situation that either of us had ever run into. He seemed to be angry with the insurance company. Perhaps he did not want the aircraft to be retrieved but wanted to be paid out in full for it. It was a sure thing we didn't know. His wife Jeanne, on the other hand, was very pleasant thank goodness. Branson's permanent home was in Parker, Arizona and it was too bad he had not stayed there for several reasons.

The following morning we were ready to leave after rechecking the aircraft for security. There was nothing further we could do until a set of serviceable wings were shipped in. They would have to be located and shipped as quickly as possible because the summer season was rapidly drawing to an end. We were picked up by a south bound Wardair Otter and flown to Sawmill Bay where the Department of Transport fellows joined us for a flight to Yellowknife. We carried on to Edmonton via airline and spent the night at Dick's home which was always a plus.

The following day Dick got to work searching for wings with the best possible delivery date. I, on the other hand, went to the Airworthiness office of the Department of Transport to obtain a flight permit to ferry the aircraft to Edmonton for permanent repairs. An inspector was a little reluctant about issuing one to me. The fact that the aircraft had gone into the water, with the engine running, generated arguments against the engine being used again until it was dismantled and inspected. That thinking was supported by a theory based on the possibility that rapid cooling of an operating engine, on entering the water, could develop a crack in the crankshaft. The guidelines developed from that thinking served a purpose in slowing one down a little, providing time to consider the seriousness of a given operation and which could not or at least should not be treated lightly by anyone. However, while I did not want some one to think I was a know it all or one who charged into a situation without thinking it out, I had had considerable experience on that very subject over the previous years. Quite frankly, eventual dismantling of several engines that had met the same fate as this one, had failed to reveal any sudden quenching damage. Much thought had been given to those findings and it was deduced that by the time the water worked it's way through the engine and reached the crankshaft, it's temperature would have risen considerably. Added to that is the fact that the operating temperature of the engine drops quite rapidly during a landing approach with reduced power. Quite honestly I had, on those accidents, expected to find a crack in a cylinder head particularly in the area of the spark plug holes. Such cracks may possibly have occurred after such a submersion but I never found one. I had even checked the piston travels in case a connecting rod had been bent on a compression stroke with the cylinder head full of water. No indications of such a condition were found.

There was always, and for that matter there still is so much to learn. Experience is a great teacher as long as one does not pay too much for it. That is where theories must be used as a guide and caution taken until safety is pretty well assured. Well, I didn't get the permit but it was waiting for me when I arrived in Vancouver that night which pleased me very much. I credited the Department's delay in issuing the permit as being a safety measure in assuring themselves that I was fully aware of the negative factors.

Now the initial portion of the assignment had been completed and the final part should be underway shortly. That last portion of the salvage operation would prove to be most unpleasant and in fact, pilot Clem Bekar and myself would be deliberately put into a a very dangerous position that could have been fatal, all because of one man.

I do not recall now, why it took the suppliers so long to ship the wings to their northern destination but I was getting nervous, winter was approaching up there. It was in the last week of August that I received word that the wings had been shipped and were waiting for me. I lost no time in catching a flight to Edmonton, tools and all at 10 p.m. that same day. Dick met me and drove me to a motel near the Industrial Airport from which I would depart early in the morning. The rush was on or perhaps I should say it increased because during the previous week or two I had been on the run in and out of Yukon and other distant points.

When I arrived in Yellowknife I was utterly disgusted, to put it politely, to find that the wings had not been sent on to Cameron Bay per instructions.

They were in storage with a collect charge of several hundred dollars against them. That was very upsetting and I had to get Dick to clear them, what a mix up, and I would pay for that later and not with money either.

Continually knawing at me was the fact that summer was almost at an end and the wings still had to be shipped to Sawmill Bay and beyond. I arranged with Bob Engles of Northwest Territorial Airlines to transport them to Sawmill Bay in his Douglas DC-6B freighter along with a load of dynamite for a northern mine. On my arrival there, I needed a seaplane to take the wings on to Branson's place but all the Single Otters were away on long trips. I was stuck again. How do I and the wings get to Cameron Bay? I must say that everyone was trying to help me except Branson who was operating a Norseman seaplane. If I could get there ahead of the wings I could pick up some precious time by removing the damaged ones.

I turned to water transportation and found that Northern Transportation Co. was to transport the dynamite to the mine via a barge and they would move the wings for me. At last I had something moving but not me yet. I turned my attention to a twin engined aircraft that had a problem and which I had been asked to inspect if I had time. I made up a list of the parts needed and a damage description which I gave to Dick Hicks via phone. I had just completed that task when I received an offer of a boat ride to Plummer's Lodge on Great

Bear Lake and upon my arrival I was flown, in their Grumman Goose, to Branson's place.

Warren Plummer has always been a first class operator and ran an excellent fishing resort. I had heard nothing but good things about his courtesies and willingness to help others and this time I was the grateful receiver of his kindness. His son Chummy, had a fishing lodge on Great Slave Lake. He has the same qualities as his father and now I understand he has taken over from him. I wish him every success.

Upon my arrival in Cameron Bay I set to work immediately and moved the Cessna into position for the removal of the wings. It was now Friday August 30 and Branson was planning on closing up the lodge on Monday morning. At any rate I prepared the right wing for removal and with help, lifted it off. I received word that the barge would arrive with the wings on Sunday. Now that was cutting it close. It could have been said that I was exasperated at all the slow movements to date and over which I had had no control. It seemed that I was continually running and Branson was blaming me for the slowness. He was most unpleasant.

Well, dinner time in the kitchen was any thing but peaceful. He kept at me, with all his employees listening, until I was at the point of telling him off in no uncertain terms. However, I was restrained from doing so by pilot Bill Bryson, sitting next to me who mumbled, with his mouth full of food, "Don't listen to him Denny. He's baiting you, don't do it." I took his advice and kept on eating without even glancing up but thought--later we will see. I finished as quickly as possible and went back to work for as long as I could, then to bed. I was back at the machine by 7 a.m. and had a helper for part of the day. The left wing was removed as were the ailerons and flaps of both wings. I had brought in fresh magnetos and spark plugs in case they were needed and now I had time so installed them while waiting for the wings even though there was no need to do so.

I would still be all right, I thought, if the wings arrived the next day. It would be a mad rush to assemble, install and safety them but it could be done, I was sure. The lodge guests would leave tomorrow but I could see a weather change coming and it would not be for the better either. Maybe, I thought, I'll get lucky and the camp closing will be delayed. It was 10 p.m. when I quit and fell into bed after 13 hours work. Next morning a radio call advised that the barge had been in the area during the night darkness but couldn't dock to discharge my load so had proceeded on to the mine and would not arrive at Branson's until Monday. It was just another set back. Why should I expect matters to change in my favour? Meantime, the weather continued to deteriorate which might be a blessing in disguise, for me, by preventing any flying and camp closing.

Well, Monday seemed to come quickly. I was up at 4 a.m. hoping I would see the barge. A weather forecast was not needed to describe the conditions. They were bad. There would be no flying in that stuff. There was nothing more I could do on the Cessna until the wings arrived and I caught myself frequently looking across the lake for signs of the barge. Rather than stand around I helped the cook until about 6:15 a.m. then had breakfast and after that, helped him to clean up the place. I suppose, in a way, I was indirectly helping Branson but dismissed the thought. The cook had all along, been very friendly and helpful to me and now I had a little time and it was my turn.

The weather continued to worsen. The wings arrived at noon and the rush was on. Replacement units were removed from the crates and the damaged ones put in for shipment via the barge to Hay River. Bill Bryson helped me install the ailerons and flaps, then with a few minutes of extra help everything was quickly up in place on the plane. I was actually running most of the day in a very cold wind.

Branson continued to tear hell out of me for the delays in the salvage operation and intended to sue the Insurance Co. I kept my mouth shut which, I might add, was extremely difficult to do. I wouldn't give him the satisfaction of a reply. Sometimes silence is stronger than words. Perhaps that annoyed him. I don't know if it did or not and I didn't care one way or the other. I worked until 11 p.m., a full 19 hour day.

On Tuesday morning I was up at 5 a.m. and it was snowing hard. The surrounding hills were white. It was seldom, in all my northern travels, that I heard wolves howling but on that day, across the bay, they were surely singing. The snow didn't improve the working conditions but I was not complaining. Branson couldn't fly out and that was good for me. The wing installations were completed and Branson's aircraft maintenance man had helped by connecting the fuel lines and which would come to haunt me later.

The engine was given a thorough run up, a magneto was retimed and two spark plugs replaced. The fuel tanks were filled, a final overall inspection was done and all was ready to go at last. It was confirmed through a radio call to Yellowknife that Clem Bekar of Ptarmigan Airways would come in early next morning to fly the aircraft out. The weather was improving a little. Looking back, it was fortunate that I had no idea what fate had in store for us.

During the morning of that day Sed Mah, a well known bush pilot, arrived with a Gateway Aviation Single Otter to have Branson's engineer Ray Cox do an inspection on it. It was good to see Sed again.

That afternoon a Native Indian named Joe, a fishing guide, came by to see how the work was going, he was carrying a rifle and heading in a direction away from the lodge. I asked him why he was going hunting when they would be breaking camp the next day. His reply was that Branson had told him to go out and shoot a bear. I asked him if he had seen one around because I had been out there all day and hadn't seen or heard any. He said "no, but Branson had said to go out, find one and shoot it." Well, that took me aback I must say. Then I said "Joe, everytime I have needed help to lift something or help in one way or another, you were ready and willing, for which I have been so grateful. However, if I hear a shot I will be there as quickly as I can, with a camera. I will take your picture and that of the bear then when I am back in Yellowknife I will report you to Art Look, of the government game department." Joe looked at me in a strange stunned way. He didn't say a word but his eyes seemed to say how could you and why would you do such a thing to me?

He deserved an explanation so I quickly gave him one. I reminded him that the land with it's game and fish were his and mine, not Branson's. Those things were, by way of living, more his than they were mine. If the fishing and hunting ever became too poor to attract wealthy tourists, Branson and others like him would leave the country bare and return to the States. You, Joe, would then be left with little or nothing. He seemed to understand what I was saying. I also told him that I was as good in finding my way through the brush as he was. I would find the bear.

Sometime later I saw Joe coming back and I hadn't heard a shot. He went out of his way to come by me and with a grin he said, "no bears" and continued on up to the lodge. Perhaps Joe had learned something about the other side of the plan wherein Branson felt he was protecting his buildings from later bear break-ins by shooting the animals before he left for the winter. I hope so.

I saw photos showing Indians skinning out bears to the delight of tourists in Canada's Wild North. There were, throughout the northern areas of Canada, too many tourist and industrial sites where garbage disposal was too close to the camps. Bears were attracted and when certain people thought the animals were getting too close they considered it their right to shoot them.

I have always resented people having such a high disregard for wildlife.

I did not witness the action but several fellows in another of the northern camps, I had been in for a short period, spoke about lake trout being hung from the limb of a tree so bears would stand up to reach for them. It was said that was done to entertain tourists.

While I was at that camp we heard what sounded like a rifle shot and a young camp worker from Yellowknife cried out "Oh no, not yet" and ran outside. He quickly returned and said the noise was from a fire cracker used to scare off a bear. I then heard about the bears being used for entertainment and the plans for their demise when the camp closed.

It is my understanding that those thoughtless and don't care attitudes of 25 to 30 years ago have changed for the better. I hope so. There seems to be a lot of support to catching fish and letting them go. That is excellent.

The weather next day, September 4, improved a little and Clem Bekar was dropped off early at the camp as planned and we prepared for the flight south. The engine had performed very well on all the previous run ups but now we had a problem. One cylinder was intermittent in it's operation. It would cut out with a decided loss of power for a short period and then operate again in a normal manner. It was not something to be treated lightly. I determined, by a process of elimination, that the problem was probably related to a sticking hydraulic valve lifter or perhaps a valve.

We had a cloud ceiling of about 2000 feet and the temperature was dropping. In the meantime I had been too busy to realize exactly what was going on at the camp. I was therefore shocked to see that Branson had finished closing up the lodge and had loaded all his people into a couple of aircraft moored at the dock. They lost no time in shoving off. I had known that they were going to leave that day, weather permitting, but then it suddenly dawned on me that they were leaving and no one had come down to see if we were ready to go. Our aircraft was still up on shore with it's nose toward the water.

Branson was in the right hand front seat of a Norseman float plane that taxied by, as closely as the pilot dared. He opened the door and while hilariously laughing at us he yelled, "See you down south sometime!" and he left us.

The camp was completely locked up. He had not even had the decency to come over to us to see what our position was. He had to know we had trouble and there was a strong possibility of us being stuck there. He knew we had no food of any

kind and we were sure that in closing up, a certain amount of food had been thrown out but he didn't offer us any. We had no camping equipment or sleeping bags or shelter of any kind except the seaplane. Had it not been a wrecked machine, it might have contained emergency equipment. Branson also didn't come and ask us if we wanted a message taken to Yellowknife. The radio equipment in our machine was inoperative.

He just left us stranded and that in our north country was a no-no in the unwritten laws of the north. He could have found himself in trouble, with the Authorities, had an air search for us been needed. Branson, with his evil mind, found it amusing to see us stranded. If either of us had been cheeky or mouthy to him he would have had an excuse, as poor as it might have been, to do what he did, but we had not said a word to him.

I should say that I had not approached him about us possibly being stuck there nor had I asked him to take a message out for us for the simple reason that I wasn't looking right or left, I was completely immersed in the mechanical problem. Quite frankly, I didn't realize Branson was ready for his departure until I heard the engines of the other aircraft start running and the seaplanes quickly left the dock. During that frantic period of trying to clear up the problem I was so sure, on each run up of the engine, we had won because normal power lasted longer each time before we had a loss of power.

The engine performance continued to improve

but I had to admit to myself that to eliminate the problem completely, some parts would have to be removed. We could have one or more hydraulic valve lifters sticking intermittently or worse than that, a valve in one of the cylinders could be sticking in it's guide. That would be a major job up there at that time.

The temperature was dropping, the wind was getting stronger and we didn't have any daylight hours to spare if we intended to try flying out. It was agreed that we had no time to do any engine disassembly and fly out that day. We also considered the fact that if we remained there that night, the weather could close in for an indefinite period and we would be in a disastrous position re food and accommodation, to name only two conditions.

I found out later, that the weather had blanked that area out for some time as Clem had feared it would. We didn't spend any time discussing our alternatives. We agreed to give it a try for Yellowknife. If, after take off the weather conditions were too marginal or the engine performance proved to be unsafe, then we would return regardless of the rotten conditions we would be in. However, if we had to return we would find it necessary to break into the lodge for survival and on reaching Yellowknife later, I would submit a full report to the R.C.M.P.

It came as quite a surprise to find another problem raising it's ugly head in the form of a fuel leak, after the aircraft had been moved onto the water and in a level position. I had had Branson's aircraft engineer, who does not live in Canada anymore, help me with the installation of the wings. He did the connecting up of the fuel lines but did not tell me that the fitting or connection on the frame of the aircraft did not match the mating right hand gas tank fitting. That joint was in the balance line between the two fuel tanks and the leak didn't show up earlier because the aircraft had not been in a level position.

It was a seepage type leak and would stop after a small amount of fuel was used as the tube was connected to the tank near it's top edge. We could have drained off some fuel but wanted full tanks in case we had to make the flight longer than planned. We couldn't find a container to drain off fuel and take it with us so we could land and refuel if need be. That was risky because at that time we could be over rough country and in bad weather too. So the leaking joint was wrapped with a bundle of rags. Now we had some fumes to contend with for a while instead of a liquid leak. I was angry over the fact that I had not been told that the fuel line connection was not safe. I was also mad at myself for not checking his work regardless of the rush I was in. We had no electrical equipment, radios etc. that were operational, which under normal conditions, might have been a problem.

Now, with our door windows open we started the engine and taxied out onto the lake. The engine was performing very well, then Clem, with a big smile of satisfaction, opened the throttle and we were on our way. The engine performed in a normal manner during the aircraft's take off run and the lift off from the water, into the air. Then, as Clem was about to bring the aircraft into level flight, the engine lost some power and the airspeed dropped. It felt like the aircraft was coming to a halt in mid air but we limped along for a little bit without losing any altitude then suddenly the engine regained it's full power and the aircraft lurched forward. That performance was repeated throughout the trip to Yellowknife.

There was however, a little humor that went along in the first part of the trip. Clem had a problem--he wanted to have a smoke. He had a cigarette in his hand and looked at me. I shook my head--no. He pretended he was unhappy but was only teasing me. I'm not a smoker so it was easy for me. As soon as the rags around the leak were dry and the fumes had dissipated it was time for Clem to have a smoke but with the windows still open.

The weather became worse with the clouds forcing us down lower and snow showers reduced visibility to a minimum and at times zero for short periods. Clem kept saying that we had to keep the mountain range on our left as we went south. At times we had only 200 feet between the ground and the base of the clouds.

I have always maintained that it is so important to have a well experienced pilot with a good knowledge of the country for that type of operation. Clem is such a pilot.

We arrived in Yellowknife about 5 p.m. It was one flight I was glad to see finished. Clem, his wife and I went out for a very nice dinner and a most pleasant evening. Times like that cancel out much of the unpleasant situations, at least for a while anyway.

Next morning I phoned Dick Hicks and brought him up to date on my progress and found out I was wanted in the Yukon and over on Vancouver Island on more problems. I worked on the engine, checking it thoroughly until I found an intake valve hydraulic lifter, in one of the cylinders, frozen in it's flat position. It would have prevented the gasoline\air mixture from entering the cylinder, thus no power, it was dead. The lifter was dismantled, polished, lubed and reinstalled.

A repair was made to the fuel line by using a borrowed flaring tool. An inspection of the airframe and engine satisfied me that nothing else needed to be done so we did a test flight. It was a great feeling to have the engine operating smoothly and efficiently.

I took time out to see the R.C.M.P., the Government Game Department and Tourist Travel Agency. I provided them with a brief rundown on events, no opinions, just straight facts. I was back in that area a year later and learned that the lodge had been asking for tourists to be directed it's way. Apparently, none were. Perhaps the score was evened up a bit.

I had never had occasion to do something like that prior to that time and I am happy to say that was the last time too. However I was sure worked up for retaliation every time that engine lost power and the aircraft felt like it was coming to a halt in a heavy snow storm.

The aircraft was now ready for the final leg of the ferry flight to Edmonton and this time it was Bill Hetterich who did the flying. The weather was good and we had one refueling stop, at Ft. McMurray. Prior to leaving for Edmonton I received word that someone was busy knifing me -- guess who? I was told that he didn't gain anything and in fact, did himself a lot of harm.

We landed on Cooking Lake in Edmonton and Dick picked us up. We left the aircraft on the lake for the Accident Investigation Department to test fly it to complete their investigation. However they didn't do so and in a round about way, I heard that they felt it lacked a few instruments.

I left for Vancouver, arriving there Friday, Sept. 6. The next morning I left home for a flight to Watson Lake, Yukon north to Canada Tungsten Mines. Don Douglas, of the Western Division of the Accident Investigation Department in Edmonton, heard I was on my way and waited for me at Watson Lake but that is another story. I must say that Don was and still is a very considerate and helpful fellow.

chapter sixteen

Overcoming
Obstacles

A few days before Christmas and the rush was
on to retrieve a Cessna 180 from the frozen Dean
River in the Chilcotin Country of central western
B.C.

The description of the damage included bent
propeller blades, a broken right main landing gear
leg and the outer end of the right wing was a bit
crushed. It sounded like a fairly quick in and out
type of patch up but was it? At any rate I prepared
for the job by procuring a replacement leg and
propeller plus a few odds and ends related to a little metal work.

Some of those seemingly not so complicated
operations had their own little surprises that if one
lacked a little ingenuity he would be stuck and the
job could turn into a major or more complicated
one. You will see that, in a small way, that was one
of those types. One cannot take a shop with him
but he had better have the basic needs.

Chris Kent, of Aircraft Salvage and Rebuild, was
ready to go with me. I don't believe he had, up to
that date, spent much time out in such conditions
as the low temperatures we would be facing. I,
therefore, reminded him of what to expect and the

clothing needed. Later, I had reason to believe that he might have had a hearing problem.

We proceded to Williams Lake where Curly Nairn of B.C. Central Airmotive in Kamloops met us. Gideon Schutze of Wilderness Air Service flew us to the Moose Lake airstrip but the accident site was 10 miles from there. Arrangements were made at a sport fishing lodge for accommodation and meals. Roads remained snow bound around there at that time of year and it would take two weeks to travel to and from the nearest town or one hour by plane. That was true isolation.

We took off with Gideon and headed out to meet our challenge. He had thought of making a landing about two mile from the wreck where the ice looked safer, then it would have meant a long hike back to check the ice at the aircraft. Gideon made a couple of low passes over the river, near the wreck, to get a close look at a possible landing spot and was sure that it would be safe to land on.

He was determined to prove that the ice was safe and did that by approaching the intended landing area with added power and bounced the aircraft off it. Another pass over the ice failed to reveal any signs of it failing so a successful landing was made, much to our complete satisfaction. We were anxious to get the repairs started.

The damage was pretty well as I had been told except for the right wing which had more skin and several broken ribs deformed in its outer end than I had expected. It was also frozen quite solidly into the ice as was the tail with the right elevator and stabilizer firmly held. The left wing was high in the air, a perfect target for a strong wind to tear apart.

Curly and Chris went to work on replacing the leg and I took on the job of freeing the machine from the ice which was accomplished by much chopping and cutting. A tripod was erected to lift the front end of the aircraft so that the gear leg could be installed A tiger torch provided the heat needed to melt ice in the wing and tail units. That took time because the flame couldn't be applied directly to the aluminum metal for fear of damaging it.

The owner of the aircraft wanted to fly it out when the repairs were finished and was to help in getting it ready but was apparently too busy.

We had Gideon stay with us and paid him a daily rate on his aircraft plus his time to help us which was much better. It was out of the question to have him coming in and out from Williams Lake to transport us morning and night. Setting up a camp out there for two or three days would not have been a very practical plan.

As the end of the short daylight hours approached it was starting to cool down rapidly with a stiff breeze. Just about that time one of our party surprised us with his hidden talents by putting on a very original solo impromptu with the ice as his stage.

Chris was performing what appeared to be an Indian Death Dance Ritual. He had been moving very quickly while working but now his movements were steady with graceful contortions and positive foot stomping to the beat of an Indian drum that only he could hear. He was so good that I am sure it would have been his ticket to an Indian Potlatch but I was sure he had already been to one and graduated in their finer arts.

I called and asked where he had learned that dance. He had a quick reply. "Denny, I'm so cold. I'm trying to get warm." It was then that I knew he hadn't been listening to me in Vancouver. He, unfortunately, was learning the hard way.

We were soon on our way back to the lodge before darkness fell. It had been a successful day.

Next morning we were up well before daylight and right after breakfast it was back to the job. The outer end of the right wing had several ribs that were flattened on their top side and of course the sheet metal covering was distorted. Luckily, the spars were undamaged.

It would not be a problem to fly the aircraft without the wing tip cover but the contour of the upper wing surface had to be regained somehow. We had given some earlier thought to that and came up with the idea of using pine 2 by 4 inch lumber that was cut to length for a snug fit between the spars and the upper edge contoured to regain the airfoil curvature. Those pieces were then placed against the crushed ribs, stretching them back out to their full size, top to bottom. The upper and lower metal skin surfaces looked good.

The top and bottom metal skins were secured by nailing them to the new wood formers with rough shanked nails and penny washers under their heads.

Gideon had, earlier, gone back to the lodge to phone the owner of the aircraft at Anahim Lake to inform him that his aircraft would be ready next day. He brought two fellows back with him, Jean Jack and Johnny Blackwell who were so willing to help us.

I believe it was Johnny who said he was a whittler. Just what we needed and he had his knife with him. He carved out a perfect fitting rib to blank off the very outer end of the wing. It was also securely nailed into place.

The propeller had been changed and about the last thing done was operate the engine which passed with high marks.

It began to snow heavily and night was closing in so back to the lodge we went. We hadn't even stopped for lunch that day. We were back out to the aircraft next morning and prepared it for a flight while Gideon went to Anahim Lake to get the owner who flew the repaired aircraft to Nimpo Lake, the first stop en route to a repair shop. We also went to Nimpo so I could get a written pilot statement and log book data for insurance purposes, then away to Williams Lake. Weather blocked our flight at Alexis Creek but Gideon arranged a ride for us via road to finish our journey and catch a plane for home.

Another successful job completed with a competent and harmonious crew.

That job was brought to a successful conclusion by, to a great extent, substituting and making do with materials foreign to the design standards of that aircraft. There are of course limits on how far that deviation from standard practices is taken but it can be very effective with subject knowledge and caution.

I remember two occasions when the only item needed to complete a salvage job was enough sheet metal to cover a fairly large opening between two nose ribs in the leading edge of a wing. We were, in each case, a long way from a source of aircraft sheet metal.

We were in a remote area of the Yukon the first time that happened. A nearby cabin had one of those large Borden Powdered Milk cans that happened to be empty. The metal from it was perfect and already rolled into shape for the job. The name of the product was on the outside of the curvature when it was installed on the wing. It was easy to read and a few comments were made back in civilization.

A second similar situation arose, also in the Chilcotin Country. That time, the only material available was a stove pipe from a cabin. It also worked very well and pulled us out of a jamb.

It was in February of 1973 that Canyon Airways unfortunately put a Cessna 185 over on its back in deep snow during an attempted take off from Tsacha Lake, about 120 miles west of Quesnel B.C. A description of the damage, received via phone from the pilot Ernie Onofrychuk, indicated that it was minimal. I rushed up to Quesnel with a few bits and pieces for the aircraft plus a good propeller from West Coast Air Services.

Daryl Smith, an engineer from Coast Mountain Flight Services and myself flew, via Highland Helicopter, to the downed aircraft with tools and a small amount of repair materials.

Ernie had damaged a ski on the Cessna then removed both of them. He had local help in ploughing a strip out of the deep snow that proved to be not long enough for a take off on wheels. We used the helicopter to assist in turning the aircraft back over onto its wheels. While we were making temporary repairs Daryl and Lance Durand, the helicopter pilot, thawed out a tractor engine and ploughed out a longer strip.

We used all the aircraft metal we had brought with us to reinforce damage to two wing spars that we hadn't known about. I had found those problems by using past experience in examining the aircraft. Pilot Ernie would not have suspected problems inside the wings.

We had no sheet metal left to cover an opening between two wing leading edge ribs.

Our thoughts turned to a summer cabin not far away. The only metal in or around the cabin that seemed practical for our use was a stove pipe. It was already curved to a degree which helped in forming it around the front edge of the wing so a section of the chimney pipe was borrowed. The owners of the cabin were contacted upon our return to Quesnel, informed of the borrowing and well paid for their inconvenience.

Solving our problem in that manner saved us from having to make a trip to Quesnel for metal and extending the job another day with a possible weather change holding us up even more.

Daryl, at the onset, had not thought the aircraft could be made ready for flight that day but it was. I signed the log books stating it was fit for a ferry flight and Daryl made a good take off for home. We had made the machine as light as possible and therefore I did not go with him as was my normal practice. We followed in the helicopter. Later, Daryl flew the machine to West Coast Air Services in Vancouver for permanent repairs.

There were, as expected, comments of surprise from maintenance people on its arrival in Vancouver. It is amazing what can be done in an emergency with a little practicality and ingenuity.

Somehow but not surprising, John Gladstone, the Western Manager for the British Aviation Insurance Company that held the insurance coverage on the Cessna, had heard that Accident Investigation for the Department of Transport had objected to me using other than aircraft approved materials to patch the wing He was quite firm in telling me to provide him with the details.

I have a copy of the Speed Message sent to him on the matter and it reads as follows.

SUBJECT: Salvage of CF-GPL.

The Accident Investigation of Department of Transport made it their business to ask the Department of Airworthiness to check my temporary repairs for salvage and ferry. I went looking for them and explained that they had no one in a position who could criticize me and they agreed.

Airworthiness politely told them it was none of their affairs. Seems they didn't like stove pipe being used. Silly guys didn't mention the areas I thought important. Anyway all seems OK now after I remarked that lack of a thorough knowledge of a subject generally creates uncertainty and doubt in one's mind. I estimate it would have cost another $1,000.00 re helicopter etc. if not done in one swoop.

Signed: Denny

The enclosed verbatim memorandum illustrates that this industry also has its second guessers.

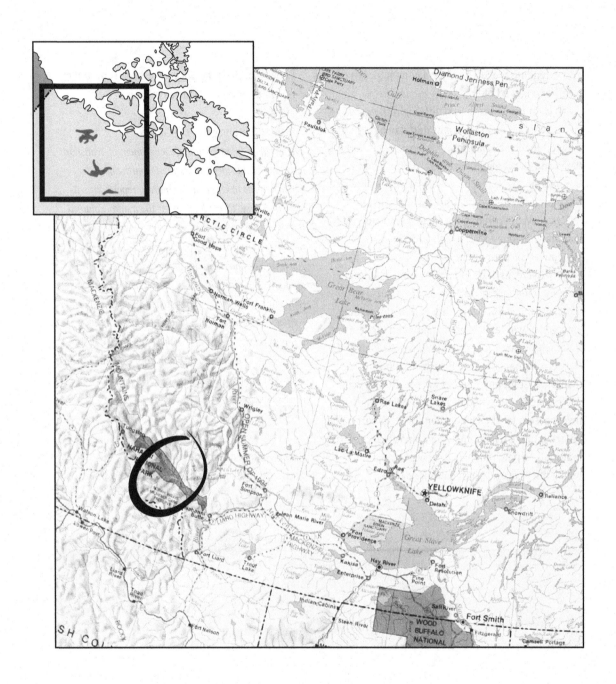

158   picking up the pieces

chapter seventeen

Nahanni
(Headless Valley)
Major Beaver
Patch Up

I received a phone call in January of 1962 from Dick Hicks of James Taylor Company in Edmonton asking me to leave immediately to accompany him to the Nahanni in the North West Territories.

Dick had been assigned, by the British Insurance Company, to investigate an aircraft accident involving a De Havilland DHC-2 Beaver that had come to a sudden stop in the trees on the bank of the South Nahanni river.

Dick was an insurance adjuster who specialized in aviation accident insurance claims. He wanted me to assist him from an engineering point of view, to make up a detailed description of the damage, set up an approximate cost of repairs and look into the feasibility of making temporary repairs for a ferry flight out to a shop.

I was always happy to receive such calls because it meant work for me. However, quite honestly, when I heard we would be going into the Storied and Legendary Nahanni, my mind became preoccupied with thoughts of adventure and the stories of unsolved mysteries. The South Nahanni River country had, by that time, been credited with so many mysterious, strange unexplained deaths and mishaps.

Dick is a very perceptive person and I was sure he sensed that my thoughts were not completely on his problem but he said nothing.

I arrived in Edmonton that evening and we left for Watson Lake, Yukon, the following morning. It was there that B.C. Yukon Air Services had its main base of operations and in fact the Beaver, involved in the accident we were to investigate, was part of its fleet.

Hal Komish, the owner/operator of the company and Walt Forsberg, the pilot in the unfortunate accident, met us. Walt was set to go to Whitehorse for a replacement aircraft for their fleet and in which he planned to fly us north to the accident site. We noticed that he had one foot in a cast and appeared to be in much pain, walking with a very bad limp.

He was most anxious to provide our transportation needs but we could not wait for a day or two until the replacement machine arrived.

His injuries may not have hindered his ability to make a safe flight, however, we were going into a location that had proven that it had the ingredients for an accident and a little caution occupied our thoughts. Through our business of investigating such problems, we had developed a self-preservation attitude of wanting, where possible, all the odds in our favour.

The following day we had Jim Close, of Watson Lake Flying Service, fly us into the accident site, using a ski equipped Cessna 195, owned by a Bud Harbottle, a well-known northern pilot. It was a good flight, ending with a very professional landing, in deep powder snow on the frozen Nahanni River about a quarter of a mile above Virginia Falls.

An American visitor in honor of his daughter named that great waterfall, in 1928. The Native Indians called it *Na ili Cho* or "Big water Falling Down."

The Native name would seem to be more appropriate somehow.

The temperature was -22° F., cool but not unpleasant as I recall. Dick, of course, was accustomed to such weather where as I, from the Vancouver area, felt the lower temperatures a little more on first contact with the cool air.

The Nahanni River runs down through the southwest corner of the Mackenzie Mountains in a spectacular setting. The name, "Nahanni" came from the Slavey Indians of the Lower Liard River, into which it drains. They were referring to the Indians, living farther up the river, as "people from there far away."

The wrecked Beaver, CF-HGY was in the trees with the propeller almost touching a vertical piece of the landscape and about one hundred yards from the river. The damage was very extensive in the wings and empennage (tail section).

The accident had occurred during an attempted take off from the deep snow covered ice. The aircraft had struck a cable that had been strung across the river by Water Survey of Canada to enable them to maneuver a boat on the fast water and hold it in position while readings were taken during ice-free periods. The aircraft had been parked near the cable while Alex Van Bibber; a government water surveyor metered the water through a hole in the ice.

Both the vertical fin and air rudder had been sheared off within a few inches of the fuselage (the body of the aircraft.)

When Walt was asked, by the insurance adjuster, why he hadn't, following contact with the cable, made a landing straight ahead in the deep soft snow, he replied. "I thought you could fly an aircraft without a rudder." Well possibly, with some small type aircraft under certain conditions such as weather and location, to name a couple, that might be accomplished with heavy use of the ailerons. However, in his case, both the rudder and fin had been cut off. Walt said that at the time, he didn't know that he had lost the fin as well as the rudder.

The tail of the Beaver is small and heavy use of the rudder is needed to offset the high torque values of the propeller during take off. Without a rudder the aircraft would go into an uncontrollable right turn. The loss of the fin would magnify the problem and the relatively narrow valley limited

Beaver as first seen - sad sight.

the final manoeuver of the aircraft.

I recall Dick saying, after a quick look at the aircraft, that it looked like a total loss and I must say it did look bad. Its location and position didn't help either. We did some rough mental calculating and could see that it could possibly be repaired well within the value of the insurance. We would, though, need more time to dig deeper into the damaged areas and darkness was approaching to end the northern short day of winter daylight.

We helped Jim maneuver the aircraft into position for a take off by us pushing the tail around in the deep snow with the propeller turning at high speed and blasting us in a blizzard of powder snow.

We returned to Watson Lake and after dinner, spent a nice evening with Bud and Jeanne Harbottle. Bud had lived in Yukon all his life and in his earlier years he had, during the winters, operated a Cat Train [a tractor type unit pulling sleighs] between Whitehorse, Dawson City and Mayo, hauling supplies. He served in the R.C.A.F. during WWII and after the war he continued flying as a Bush Pilot in Yukon. Jeanne was from California and formerly married to a big game hunter and trapper named Tom Connolly who taught her how to hunt, trap and survive in the wild of Yukon. I first met Jeanne in Ross River at her Trading Post and, come to think of it, that is where I also met Bud for a charter flight.

Jeanne wrote about her experiences in a book titled "Woman In The Bush." It is very descriptive and well written. Recommended reading.

Jim Close flew us into the accident scene again the next day to complete the inspection and photo work. It was a pleasant day with light blowing snow and a temperature of only -14° F.

Upon returning to Watson Lake we caught a C.P.A. flight to Edmonton and during which we worked on preparing approximate repair costs for the Insurance Co. I continued on to Vancouver and upon my arrival home, a message, from Dick, was waiting for me with instructions to prepare for and carry out a salvage operation.

While making the preparations for living and working, for a period of time, in that isolated and hostile environment, I thought about the unknowns and legends of the Nahanni Valley.

An expedition into the Nahanni in the middle of winter and remaining there for a period of time in isolation, so far from habitation, would be a first for me. More than just a few questions came to mind.

While in Watson Lake I picked up a little background on what would be our destination and learned that there had been a dozen or more deaths associated with the Nahanni. Some were of a mysterious unsolved nature, such as the McLeod brothers, Frank and Willie, found in their bedrolls, on the riverbank, minus their heads.

That was the start of the mysteries beginning about 1905 and the name "Headless Valley" was born.

Other fatalities had resulted from starvation and

in the same year as my adventure took place up there; it was said that a group died because a charter pilot forgot to return for them. I heard of a prospector found dead on the steps of his cabin and a dead grizzly bear, with a serious bullet wound, next to him. Evidently, the bear had gone for the man after being wounded and caught him just short of safety, then also died.

Those stories delivered a message on the importance of self-preservation and drove home the fact that mistakes and foolishness would not be excused or overlooked by Mother Nature.

The book titled "Nahanni" by Dick Turner is very descriptive and informative of that intriguing country. Also recommended reading.

Projects, such as I was about to take on, required a lot of planning and preparation. It was mid winter in Yukon and the North West Territories and I anticipated temperatures would likely reach down to around -35˚ F. as we later experienced.

The planning was so important because it formed the foundation for a successful operation, which was so dependent on even the smallest details. Poor planning could result in anything up to and including a disaster.

We would not be able to depend on radio communications to order in materials, parts or other supplies. We would be camped on the north side of the high McKenzie Mts. that would make radio contact difficult if not impossible most of the time.

It was not to be a cost plus operation. The plans had to include a minimum, not a maximum of food, manpower, equipment and parts for the job to be done as efficiently as possible.

I had photographed the Beaver and damaged areas in detail, using slide type film. The slides were then projected on to a screen and the exact locations of the damage could be determined in a wing for example, by counting the rivets and ribs from one point to another. That data was then applied to a good wing and a blueprint to obtain measurements in inches. Repair sections such as would be required for temporary repairs were then made up.

Plans were carefully set out on paper as the thoughts came to mind. Besides myself, the manpower would consist of a top notch airframe technician and one camp man who would do the general camp duties such as cutting wood, doing dishes, cooking and assist as needed.

I was most fortunate in filling the technical needs. When I asked Ron Rogers to go with me, he readily agreed. I was very happy about that because he was well known around the Vancouver airport as an extremely capable aircraft structural technician. He was from England where he had obtained his aviation training and experience in the Fleet Air Arm of the Royal Navy during WWII, a section of the military with which I also have some background. He had a terrific sense of humour that, later, proved invaluable especially when we ran into unexpected major problems.

The third man, Bob Marineau, thought the wide open outdoors was the way to live and looked at the trip as a great adventure, right up his alley, nothing to it. He was informed of the hardships he could be facing and possible consequences of failure but he wanted to go. I would not have considered taking him but there was family pressure, not my immediate family, and I weakened, when I shouldn't have as I learned later. What a surprise he was in for.

We loaded a flat deck trailer with a large tent, tarps, tools and parts. It was hooked up to our family 1957 Pontiac station wagon and we took off for the 1700 mile trip to Watson Lake, Yukon. The trip was, for the most part, uneventful even though ice and snow covered the road most of the way. Tire chains were not used because once we were

into the low temperature areas the tires remained as cold as the road surface and we had good traction. Even truckers didn't use chains on hills when the temperature was -10 degree Fahrenheit or colder. The tires ran white, no heat build up as in warmer conditions, thus no skidding.

Upon our arrival plans were made to fly via Beaver, to a spot on the Nahanni we were to call home for a while.

Walt Foresberg took us in with a Beaver. It was a good flight that ended in a nice landing in the deep snow. We tramped down a large flat spot near the river bank and unloaded the aircraft.

We then assisted Walt by pushing the tail of the aircraft around until he was lined up in his landing

(left); Our home with the unhappy Beaver. (right); Ron Roger leveling up the aircraft.

tracks for a take off which was a good one. The other fellows had their introduction to propeller snow blasting.

When we could no longer hear the aircraft engine we knew we were all alone and totally on our own. The deadly silence gave me a strange feeling and the -42˚ F. didn't do anything to help either.

We chose a spot for our tent then tramped out an area and set it up. We were actually on a frozen pond. It was a convenient location, close to the aircraft. Everything was packed up from the river and stowed or systematically stacked and their locations marked with a pole in the snow so nothing would be lost or misplaced. Nothing was to be laid down on the snow otherwise it could be covered with snow and lost.

A deep bed of spruce boughs formed the base for each of the three beds on which foam mattresses were placed for the sleeping bags.

Ron made supper by candle light, on a Yukon stove, which is a collapsible wood burning type that held enough wood for only 1/2 hour of burning after we had gone to bed. No heat all night. Ron, by the way, was an excellent cook.

We were up by about 6:30 am. The thermometer showed -35˚ F. and the bathroom was in the wide open spaces with Mother Nature and her deep but soft snow blanket.

That was quite an introduction to the North West Territories for all of us and a little more so for the other two fellows. Such conditions and situations would be repeated in the many mornings to come. That first cool night and cold morning did not encourage anyone to drink tea or coffee in the evening and suffer nocturnal trips out into the snow.

I should mention that we were using Woods 3 Star eider down filled sleeping bags with metal fasteners, not zippers, because a broken zipper could have been a disaster. The bags were lined with a Hudson Bay wool blanket and still we found it necessary to wear our heavy under clothes, socks and a toque for warmth. Eider down has the highest insulation qualities of any materials known to or designed man, even to this day.

The Eider Duck is found in Eastern Canada and plucks the down from its body to lines its nest. Down is collected in small amounts from the nests, which the duck replaces during the egg hatching season and more is obtained after the chicks leave the nest. Just thought I should add that bit of information about a product of nature.

In the morning the openings at the head of the bags had a heavy coating of ice (not frost) from our breathing. That had to be thawed out and dried before rolling them up for the day.

On the first morning of work we could see that the aircraft should be leveled up and several items removed for major repairs, especially the right wing. We did some planning on our approach to the repairs then got started.

A tripod was erected, using spruce trees, and the aircraft was lifted into its upright position, which made it look a lot better. Then a work shop was built by lashing spruce poles together, forming a framework that was covered with plastic sheeting. Structures, not unlike saw benches, were constructed from poles and on which a wing would be repaired.

Both the front and rear spars at the root or inboard end of the right wing were broken. The outer end of that wing was also torn up with spar damage from tree and ground contact. That damage would be a major part of our work.

A day or so later, Walt brought us a Herman Nelson heater and a power generator. That equipment was very much welcomed because it had been cool in our shop that had one end open to the elements. Hand drilling had its draw backs too.

We had rented those units in Watson Lake and within two days the generator failed. Much time was lost in making repairs to it. However, it failed again after a few days so it was back to hand drilling. I would find it so very difficult to explain the frustration that caused.

I was so fortunate to have had Ron Rogers with me. Adversity bothered him as much as it did me but he had a good sense of humour and dug in to make the best of a set back. "We mustn't complain," he would so often say.

Mother Nature must have seen our plight because she favoured us with a few days of warmer temperatures during the daytime but it also brought snow, which did not hamper us in our shop. It was a bit of a relief because without a generator we could not operate the heater.

In the meantime, Bob, in charge of camp chores including wood cutting, was finding that the northern experience was not as thrilling and exciting as he had earlier imagined it would be. I can honestly say that he had been told what to expect but he must have thought I had been exaggerating because, in spite of the warning he had still wanted to go along. He was a friend of my sister who thought he should be given the opportunity to go. I knew, and it was later confirmed, that I should have hired a man from the Watson Lake area who was accustomed to roughing it in that part of the country.

One day he wandered a little farther into the woods to find dead, dry trees and came upon fresh animal tracks that I identified as being wolf and bob cat. Another time he discovered that a few wolves were watching him from a distance. It was reasonable to expect him to be more than a little concerned and I didn't joke about it either.

I told him not to worry about wolves but if he saw a wolverine, he had better back off slowly and get back to camp because that small bundle of fur could be very volatile if he is disturbed while eating. Then he was given a description of the animal and it's habits, also why it was called a skunk bear.

We did what we could to help him adapt, even to cutting some of the wood and we were having problems of our own with the repairs. The trees were frozen for about 2 inches inward from the bark so I showed him how to cut them without chopping off a leg. An axe will glance off such a tree very easily. We needed a large wash tub for him to stand in but didn't have one.

I explained that we all depended on one another for survival and, to which, part of each day was donated. Mother Nature who seemed to be waiting for such invitations to teach us a severe lesson did not over look carelessness and mistakes.

One evening, just after supper, something from outside struck the tent at the side, next to Bob's bed. It startled us all. I told him to go out and prove his survival ability by shooting whatever it was out there but he was frozen with fear. So I pulled on a pair of heavy moose hide mitts and went out with a hunting knife and a flashlight and saw nothing except wolverine tracks. I imagined that the animal was watching from close by. It was perhaps a brazen act on my part but I was trying to prove a point that existing in a location such as that was not a piece of cake.

I should mention that those animals, while they are comparatively small, have been known to drive a bear away from its meal. They can also climb trees to bird nests. They are called skunk bears because they urinate on food caches and animal food, leaving an odour that is revolting to other animals and man. That is their way of protecting their food.

Our man continued to be careless in many ways and I had to explain to him that in the event he was seriously injured it would be disastrous because our communications with the outside were in fact, zero. An accident could result in a person bleeding to death before help arrived. Then his body would have to be placed out beside the tent; face up with no covering, in cold storage with whatever there was that had hit the tent that night.

I suggested that he keep in mind that there was a good reason why the area was called Headless Valley. I must say I didn't like talking that way but better it was said than wait for a disaster. We could see, in the next few days, a decided change in his approach to life and working safely, which pleased us very much.

Following our short interlude of snowy weather the nights turned snapping cold with temperatures of -35° and -40° F. A full moon was so bright in the crystal clear air that it made the snow sparkle like millions of diamonds. The shadows of the spruce trees on the snow, right down to the tips of the smallest branches, were so sharply outlined like black on white. It was as if a giant artist had been at work. That was fascinating to us, coming from Vancouver.

I usually walked down to the river before going to bed and each time, as I gazed across to the other side, I was so sure that I could see Old Mother Nature over there and heard her saying "Make a mistake and I'll have you."

It was, no doubt, that constant concern for safety and well being that kept me reminding all of us of its importance.

In the meantime, we had been trying to get a

radio message out to Watson Lake or Canada Tungsten Mines, both on the other side of the Mackenzie Mountains, with a message about us needing another generator, all with no luck.

We continued with hand drilling and candle light to cook supper.

I remember one evening that Ron was cooking supper (as usual and so very much appreciated). He had made up a batter that he set within arm reach from the small stove and at the edge of the tent. When it came time for him to use it in the meal preparation, I heard him loudly yell "Core, (an English term of surprise), the batter is frozen". Keep in mind, the batter was inside the tent, not outside.

The repair work had been slowed down considerably because of the generator failures and we were getting low on our rations as well.

It was about that time we received a visit from the Water Surveyors, Monty Alford and Alex Van Bibber. It was so nice and a relief just to see them. They called Watson Lake re our need for another generator which was wonderful, believe me. Our battery was too weak for transmission.

Prior to them leaving, they gave us the rations they carried with them which included steaks. I have so often thought of that fine gesture, it sure perked us up. Monty Alford's book "Yukon Water Doctor" is recommended reading.

Walt arrived the following day with another generator then we were able to set a date when we would be ready to fly out. Ron said. " Now we can

get cracking." We worked until midnight and finished the metal repairs. We had replaced metal sheeting and support structure for about a quarter of the wing. Maintaining the alignment was a constant concern. It had to be reasonably accurate because there would not be any test flight and return to the shop for adjustments. Therefore, even though it was a temporary repair that would be completely redone in the final repairs, we could not afford to take short cuts and hope for the best. That could be a suicidal action.

It so happened that we had no sooner finished the metal repairs, when the replacement generator failed, but now it was chiefly assembly work or, so we thought. Needless to say there was an exchange of words later at the rental shop. I never rented some else's junk generator again, I bought a new one.

It did not always happen, but one had to expect unforeseen problems to be discovered even when all seemed under control. I had thought we had had our share of nasty surprises with generator failures. Such wishful thinking.

We were moving right along toward the finish line when I discovered, to my horror, a crack in an upper leg of the tubular designed engine mount. That was indeed serious. The aircraft definitely could not be flown without a repair of some kind to the mount. But repair it with what?? Discovering damage to an engine mount was worse than a crack any where in the airframe. We had no idea what we were going to do about it but we had sev-

168   picking up the pieces

eral other things that needed our attention so we got on with them and let the horror problem set for a while.

I had learned, on other salvage jobs, that as soon as a matter has been thoroughly thought out, with no resultant solution, it does not help to stew over it. The problem remains in one's mind but should not be allowed to totally occupy it.

We did not discuss the mount problem any further. We had plenty to do in the tail area that pre occupied our thoughts.

One day, while rooting through a tool box for some bolts, my eyes came to rest on a cylindrical shaped handle of a strong arm wrench for a half inch socket set. I, without stopping to think, yelled. "I have it. I have it".

Ron came running around the end of the aircraft calling loudly, "WHATS UP?" and I said, "Look". He came back immediately saying, "An inside sleeve for the mount leg? Do you think it will fit?" I replied, "It's perfect". He then wanted to cut the leg to check it. I said; "No" and he asked me if I were afraid it wouldn't fit. I answered "Yes." At that moment it seemed too good to be true, yet I was sure it was the solution even though I did not know

the inside diameter of the tube and I had not measured the thickness of the tool handle. It was as if some one had said, there you are, that is what you need. The thing that was so strange, and I have thought about it so often since then, is the fact that I was not even consciously thinking about the mount at that time. My mind was on a problem in the tail that required some longer bolts that were found after I had settled down.

Well, another day or two went by and I asked Ron if he would cut the mount and check the tool handle for fit.

He did and very shortly I heard him yell. "CORE", his terminology for surprise and excitement, "its perfect." The sleeve fitted like a piece that had been machined for the tube. I do not believe in miracles but I do not know what else to

(left); Northern major repair shop with Ron Rogers rebuilding the wing.

call something like that. It was not to be the last of such experiences either.

When we were sure that we had no further need for the tool, it was fitted into the leg and four quarter inch bolt holes were hand drilled to secure it. That took a bit of doing too but we were happy the mount was repaired.

Those who did the permanent repairs later in Vancouver, could not believe their eyes when they saw the mount repair.

Our work was finally finished except for the installation of the wing. We decided to use the height of the river bank as an assist in holding the wing up in position for its installation. The aircraft would eventually have to be winched to the river bank then down onto the ice so why not do it at that stage and minimize the struggle of lifting the wing into position.

We froze large stakes into the river ice as anchors for winching the machine down the slope and positioning it. A rope, secured to the tail ski assembly and paying it out from around a tree, prevented a fast slide down the embankment. The ground level above the river was a perfect height as one man could sit on it and hold the tip of the wing on his lap and keep it level.

It was not long until the assembly of the aircraft was completed and we were ready to run the engine, which would firstly have to be warmed up from an external source of heat. We were blocked again because our power generator was inoperative and the heater couldn't be operated without it.

To make matters worse, the Beaver had not carried a portable blow pot type heater in it. So we were stuck until the other aircraft came in to pick us up.

However, little did we know that that was a minor matter as compared to what fate had in store for us later, on the ferry flight to Watson Lake.

During our stay at that site, wolves had been traveling up and down the centre of the river and had made a single path about two feet deep as they ran single file. The powder snow, over three feet deep discouraged wolves from spreading out. However, it well suited the long legged Moose and Caribou until sufficient crust was formed on the snow to support the wolf. Then the larger animals were at a disadvantage as the wolves could run alongside them and eat on the run, slashing at the hind quarters and other parts until the animal slowly died.

Walt and Bud Harbottle arrived on schedule with a Beaver. Bud appeared to have something bothering him but he dug in and worked like a Trojan warming the engine with a plumber's blow pot, in preparation to start running it.

I learned at a later date in Watson Lake that Bud had wanted to fly the repaired aircraft out as a favour to me but he had been told, as they neared our camp, that I had said that I did not want him to fly the aircraft. That was, of course, a lie because in my earlier talks with Walt, the pilot for the flight out was never mentioned. Apparently, Walt was determined that he was going to do it and had told others of his plan.

Bud must have been very upset to think that I would have said something like that. He was made of good stuff because it didn't slow him down and to his credit he didn't make an issue of it. That would have developed into unpleasantness that was not needed at that point.

Bud had wanted to fly the aircraft because he felt he owed me a favour for a variety of information and engine installation photos I had sent him in the past. I never did think that at all, just happy to help. The subject came up later in Watson and he said that if he had been flying the Beaver into our camp, when he was told the fib, he would have turned and gone back to Watson Lake. We would have been in big trouble if that had happened. I shuddered to think about it.

We loaded both aircraft, putting the heavier items in the good one and lighter things in the repaired machine. The tent had become frozen into the ice so rather than tearing it out I left it for any one to take later on. We also left the Herman Nelson heater that I went back for, later. I felt like leaving the generator too, permanently, but didn't.

Walt took charge of the repaired H.G.Y. He and I took off ahead of Bud who was to wait until we were clear and on our way. We had been camped for 21 days and were now looking forward to the luxuries of a hotel.

The aircraft was performing very well with no abnormal pressure needed on the control wheel. I felt very satisfied and relieved of the tension that

one has on that first take off after such major temporary work, even though I felt good about the quality.

It was the proof of the pudding so as to speak.

We lifted up over the Mackenzie Mountain tops, which are high above the tree line. The landscape, below us, of jagged rock and barren valleys was awesome. It looked, for all the world, like a huge grave yard full of enormous statues.

The thought of the possibility of a forced landing on a ferry flight was always in the back of my mind and one in that area with its solid vertical rock walls would be fatal. Strangely enough, Bud, later spoke of that area in the same terms.

Little did I suspect, at that time, that after about 1 hour's flight, we would be doing just that, making a forced landing.

Ron and I had double checked our work physically and mentally until we were positive we had not overlooked anything and satisfied ourselves that we should not have any in flight problem. However, as per my habit on those flights, I watched the engine instruments like a hawk, kept an eye on the repaired areas and alert for any abnormal vibrations or smells such as burning oil would produce.

We had been in the air for close to an hour and starting to leave the mountains behind us when I noticed the oil pressure fluctuating, then it dropped to a lower reading and stayed there. Walt had seen it too. During the next few moments the oil pressure fluctuation was repeated, ending with still a lower reading.

I quickly removed the oil tank cap/dip stick that showed we had lost considerable oil. Fortunately, the Beaver had been designed for bush flying and the ability to measure oil quantity or add oil from the pilot's position was one of the many special design features that only De Havilland would think of.

It was a life saver for us and I have good reason, even to this day, to be thankful for practical thinking of Punch Dickens who is credited with that innovation.

With the oil loss we were in a serious position. I rushed to the rear of the cabin, stumbling over tools and equipment, for cans of oil left over from the fill up at camp.

I recall that I found about 2 gallons, in quart cans, and in spite of rough air and no funnel, most of it went into the tank. The pressure immediately went back up and we felt greatly relieved. However that period of great relief was not to last.

The pressure, in about 20 minutes time, started to fluctuate and drop again. During that short period I mentally went through all our pre flight checks trying to sort out a possible cause for the oil loss. I was satisfied that every thing and in particular, the oil drain plug had been secured, and double checked. Also, one of the most experienced and qualified northern operators, Bud Harbottle, had helped me prepare the engine for the flight.

Through a process of elimination I narrowed the problem down to a leaking oil cooler or a failure of the super charger blower seal. A failed seal would permit oil to escape from the crankcase, into the induction system where it would be burned in the cylinders.

The oil loss was quite rapid so I was sure the seal had failed. The remaining oil would not last long, then the engine would seize up instantly. There was no other indication of a problem, the engine was running smoothly and the instruments, other than the oil pressure gauge, showed that the engine was performing in a normal manner.

The cylinder head temperatures had remained constant and it seemed possible, that with enough spare oil to keep the tank level up, we might have been able to baby it along, even as far as Watson Lake but we did not have the oil.

We were clear of the rock pile but we were now over the winding crooked Coal River with no straight stretches long enough for a safe landing. A small lake was spotted and I was determined that we should land on it while we had engine power and full control of the aircraft. Walt did not agree and was determined to proceed farther down to the Highland Valley which no doubt, would have been a better area with more choice of places to land.

However, I had calculated about how long the oil would last and it would be utterly impossible to reach Walt's preferred spot so I dug in my heels. I was determined that we were going to land on the lake and reminded him that as the representative of the Insurance Company I was responsible for the safety of the aircraft as well as my own hide.

He continued to argue but I had lost my control and loudly supported by thoughts by shouting, "When that engine seizes up and it is quickly heading to that point, the aircraft will take over full control and choose the spot for a crash, not a landing."

Suffice to say that a good landing was made even though the lake was quite small.

Bud was following and would be looking for us so we hastily tramped out, in the snow, the words, NEED OIL. He came in quite low, apparently got the message, then left.

We moved the aircraft up on to Spruce boughs to prevent the skis from freezing to the snow. Following that, I checked the engine exhaust tail pipe. It was very oily and heavily carboned up. The oil quantity dip stick indicated that the oil level was only a thin line above the empty mark.

My diagnosis regarding a failed blower seal had been correct. We could not have stayed in the air for more than only a very few minutes longer before the engine failed completely.

It was then that Walt saw the wisdom of landing on that lake. I didn't have to say anything more to convince him. I had already said more than enough.

Bud returned with oil. He explained that he had taken off from the Nahanni shortly after we did and at 10,000 feet he could not see us even though it was a clear, sunny day. The first sighting he had

was a flash of light way down below him which, he guessed, came from a sun reflection on the new metal of the repaired wing.

He said he couldn't imagine why we were that low so he dove down as rapidly he dared and quickly saw us clearly with a long trail of smoke coming from our aircraft. Bud said he had a horrible feeling we were on fire. It reminded him of the war as our machine looked like one that had been set ablaze by gun fire.

His description of the smoke trail confirmed that it was, indeed, the blower seal that had failed, permitting oil to escape into the cylinders where it was burned and produced thick black smoke that poured out the exhaust.

I had had that very same experience a few years earlier while ferrying out an aircraft with Jim Lougheed on the west coast, north of Campbell River.

We lost no time in filling the oil tank and Bud had brought an extra lot of oil that would get us to Watson, if we could get back into the air.

Try as I might, I could not get that engine operating at its peak performance and to my satisfaction. The head temperatures of the cylinders remained too low. That was an indication that too much oil was getting into the heads and preventing complete combustion of the fuel with a resulting reduction in power.

Walt then ran the engine while I stood off to one side to listen to it, and he was completely satisfied with its performance. I thought he was wrong and told him so, because the engine had not sounded, to me, like it had reached its top performance. However he was the one who had been reading the instruments on that run up but I was still a Doubting Thomas.

We were now not very far from Watson Lake and desperate thinking suggested that with plenty of extra oil and good engine performance, it was reasonable to feel we could finish our flight. The key to that thinking was "good engine performance." Walt couldn't see why I hesitated.

Then I agreed to try it. So down to the very end of the lake we went, turned around and started a take off run. I watched the instruments like a hawk. At about the half way point of our run I didn't like what I saw. The R.P.M. was not high enough and the head temperatures were still low. The engine did not have that top power sound that gives one the needed feeling of satisfaction and confidence.

As we rapidly neared the end of the lake with trees suddenly looming up in front of us, we were still on the snow with no increase in engine performance.

I was much more than a little concerned because we now had no chance of missing the trees even if we did get into the air so I, without uttering a word, quickly reached up and pulled the throttle and propeller controls back, to shut down positions. We came to a stop near the trees.

I then turned to Walt and said. "That engine did not produce full power in the static run up as you claimed it did." He replied by saying "well, it almost did."

That finished me and afterwards I was surprised at myself that I hadn't expressed my evil thoughts on the matter. If that flight attempt had continued we would most certainly have ended up in the trees and no doubt, with injuries, if not more than that. Bud later echoed my thoughts. The aircraft was secured with spruce boughs under the skis to await our return.

Too much oil had been getting into the combustion chambers, and fouling up the spark plugs. That had prevented the plugs from producing complete combustion needed to develop full power. We needed a replacement engine so we flew back with Bud to Watson Lake where I put our Bob on a plane for home.

Never, in all my years of flying out in patched up aircraft, did I find it necessary to interfere with a pilot's flying procedures, or have reason to do so, as I had on that ferry flight.

I had, at the time and since then, often thought how fortunate it had been, especially for Walt, that I had followed my practice of flying out in the temporarily repaired aircraft to monitor its performance and provide, at least moral assistance, if it became necessary.

I should also say that I, besides saving my own skin, had an obligation to the owners of the aircraft and those who insured it by doing my best for a safe flight. They put a lot of trust in me.

Slim Knights, a very experienced wartime and

post war West Coast pilot had arrived to fly the Beaver to Vancouver so we moved into rooms where he was staying. I will not try to describe how luxurious it felt to be in a motel and have a hot bath.

Later, Ron and I went to visit Slim in his room and found it to be far too warm for us. We therefore opened the door and all the windows to cool it down. I can still hear Slim pleading with us to "please" close them. He said he realized that we had become winterized and he was sorry the room was too hot for us "but – PLEASE".

Preparing Beaver for flight. Left to right: Bud Harbottle, Walt Forsberg and Ron Rogers.

How could we have ignored his plea? We couldn't and we didn't. So we suffered in silence.

Next day we made inquiries about a replacement serviceable engine, around there, that we could get on loan. Hal Komish, owner of the Beaver, helped us by letting us have an overhauled one. The engine would not fit into a Beaver cabin unless we firstly removed some cylinders that I was opposed to doing on a new engine. We were lucky that Bob Engles of North West Territorial Airlines was in the area with a De Havilland Single Otter. It was the same aircraft that he and I had ferried up from Bogota, Columbia, South America, to Calgary, about 3 months earlier in December 1961. Bob agreed to transport the engine into where the Beaver was stranded. It was loaded as a complete unit and flown to the lake that was to be Ron's and my home in the deep freeze again for a while and the Beaver would be our sleeping quarters.

We spent another 5 days changing the engine. A tripod was erected over the aircraft and the old engine was removed and lowered to the ground. All the accessories, the mount, exhaust system and other items were transferred from it, to the new one. The complete fresh engine was man handled into position below the tripod then lifted up and bolted to the aircraft after which the propeller was installed. That work involved an awful lot of heavy bull work for the two of us as we had nothing but hand tools and a small chain block.

nahanni (headless valley) 175

The day temperatures were well above freezing and down to 0˚ F. at night. No complaints about that. However, one day we were hit by a storm of strong wind and sleet that forced us to stop work. Next morning we were up at 4:30 with a temperature of 0˚ F. and back to our task.

We kept working long after dark by camp fire light. The Northern Lights, some nights, lit up our area as they steadily flashed across the sky in broad bands of bright colours. That made our situation a little more pleasant.

We slept in the aircraft and cooked our meals on an engine blow pot heater, with engine cowlings shielding it from the wind. It was a first class kitchen. Perhaps I should explain that the heat for cooking came from a vertical gasoline fired unit used by plumbers to melt lead.

Finally the engine change was finished, it performed 100 percent and we were ready to go. Radio contact with Watson Lake could not be made but Canada Tungsten Mines picked up our message and passed it on to Bud Harbottle who lost no time in getting to us. Such co-operation was an example of how people up there were so willing to help.

Cantung, as it was also referred to locally, assisted me in the same manner on several different occasions when I was in desperate need of help. That northern atmosphere was so different to the big city but there was the very odd exception.

The last time they helped me, I was camped out on a patch up job, just south of the Nahanni and was to be picked up by a certain pilot, whose name I shall not disclose, from B.C. Yukon Air in Watson Lake on a specific day which came and went with me still there. Two more days went by with poor radio conditions between there and Watson Lake. Then I received a grateful reply from Cantung and they immediately went into action for me.

I was short of food and very angry about the delay. Again, it was Bud Harbottle who came to my rescue.

Later, the pilot's excuse was that, in flight, icing conditions made him turn back. Others, in Watson Lake, said that the ice was in a glass and the condition was developed in the early morning hours of the bar in the Watson Lake Hotel. I never flew with him again and I was thankful that I had a radio or two days may have been extended indefinitely but now, back to my story.

Ron and I had partially disassembled the old engine then it and all our gear was loaded into the two aircraft and we left for Watson Lake.

I recall, on our arrival, that Hal Komish expressed more than just a little surprise at the excellent condition of the aircraft and he did not hesitate to say so. Ron and I were very pleased to receive that compliment and because of my position in the overall picture, perhaps it would mean even more to me in the long run. The skis were removed from the Beaver and after another inspection and I had again signed the log book, certifying it as being fit for a ferry flight to Vancouver, Slim was ready to go. He and Ron had a nice trouble free flight home.

We still had some equipment on the ice in the Nahanni, such as the Herman Nelson heater. I left Watson Lake in a D.C.3 with Bud and Gordy Bartch, to meet up with Bob Engle at the Cantung Mines. Next day, Bob, a Larry Wilson and myself flew into our old camp on the Nahanni. Bob parked his aircraft on the river next to the encampment and in water overflow caused by the warmer weather. My feet were soaked, cold temperatures would have been better but Spring was on her way.

During the loading of the heater I was lifting and pushing the unit up, into the aircraft from my position on the ice. At one point it was tilted enough that the diesel fuel spilled out of the tank and over me from the shoulders, on down. I was very uncomfortable, to say the least, during the flight back to Cantung.

I worked until 11 p.m. on our return to the Cantung airstrip, inspecting and servicing Bob's Otter then arose at 3:30 a.m. next morning and helped him get away on another trip.

Later that day, Gordy Bartch who was hauling freight into the mine, did me a favour by taking me and my equipment on a back haul to Watson Lake at no cost.

I haven't the words to express how good it felt when someone helped me like that. I should also mention that Roy Lambert of Cantung was also a great help during their mining preparation days and I have never forgotten the invaluable favour he and Max Ward did for me on one particular occasion at that mine.

The morning following my return to Watson Lake I loaded my trailer and started south. I had gone only a short distance when I had a trailer wheel problem. It was Jimmy Close of Watson Lake Flying Service who helped me overcome that one.

I hope, by mentioning these several tremendous courtesies, I have been able to depict, for the readers who may never have been into those northern areas, the humanity that prevailed through out the north.

I left Watson Lake on April 13 and it was 3 tires, one wheel and 1600 miles, of which, 1,000 were terribly rough, that I arrived home at 8 p.m. on April 15. The roughest piece of road was in B.C., between Dawson Creek and Prince George. It made me furious to see a road grader off to the side of the road apparently needing maintenance and the road below it so badly in need of grading. That sight was not, in that stretch of the road, at all uncommon.

I had left home Feb. 27, a total of 48 days.

I was so fortunate to have a wife like Dot, waiting, worrying but no complaining. Many aviation wives were and are of the same qualities, however there were others who were not.

chapter eighteen

Perry Linton's Helio Courier

Major Patch Up

Perry Linton had the misfortune to have a forced landing, due to weather, on what he thought was an air strip on the horse range. That was a spot some distance south of Watson Lake, Yukon where some outfitters (big game guides) put their horses out to range during the non hunting periods.

I was not an insurance adjuster at that time but did work for insurance companies as an aircraft engineer specializing in patching up damaged aircraft in out of the way places.

Stan Bridcut of Watson Lake Flying Services and I flew to the accident site and located the Courier close to the air strip that Perry had tried to locate. It was a sad sight. The rear half of the fuselage was completely buckled downward about mid way between the cabin and the tail. The aircraft had come to a stop with the main wheels on a small mound and the tail wheel on another, separated by a depression with the fuselage buckle down into it.

I had not been asked by the insurance adjuster in Seattle to do anything more than see about salvaging the aircraft and I did not report beyond that. However, I was naturally curious about how a buckle like that would happen and I could think of only one thing, a full load and a rough landing. The aircraft was empty with no sign of the cargo, which Perry later said had been potatoes and his brother Beacher had done the loading.

I returned to Vancouver and provided Jack Mitchell in Seattle, the western representative for Leo Leclerc of Montreal, with a damage description and cost figures. Instructions were quickly received with a request to get on with the salvage operation. Tools, camping equipment and repair materials were loaded into our family station wagon and about three or four days later I was in Watson Lake ready for work.

Meantime, I had ordered a certified replacement rear section of the fuselage from the Helio Courier dealers and parts suppliers in Edmonton. It would reduce the bush work considerably by installing another unit instead of making a very major type patch repair on such a badly broke up assembly. A shop would no doubt use a replacement for the permanent repairs anyway.

Perry was a good worker on the salvage operation and nice company too. When we thought we had waited long enough and the shipment from Edmonton had not arrived, Perry and I left to go to work. I would have preferred to see what we were getting before going into the bush but we had a big job ahead of us so off we went. Watson Lake Flying Service flew us and all our gear to the horse range. We were not long in setting up a camp and erecting a tripod over the cabin of the aircraft to support it during the repairs.

The end of an unhappy landing

The task ahead of us would have been classified as a major one in any repair shop but a bush operation magnified it tenfold.

Everything had to be stripped out of the rear half of the fuselage including the cables for the elevators and rudder that also had to be removed with all their fittings. Needless to say, all that had to be reinstalled in the replacement unit after it was in place. The front and rear halves of the fuselage were joined together just behind the cabin and that is where we drilled out all rivets to separate them.

Bud Harbottle tried to fly the replacement tail cone into us as soon as it arrived in Watson Lake but was unable to handle it with his aircraft. A helicopter transported it as a side load on its carrier.

We quickly found that the unit could not be used as received. I had expected and rightfully so, to get an assembly that was complete and ready to install. It upset me to think a parts supplier would send something like that to someone out in the bush.

At a later date I confronted the individual on his thoughtless action. His reply was. "I knew you had a "B" license and could do what was necessary."

Perry and I continued with the work of installing the replacement assembly. It was awkward to attach it to the cabin because the rivet holes in both pieces did not match up. It is extremely important, in doing temporary repairs, not to enlarge any holes that will be used for the perma-

nent repair or drill any extras. We overcame that poor manufacturing feature by inserting a narrow splice strip between the two sections and used the holes as they were. The splice was completed with many machine screws and blind pop rivets.

When we had overcome the main obstacles and could see we were gaining ground we stopped work an hour before dark one day. Not far from us was a creek down in a small valley where beavers were building a dam to form a pool. We looked down on them for a while, watching them steadily going about their business of towing branches through the water to the dam. Too bad we couldn't have given them a hand but at least we did not disturb them. Watching them made me feel better to think we weren't alone in having to work hard. I hope they have never been disturbed by anyone.

Slowly but finally the assembly work showed pleasing results and Perry was certainly doing his share and more. We arrived at the point where we could start preparing the aircraft for flight, which called for a general inspection of the remainder of the machine. I came across three or four items that needed attention and which were indications of poor maintenance. That surprised me so I asked Perry about it. Apparently he had not had the aircraft very long, having taken delivery of it only a short time back and had not flown enough to need an inspection. I seem to recall that the suppliers of the tail section had also sold the machine to him.

Those extra items needed the same attention as

the accident damage to prepare the machine for a safe flight. I then made the required entry in the log book certifying the aircraft as fit for a ferry flight. Additional entries regarding other none accident related work were made with a recommendation that the aircraft receive a 100 hour inspection for recertification. I was evidently not very popular with a certain shop operator in Edmonton as a result. The entries could not be not be ignored by anyone, especially the Airworthiness Division of the Department Transport. Perry's interests had been taken care of and to his benefit. I had never taken such a stand prior to that or since then because I had no need to do so.

The aircraft was moved the short distance to the airstrip and Bud came in to pick up our camp and equipment. Prior to leaving there, we put the damaged tail cone up on end, off to the side of the airstrip securing it with wire and rope.

Some time later, Stan Bridcut said, "I was flying over the strip and saw something that made me think. Oh my gosh some one has crashed head first into the ground." He continued. "I turned and made a low pass for a close look then it dawned on me, Denny McCartney had been there."

The flight to Watson Lake was uneventful. It had been a very different but interesting type of salvage operation with good company. Perry flew his machine to Edmonton for permanent repairs and I returned to Vancouver.

(top); Rear half of aircraft removed. (above);
Helicopter with replacement part for Helio

chapter nineteen

Bottom's Up

As soon as the salvaging of a Cessna in the Fort
Smith area was completed, Curly Nairn, his son
Rob, my son Murray and I went directly to
Plummer's Great Slave Lake Lodge.

A Grumman Goose (a fairly large amphibian aircraft) was on its back at the side of a sand airstrip.
A brake had seized during a landing and the wheel
had dug itself into the sand causing the aircraft to
nose over on to its back.

We arrived about 5 p.m. and moved all our
equipment to the accident site with a truck from
the Lodge. Then I left for Yellowknife to pick up
propellers and other parts and materials that had
been shipped up for the job. There was nothing
missing in the shipment. The crate containing the
replacement air rudder was broken but, thankfully
the rudder was not.

That rudder was the only spare in Washington,
Oregon or British Columbia and I had been lucky
enough to get it on loan through a fellow I knew in
Seattle.

I had of course been giving a lot of thought to the
challenge facing us. I had successfully uprighted
quite a few aircraft, that had become inverted on
dry land, without having to disassemble them.

None of them had been the size and configuration of the Goose which offered us a new challenge. However, there were several pleasant and positive factors that played a big part in the success of that operation.

Curly was a very experienced Aircraft Engineer and the Goose was no stranger to him. He had spent a number of years maintaining them. Chummy Plummer was always most pleasant and ready to help us in any way he could. It was like white on black in strong contrast to another Lodge I was at two years earlier on Great Bear Lake. Another big factor was that we had our meals at the Lodge and went back and forth to it with a boat and outboard motor supplied by Chummy.

While I was away the others had eaten, the tents were up and Curly had made a start on the repairs. A very good beginning.

The aircraft had come to its stop on the airstrip and had been carefully moved off to one side to keep the strip operational. It was then in an ideal location for what we would have to do in turning it over on to its wheels.

Some of the damage was quite serious. The blades of both propellers were bent, one engine mount and its airframe support structure were broken, damage to one wing tip and both the vertical fin and the rudder were crushed.

The methods of repair were easily agreed on as was the thought of doing as much of that work as

A rare position for a Goose.

we could while the machine was in its inverted position. It would be much easier for us to work on some of the damaged areas with the aircraft in that position than when it was sitting upright on its wheels.

The most serious damage that got our immediate attention was the broken prime structure in the left wing, that included the fittings to which the left engine was attached. If that could not have been repaired sufficiently to safely support the engine and its propeller in flight, the machine would not have been flown out of there. We would then have had a major problem.

I had, on my first inspection of the aircraft, given that particular damage some very serious thought and was convinced it could be repaired satisfactorily. Accordingly, the materials and parts, needed for that work, were brought in with a positive approach to repairing.

I had always found it most important to check out all possible alternatives in the various phases of a planned salvage operation. The ground method of transporting the aircraft out to an overhaul shop south of there would consist of barging it down the lake then transporting it via rail on a flat car. The aircraft would have to have been extensively disassembled and crated, all of which would increase the costs considerably plus a huge increase in the out of service time, an added hardship on the Lodge but there would also be a very great risk of shipping damage.

Curly turned his attention to the engine mount attachment support with his son Rob helping, while Murray and I prepared the propellers and left engine for removal. We were well started and on our way.

The work progressed favourably but I must say there were times when Murray couldn't be kept busy enough and he became restless when I was on a one man part of the work but he worked hard at everything he was asked to do. That energetic go, go trait has paid off for him as he is now President of a very successful oil and gas company in Calgary.

A day or two had passed, then we were hit with heavy rains and little or no shelter while working out in the open. We went to bed feeling a bit damp.

The engine support frame repairs were successfully completed as were several other major metal damages and we were then ready to start turning the aircraft over.

As would be expected, we were now faced with obstacles that hadn't arisen on previous retrievals but there was nothing new about that. There was usually something new or different on every job which, at times, was a worry because of limited equipment and resources in the wilderness.

It was apparent that we could not pattern that turn over off previous successful similar situations because the tail of the Goose would have to be raised to quite a height, with the full weight of the aircraft concentrated on its nose. That could very well have damaged the hull and there would have been no way in which we could have used man power to assist or restrain any movements. To add to the challenge, a strong gusting wind had developed.

The tail had to be brought upwards to move the machine over at an angle of about 45 degrees rather than the usual 90 degrees or vertical position used on smaller aircraft. The cat would provide the muscle to pull the tail upward with a line secured to the end of the hull structure but the nose of the aircraft might just skid toward the cat and cancel out the lift forces. We would gain nothing.

We pooled our thoughts and came up with a plan. We had to, for a start, have the nose set firmly at a selected spot which was done by digging a fairly large and deep hole immediately in front of it and filling the bottom with soft cushioning sand. Theoretically, the nose would slide into the hole and held in that position, burying itself, to a degree, as the weight on it increased.

Then we would need something to prevent the aircraft from crashing down on to its wheels and bottom side after it had passed its apex in the turn over otherwise additional damage could be expected. Another piece of mobile equipment with a line attached to it and the tail of the aircraft might have been used but none was available and besides that, the cable would lose its effectiveness when it started to flatten out as the tail of the aircraft began to level out and settle down.

A scheme was devised to halt the downward travel of the aircraft at about its half way point. The aircraft would come to rest on its bottom, tail still high and at an approximate 45 degree angle.

That was accomplished by building a steep sand ramp leading up from the back edge of the hole and extending well out from both sides to take care of any side movement in the final moments of the up righting.

Oh, Curly and I had it all figured out or so we thought.

We started the operation, using Chummy's cat and ran its cable out to near the top of the longest pole we could get so that the tail would be lifted upwards from the highest point possible. A heavy nylon rope was attached to the very top of the pole with its other end secured to the tail structure of the aircraft. We were all set to go.

Chummy's cat and operator provided the power needed to pull the aircraft over and we got under the tail to tilt it upwards as much as possible from its horizontal position for the start of the lift.

It seemed that all was proceeding favourably with the tail well on its way upward. SUDDENLY it dropped back down and a piece of the wooden pole came soaring through the air like a javelin and buried itself in the sand next to the tail, narrowly missing us. It was a close one.

It appeared that the heavy pull on the pole and possibly a slight jerk had caused the pole to snap. The nylon rope had been stretched to its limit and the sudden release let it recoil like a huge spring, sending the piece of post through the air like an arrow released from a bow. We, at the tail end were, to say the least, lucky. I was one of them and can still see it hitting the sand close to me. An inspection failed to reveal any additional damage as a result of the mishap.

The necessary changes in the rigging were made, including the use of the steel A frame that we hadn't used because it was so heavy and also shorter than the wooden pole. Height was very important at the beginning of the pull on the tail because it started it coming upward immediately, which was what was needed.

The aircraft was turned over with the damaged wing tip lightly in contact with the ground, at the start of the lift, to steady it. It worked out very well with the bottom of the aircraft coming to rest on the built up ramp with its tail high up. As we had hoped, it had settled down very slowly. It was interesting to see that its nose had actually dug into the wall of the hole and its heavy lower structure took much of the weight stress.

We got a great deal satisfaction from the fact that we had been able to turn that bulky aircraft over exactly as we had planned and, I might add, with not even a dent of additional damage. Lucky? I do not think so but perhaps a little nervous at times.

The hole was filled in and with a rope bridle on the landing gear the cat pulled the machine forward until it was sitting on all three wheels. Had we been some place where a cat was not available the job would have been so much more difficult using a well anchored heavy B-B winch [a common type hand winch].

Metal repairs to empennage (tail) and the wing tip plus the engine and propeller installations kept us very busy for the next few days. The left engine had not been reinstalled earlier to avoid possible damage to it during the up righting of the aircraft. Sometimes it was quite difficult, in those bush operations to work on something that was out of reach. Such things as ladders or stands didn't exist. It was a matter of using what was around and so often, 45 gallon fuel drums were the answer. The problem out there on the lake shore was solved by grading up a sand ramp to

Successfully uprighted. Left to Right: Murray McCartney, Curly Nairn, Rob Nairn.

assist us in gaining sufficient height to install the engine on that high wing.

Chummy's cat was, of course, a great help in lifting the engine up into position by hanging it from a sturdy pole secured to its grading blade.

The repairs were drawing to an end and much of our equipment was no longer needed, so when Chummy said he was going to Yellowknife and offered to take our heavy items as well, I was delighted.

I had heard nothing but good things about Chummy and his father, Warren and it was very plain as to how they had gained such a good name.

The cowlings (engine covers), having been crushed out of shape, required a lot of work to make them fit reasonably well. The aircraft was refueled and run ups were done on the engines to our satisfaction.

The last item was the right wheel braking system. The aircraft had been given an inspection, by an independent maintenance shop, a short time prior to the accident and the quality of the brake certification was questionable.

Considerable time was involved in determining just what was wrong and we found, for one thing, that incorrect type seals had been installed. Finally, after several adjustments were made and the system bled, it was operating reasonably well.

That day was a very windy one and found us working in an atmosphere of blowing sand. Most difficult. Parts removed from the aircraft were stowed inside it for the ferry trip, then it was taxied to a parking area to wait for the ferry flight.

The following morning we packed up our camp in preparation to leave. An Otter was coming in with a few drums of fuel for the Lodge and we would return to Yellowknife on it.

I then picked up some lake trout, for Phil Clayton and John Gladstone who so often provided me with working trips into the north but few or none for themselves. Then, we left at noon, taking with us the outgoing mail from the Lodge.

On arrival in Yellowknife I provided Curly and Rob with tickets for Kamloops via Calgary. Murray and I headed for home with a stop over in Edmonton for a meeting, regarding the Goose, the next morning. Klondike Days were in full swing and Edmonton was alive in a big way.

It was then July 30 on the night we arrived home. I had been steadily on the run from one place to another after damaged aircraft since June 5th. The following day was Friday and I thought; the weekend will be great up at Cultus Lake with the family.

That was dreaming, because, the next day Murray and I were on our way to remove an aircraft from the glacier on Mt. Garibaldi and the week following I left for Saskatchewan.

In the meantime, Curly returned to the Goose with pilot, Ken McQuaig and it was successfully ferried out for permanent repairs.

chapter twenty

To The Rescue

snowmobiles rescue Cessna 310 C-FPPF

This is a story about the co-operation and help that was so often associated with the people of the North Country.

During a take off from a gravel air strip at Dease Lake, in the North west corner of British Columbia, the left engine of a Cessna 310 lost power. High terrain forced Stephen Klesenhowski, owner/operator of the Whitehorse Flying School to go into a left turn to attempt an emergency landing on the ice covered lake, which he did. However, because of the lack of power in the left engine, he was not able to lift that wing up enough to level out the aircraft for a landing and struck the ice rather hard. The nose wheel structure collapsed on contact with the ice and the right hand wing fuel tip tank caught fire.

The calendar said it was the last week of April, 1979. Spring was slowly returning to that part of the Province with ice, in various stages of deterioration, still covering lakes.

I arrived in Whitehorse via airline then south to Dease Lake, in a Cessna 172 wheel plane with Stephen. Prior to landing on the airstrip we checked the shoreline for signs of a road of some sort leading down to the lake and found one.

Prearranged ground transportation consisted of a light truck and a skidoo. The fellow driving the truck was Richard Brown a close friend of Stephen. He joined us in our venture.

A quick look at the ice didn't leave any doubt about it getting ready to leave for the summer. There was some open water along the shore and a little over flow out further. The usual beginning of ice break up.

In preparation for a trip down the ice, to the wreck, the other two fellows started roping themselves together as if they were going to scale a steep mountain side. They explained that they were playing it safe in case one of them broke through the ice.

Well, the playing it safe approach was always good common sense but the procedure, in that case, was wrong. It was not that I was so clever and had a solution for every awkward situation,

but experience with ice of questionable condition, I did have.

I suggested that they stay on shore until the condition of the ice was checked and a safe path from the shore was determined. I did that by using an ice auger and cut several holes starting from near the shore and outward for about 50 feet. The ice was about 24 inches thick at every hole, quite safe for our needs. We then drove the skidoo in a straight line to the aircraft with no problem.

Stephen's remark to Richard was something like, "Imagine some one from Vancouver coming up here and showing us how to look for safe ice." The caution he displayed at the onset was, no doubt, a reaction to the hazardous trip he and two passengers made through slush, over flow and snow drifts to reach shore after the accident.

The right wing of the aircraft had been burned out, from its tip to the engine. The aircraft had

(left); **Cessna 310, right wing burned out.** (right); **Aircraft on skiis (auto engine hoods) and towed by skidoo team.**

remained up on its main landing gear but the nose wheel support structure was crushed under the nose of the machine that was flat on the ice.

The next step was to get the wreckage on shore, from where it would be hauled away. That would have been our plan in any event but also the owners had been informed by the Royal Canadian Mounted Police (R.C.M.P.) that they were not to let the aircraft go through the ice and sink in the lake.

The method to be used for its removal was quickly decided. There were no helicopters in the area large enough to lift it or even skid it to the road.

We had no time to lose because, if a strong wind struck the lake, the condition of the ice would change rapidly and not in our favour. The aircraft had to be skidded down the ice, some how, to the road.

My two cohorts knew pretty well everyone in that area and thought that they could get some skidoos to tow it down the ice. Now, that made good sense and was certainly an original idea. I was very pleased with that suggestion.

My donation to the plan was based on past experience wherein 45 gallon steel drum halves were used as toboggans under an Anson's wheels. That led me to thinking about using light truck engine hoods that had deep fronts or noses.

The other two knew where an auto wrecking yard was so off we went and found three good ones. While in the small town, they arranged to have their skidoo friends help us.

The engine hoods were made secure under both main wheels and the crushed nose with sticks of wood placed under them to prevent them from being frozen to the ice. We worked until quite late in the evening and were up at 4:15 next morning after a short night's sleep, then out on the ice by 6 a.m. We had no sooner completed a brief check of our project when we saw three skidoos coming down the lake to do a job for us before they went to work.

Each skidoo was independently attached to the landing gear of the aircraft by a long rope. The trip down the lake with four skidoos pulling the aircraft was quite a sight, perhaps an original such operation. All the drivers were excited about doing it too which made it a pleasant task.

Upon reaching shore the skidoos were then on an up slope and could go no further in their towing. Fortunately for us, we were able to beg the use of a government truck and its winch to pull the aircraft through the near shore overflow and poor ice until it was safe on shore. However, the trucker had a problem after he had helped us. He became stuck in the road and could not get back up to the main highway until other government road equipment pulled him out.

I was very sorry about the trucker's misfortune in the face of his generosity in giving us the help we had so desperately needed.

Pacific Aircraft Salvage provided the assistance to disassemble the aircraft then transported it to Vancouver without further problems.

chapter twenty-one

Belly Landing

Hawker Siddeley lands on Hudson Bay Ice

At approximately 3 p.m. Bill James of Reed Stenhouse in Calgary, phoned to say that Calm Air's British Aerospace Hawker Siddeley H S 748 airliner with registration C-FMAK had blown both engines shortly after take off and the pilot was forced to make a belly landing on the ice covered estuary of the Churchill River in Hudson Bay. - They wanted me on the job immediately and had already booked me on Air Canada's 5 p.m. flight to Calgary.

That really put me on the run. That was the shortest notice I had ever had to get home, pack Arctic clothing etc. and be out to the airport for a flight that would leave in 2 hours. Panic rushes had happened so many times and I was lucky my wife Dot was a very good packer and knew exactly what I would need. Her calm capacity to get things organized made it possible for me to meet my deadline.

Bill and Gord Smith, also of Reed Stenhouse, were waiting at the Calgary airport and took me directly to a Lear Jet executive aircraft for continuation of the trip. Another first for Denny; my first and only such executive type flight and I thoroughly enjoyed it.

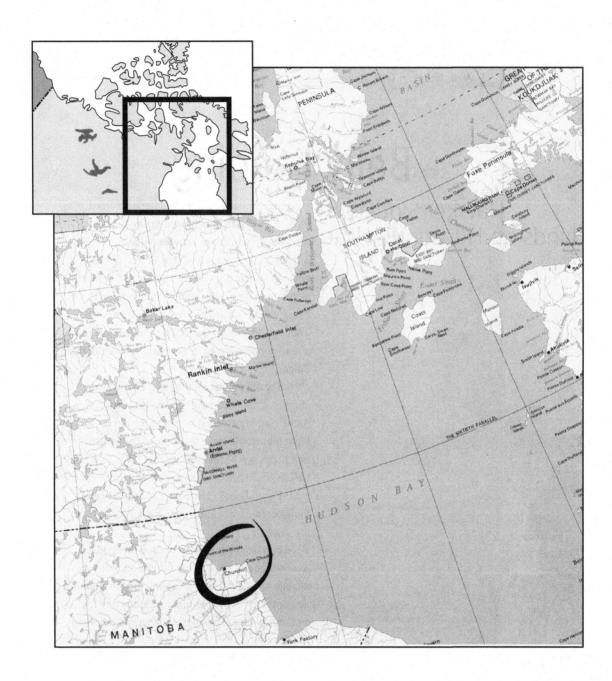

192   picking up the pieces

A short stop was made in Saskatoon to pick up insurance adjuster Hank Eisler of Stinson Eisler who normally serviced that central area. My participation in the investigation was based on my engineering and salvage background.

It was a little under 10 hours from the time Bill James had blown his starter whistle until I was in a Churchill hotel. It was spring time in Vancouver and a bit of an expected shock as we left the jet with 0° on the 'old' scale and a strong wind in the face. We had arrived within one half hour of Transport Canada's Accident Investigators from Winnipeg and investigator Joe Bajada from Ottawa.

Early next morning we and the Government Inspectors used skidoos to reach the Hawker Siddeley and start our investigations.

That model twin engined aircraft was a good sized one with a seating capacity of 61 and a gross load weight of 46,500 lbs. It was quite some distance out from shore, flat on the ice with extensive damage to its lower side, propellers and engines.

Pilot Ken Towers had reported that just after take off from the airport the right engine quit and shortly after that the left engine failed. He had made a good wheels-up landing on the ice with a full load including 19 passengers and no injuries or freight damage.

One of the passengers, an Eskimo Lady with a 4 day old baby, was not at all excited about the experience and seemed quite contented as she waited to board another aircraft for her flight north

and home. No passenger claims evolved from that unfortunate mishap. I have thought how different that might be today with people farther south seeking a retirement program through legal encouragement.

The pilot's descriptions of the accident led us to the water/methanol system. Our inspection revealed that it had failed in its function at a critical point in the operation of both engines. The result was a drastic loss of power that led to the emergency forced landing. The water/methanol mixture is injected into the hot turbines of the engine to lower their temperatures. This increases their power output.

The initial part of our visit was finished and we turned our attention to the major challenge of getting the machine back to the airport. A mental picture of the plan clearly showed that assistance and co-operation was required from a number of groups and their executives.

I received tremendous assistance in setting up a meeting that included representatives from the City of Churchill, Canadian National Railroad, Manitoba Hydro, Transport Canada, Calm Air and the Royal Canadian Mounted Police. As you will see, each one contributed a great deal and without help from any one of them, we would have been blocked in our efforts.

Grading out a road to the aircraft was the first item and somewhat difficult at its shore end where huge rocks the size of small buildings dominated the areas. A winding path was made between them where the aircraft could be safely pulled through. Then there was a stretch of tundra with small trees and other growth that I didn't like tearing up but there was no other choice. I hoped no one would come after me about it. The same accident situation in climate friendly B.C. would have attracted a gaggle of tree huggers.

The work on the aircraft was started by cutting away the ice from under the fuel drains in the wings. A fuel tanker was driven out on the ice, which gave us some anxious moments when it broke through tidal overflow ice nearer to shore. We had to pump out 10,000 pounds of fuel from the tanks to reduce the weight and ease the lift facing us.

The temperature ranged around -12° F. with a steady wind of 25 m.p.h. We did not, as usual, consider or calculate the wind chill factor. We were as cold as we felt and didn't need any such figures that might make us think we should feel colder than we were.

There were no lifting fittings for the aircraft closer than England and further more, there was no large mobile crane in the area even if the ice could support it and we knew that it would not.

That left us with only one method of lifting the aircraft nearly 5 feet to get it up on its wheels. Small vertical hydraulic jacks called bottle jacks, similar to a car jack but having greater lifting capacities, were used. The aircraft was lifted about 10 inches at a time then timbers were stacked or blocked up under the fuselage and the

jack reset for the next lift. A crane mounted on a truck was used to hold the nose up and keep the aircraft level as it was jacked upward.

I was most fortunate in having two of Calm Air's men lying on their stomachs under the aircraft doing that work. They, Dave Cross and Colin Sarswell, were from England and their good nature and sense of humor made the work go much faster under conditions that make saints swear. They worked hard and steady with no complaints about the cold and blowing snow.

This was a complete turn about for me. It felt strange not being involved in the hands-on work but it gave me a chance to plan ahead for the next move. I was able to continually check the stability of the aircraft as it was balanced on two jacks and at times shuddering in the wind. I told Dave and Colin about my dicey experience under an Anson balanced on oil drums while Arctic winds tried to bring it down on top of me. They cheerfully accepted any constructive thoughts I had on safety.

It was slow work. Given the cold and the wind it could be dubbed a painfully slow process. We were constantly on edge because a sudden change of weather could give us problems beyond our control.

We worked until dark then blocked the machine up solidly, tied every thing down as firmly as we could and left it for the night. It was a nervous sight to look at the aircraft sitting on stacks of wood blocks and thinking about what Mother

Nature might do to it. A perfect target for a strong wind.

All of us hated to leave it that way for the night but it would have been too dangerous to continue work in steady blowing snow and the head lights from a truck. One unseen problem could have so easily developed into a catastrophe including a fatal injury. Happily, the only casualty, and that only temporary, was Dave's beard; his breath froze it into a hairy icicle.

Luckily the wind strength had not increased nor had its direction changed which was right on the nose of the aircraft, perfect.

During the night I slept fitfully in a shack and could hear the steady threat of the wind as it whistled around the corners. Each time I awakened I got up and checked to see if there had been any wind direction change.

The fear was that if the wind swung around and struck the vertical fin and rudder broadside, it was almost certain that the machine would be twisted off its blocking. I spoke of my restless night at breakfast next morning and one of the fellows said, "You were awake all night too?"

Drifting snow had filled in the road and had to be bull dozed out again. However, the aircraft was still as we had left it and the wind hadn't slowed down the least bit.

The jacking continued and late in the day it was high enough, about 52 inches, to put large base hangar type, high floor jacks in place, under the jacking points of the aircraft. The aircraft was

A perfect emergency wheels up landing

then secured sufficiently to lower the landing gear and lock it in place. We stood looking at it for a moment with a feeling of relief.

The bottle jacks and blocking were removed and the aircraft was ready for the next phase, towing it out. I had, in the meantime procured cable and heavy nylon rope from the Harbour Board to make up a towing bridle. The rope was used for the bridal that had to be wrapped around both the main landing gear legs. It protected them from being scored or cut as would have happened if cable had been used.

That aircraft, as are other nose wheel equipped machines, is normally towed around an airport with equipment attached to the nose gear. Some thought the method should be used out there on the ice.

I pointed out that a bulldozer would do the towing and if a main wheel broke through the ice the sudden tension developed on the tow bridle could rip the nose gear out. So I planned to tow the machine backwards with a bridle on the main landing gear legs that were structured to withstand backward type loads during landings. They would stand up to any irregular shocks during the tow. We did it my way.

Bill James, in the meantime had been trying to reach me to advise that my Mother had died and he would provide a plane for me to get back to Vancouver. It was generous of Reed Stenhouse to offer such help.

I was torn. For a while I struggled with the decision. I loved my Mother dearly and wept because I had not been with her. Powerful emotions tugged at me. The importance of having that one last visual contact was so strong. Finally I asked myself what she would tell me to do and it was as if she were beside me. The words, "You can do no more for me. I am at peace." came into my mind. I talked to my very capable sister, Kathleen. She, like her mother, was pragmatic. The matter was settled for the moment by her making arrangements for a cremation and we would have a family service upon my return home. With a heavy heart I turned my full attention to the Hawker Siddeley.

That salvage job was actually at a critical stage with problems popping up that were new to everyone. I had experience getting aircraft out of unusual places and I my built in sense duty, put there by my mother, counseled me not to leave this project with so much more to be done.

The towing got under way with the tail leading the way and the nose wheel being used as a rudder; the standard nose towing gear in place and now functioning as a tiller in the hands of a man steering the aircraft to keep it lined up with the bulldozer.

I was steadily on the move from the dozer back to the nose looking for possible problems. Two young fellow were taking turns at the steering and I caught one of them riding in a truck, that was bringing up the rear, instead of doing his job. I had him out of there in a hurry and back on his job. He was complaining that it was cold and hard work. I assured him that life was not easy and that job was only a sample of what he would be faced with in the future so get on with it.

We had to stop our tow some distance out from shore because thick blowing snow had filled in the road and reduced visibility as the day was nearing its end. The cat skinner worked until 9:30 p.m. and then as usual set the engine of the cat to idle all night in the -12° F. and strong wind. That procedure is still used throughout the north on heavy equipment to eliminate starting problems in the mornings. A shut down all night could, in some cases, prevent a start up next morning.

We were out early the following day and after the cat operator had completed a road clearing run we hooked up the towline to the aircraft were not long in reaching the railroad tracks.

Railroads guard their right-of-way against all interlopers. They are especially careful about anything crossing the lines where no railway crossing is in place. The Railway Act gives them huge punishment privileges. I learned this in my youth and had it confirmed by my father-in-law; I married a railroader's daughter. So I made sure the local railway officials where fully briefed on our project.

The roadmaster responsible for the section of railroad we needed to cross was a friendly fellow who couldn't do enough to help us. He knew exactly what has to be done to get our aircraft from the wrong side of the tracks to the right side. He directed the construction of a temporary crossing. It was his suggestion that we build ramps of

(top); Raising aircraft with bottle jacks to get it up onto its wheels. (above); Towed up highway and was soon in the air to Calgary.

snow and wooden railway ties to reduce the steep grades over the temporary crossing and limit the stress on the aircraft's undercarriage .

When I expressed my concerns that the cat might cause some damage to the rails and that the rails could act as blocks for the aircraft wheels the roadmaster quickly erased them. He said his crew would make sure the crossing would be level and the rails would not even be touched by the cat or the aircraft. He was one step ahead of me.

During a short coffee break I told him my wife's father, Gilbert Murray, had been division engineer in Melville, Saskatchewan. His eyes lit up and he said anyone with double digit seniority working for the railroad had fond memories of Gil Murray. - Small world.

Our next obstacle was a wide space between the tracks and the highway that was all snow and looked level but what I didn't know was that the snow filled a 5 foot deep ditch. Luckily, the road-master mentioned that fact before we moved out onto it. He knew all about getting derailed engines and rail cars out of ditches. Railroad ties and planks were used to construct a bridge across the ditch and the cat easily towed the aircraft over it and onto the road.

That was a close one. The ditch was invisible and the snow was solid underfoot. I don't know if the cat would have gone down but there is no doubt the concentrated weight of the aircraft on the main wheels would have sunk them to a very awkward depth. The tow out of that kind of mess would have put a terrible strain on the undercar-riage. Another tip of the cap to the roadmaster.

Now the Manitoba Government Utilities people did their stuff. Power and telephone poles were cut to lower them and their wires, metal road bound-ary markers for deep snow were bent over and road signs cut off with a chain saw. The wings then had good clearance over everything.

The aircraft, with the tow bar attached to the nose landing gear, was towed in a normal manner up the highway with an R.C.M.P. escort. We arrived at the airfield without further problems. The Department of Transport airport maintenance crew took over the towing and had to bridge a ditch to move the aircraft onto a taxi way. Finally it was parked on Calm Air's apron at their hangar.

Every portion of our job benefited from some sort of assistance provided by: the railroad, the provincial government, the Department of Transport and the Royal Canadian Mounted Police. True Northern Spirit.

Gord Smith stayed out in the cold with me dur-ing all the days and was on the scene most of the time during the preparation of the aircraft for the move to the airfield. His good advice and support was always timely and it felt good to have him share the discomforts of the weather and lending a hand at every opportunity.

The last day in Churchill was spent inspecting the aircraft with a view to making it fit for a ferry flight to Calgary. Field Aviation had expressed interest in the aircraft so I suggested that Bill

Popovich come up and prepare an estimated cost for temporary repairs and a ferry flight plus some figures on permanent repairs.

The damage was extensive but the most critical airframe damage was in the torsion box which, for those not familiar with aircraft, was commonly referred to as the centre section.

The design of that specific structure was totally different from Canadian and American built aircraft that had front and rear spars in the base structure. It did however, serve the same purposes in providing a foundation for the body of the machine, support structure for the landing gear and facilities for the attachment of the wings.

I had no hands on experience with the design. It consisted of a series of bulkheads forming box like sections into a very stable and effective load absorbing structure. The damage to the torsion box was concentrated in the area of its left rear corner.

I have always based my temporary repair procedures on the basis of reinforcing a damaged section sufficiently enough to restore its strength and stress values for a ferry flight. I applied that thinking to the problem at hand but it did not sit well with the manufacturer's structural and stress engineer.

Bill Popovich and I finished our inspections then started making our way home. We flew to Lynn Lake in a Twin Otter and met Arnold Morberg the Owner of Calm Air. Then another Otter flight took me to Thompson to pick up Pacific Western Airlines for a trip to Winnipeg.

The International Hotel was short of rooms but I got one in the security section for aircrews. Next morning a very early Air Canada trip landed me in Vancouver where my wife Dot picked me up. That was the end of an 8-day successful job. I went directly to our office to get reports out to Bill James.

A few days later a meeting that took place in Calgary at the Reed Stenhouse office included Arnold Morberg of Calm Air and Jim Harworth from British AeroSpace, Manchester, England.

The discussions were centered on the future of the Hawker 748. It took hours to go through the repair cost figures and I began to feel uneasy in my determination to arrive at a fair settlement for Calm Air that was also fair for the underwriters. I made a proposal to the group that would set all the costs of airframe parts and those of component overhauls on common ground.

I felt that I had made things a little awkward at times during those few days, and no doubt I did, on not agreeing on certain proposals, but when the meeting was over Arnold Morberg said to me, in front of Bob Pincott. "If I ever have another problem like that I hope you are the adjuster."

Earlier in the day Jim Harworth, British AeroSpace engineer, and I had a private talk on the subject of making temporary repairs to the torsion box assembly. He disagreed with the thought because of its design features and said it would be best if he sent in a crew to make permanent repairs at Churchill. I did not argue the point and at that moment we had not yet arrived at any damage costs which would have a bearing on the future of the machine. I learned a great deal from Jim on the structure of that model aircraft. He did not hold back or circumvent any questions I put to him regarding the design and I surely profited from that.

Jim's airline ticket had been made out to Vancouver so he accompanied me on my return flight home. I took him around the city and up onto the North Shore Mountains for a bird's eye view of the city, then dinner in the rotating restaurant at the top of the Landmark Hotel. When I dropped him off at his hotel I said. "I have one last question." "What would you think I should do with that aircraft if it was on an Arctic Ocean ice strip that was starting to break up?" He replied without hesitation. "A point well taken." We said our good-byes and I left.

Interpretation: I think your temporary repair plans have merit but in my position I cannot say so.

I thought, on my way home, that perhaps it was not a fair question but he had handled it extremely well. He had the knowledge and experience to think, as I had, of the possibility of preparing the aircraft for a ferry flight. However, in his position he couldn't possibly agree or support me because he would be placing British Aero Space in a very delicate position in the event of a ferry flight failure.

I do not recall the details of the settlement. Hank Eisler handled the adjusting of the insurance claim and Calm Air made a deal with Field Aviation to repair the aircraft and put it back into service.

Stu Burke, Field's Maintenance Chief, called me and asked what I thought about making temporary repairs to the aircraft for a flight to Calgary. I replied. "Stu, you have me on a speaker phone so I guess you have an audience; that's O.K. - You are, no doubt, looking for moral support. Bill Popovich was in Churchill and knows what I think about repairing it and you know perfectly well what I would do if I had the job to do."

I heard laughter and Stu said. "I know that very well and thank you for your help." I would add that an uneventful successful ferry flight was completed.

That was the end of that exercise and 5 days later I was on my way to Paulatuk on the Arctic coast, about 200 miles east and north of Inuvik, N.W.T. A Lockheed Hercules C130 was badly damaged.

chapter twenty-two

A Cessna into a Power Dam

The rescued Otter lifted itself easily from the Mackenzie River at Fort Norman for the ferry flight to Edmonton and John Longden and I had a chance to enjoy a few hours of self satisfaction with the repair work we had done. John stayed with the aircraft and he dropped me off at Fort Smith to check out salvage prospects for a Cessna 206 that had got on the wrong side of a power dam.

Fort Smith is near the North West Territories / Alberta border midway between Great Slave Lake and Lake Athabaska - It is not a holiday resort.

Phil Clayton, insurance adjuster with James Taylor Company in Edmonton, was waiting for me. I checked into the hotel and got the last available room, a basement cell with no windows usually reserved for bar patrons too drunk to be turned out into the snow. Phil had not reserved one for me because he thought we might have been delayed by our poor en route weather conditions between there and Fort Norman. I accused him of being over anxious to save the company dollar.

That evening was spent checking on the availability of charter aircraft we would need and obtaining as much information as I could, about the position of the aircraft and the terrain nearest to it. The data was needed to determine what additional equipment might be needed.

Prior to my departure from Edmonton, en route to the Redstone job, I had been made aware of the Fort Smith accident and had planned to stop there, on the ferry flight south, with the Otter. Based on the accident report I had some tools, such as the portable steel "A" frame, that would most certainly be needed, shipped up from Vancouver to Fort Smith.

The weather turned bad next morning and kept us grounded for three days. Phil, on the first day, had an urgent call to go to Yellowknife and returned the next afternoon, hoping all was set to move out to our objective but we were still grounded. While he was away I saw that a Norseman seaplane was fully loaded with our equipment and gear.

The weather was good the next morning and we got an early start but the Norseman had such a load that it left no room or weight allowance for Phil and I. That was just as well because it took quite a long run before it lifted off the water, the sign of a gross load.

Phil and I were finally on our way in a Cessna 180 seaplane piloted by Bob Gauchie. It was an annoying and time consuming flight, the type of which I had never experienced before or, for that matter, since then.

We thought the location of the dam would be common knowledge, especially for charter pilots operating in the surrounding areas of Fort Smith. Wrong! We must have flown over all the sur-rounding country before we found out that the pilot, having been clearly told that we wanted to go to the dam, didn't know where it was. Worse than that, he didn't have any charts or maps of any kind with him.

We flew over some of the same areas two or three times until we were so low on fuel that we had to return to Fort Smith.

Phil was fit to be tied and so disgusted that he said "I have more to do than spend my time that way." When we landed he stormed off and caught the next plane out. I hope it was for Edmonton but I'm sure that he didn't care at the time. Phil was always a great fellow to be with but on that occasion there was nothing I could say that would cool him down.

While the aircraft was being refueled I obtained the map we needed. It was important that I get to the lake as soon as possible because all my gear, clothes and food taken by the Norseman, would be on the shore unprotected from uninvited wildlife, including bears, who do not open packages carefully, and have a taste for man's food. I had to get there. Added to that was a weather change coming in with lots of ragged cloud and showers.

We left for the lake again and believe it or not the pilot was lost once more. I took the map and acted as navigator. It was quite simple to find a river and follow it to the lake and my destination. The pilot beached the aircraft, some distance up from where a camp and operations base would be set up, and discharged the remainder of my gear, then quickly left. I was not at all happy about that. I foolishly thought that because most of a day had been lost plus any help Phil would have given me, the pilot might have helped me carry my gear the few hundred yards I had to go. I had the snide thought that he didn't want to walk too far from the aircraft in case he couldn't find his way back.

In a way I wasn't angry with him, perhaps more disappointed than anything but somehow felt sorry for him. I believed that he was embarrassed and felt uncomfortable over his performance. He was actually a nice fellow. I found out later that this was not the first time he had flight problems however. He had gone missing before for a period of time and an aerial search had been necessary to locate him.

Moving all the equipment down to the remains of an old building of some sort, near the accident site, took quite a while and it was heavy work. The day was pretty well gone by the time I was finished and didn't leave me with any time to accomplish anything constructive, other than surveying the situation and making mental plans. So to cool out my frustration over the wasted part of the day and to calm my soul, I went fishing in the stream below the dam where I caught four large trout with four casts of the line and let them go free again. Feeling good and relaxed, I went to bed.

This time I took a two way radio and started the next day with several unsuccessful calls to Fort Smith in an attempt to contact Barney Cooper who was to help me with the work. Barney had worked with me in the Churchill area in 1967 and I knew he was the right man for this job.

The wrecked aircraft was not far off the shore line which was quite narrow and at the base of a rocky piece of high ground to which one end of the dam was anchored. It would have to be lifted from its partially sunken position by using an "A" frame and winch, both of which I had brought.

The assembly of the frame, consisting of a number of threaded heavy steel tube sections, was completed as far as I could go by myself. Then with a Cobra rock drill, that I had borrowed from the Water Survey people in Fort Smith, holes were cut in the rock for the bottom ends of the frame when it was erected. Farther back, steel pins were set into deep holes to be used as anchors for the frame in its upright position and the winch.

I had gone as far as I could without help. It was now Sunday morning, I had been there two days. Barney was obviously away on a charter flight somewhere and weather bound or he would have arrived by then. Calls to both Fort Smith and Uranium City were made with no luck on the static filled airways.

However, I was not totally alone. Masses of flies and mosquitoes were at their peak and busy at making a determined effort to be friendly and keep me company.

Late Sunday afternoon, with nothing left to accomplish, I sat down in the sun and I guess, dozed off for a bit. I remember being wakened up, with a start, by a sudden noise of movement. A bear? No it was a large jack rabbit that had skidded to a stop in the brush nearby and was then sitting upright looking at me.

More radio calls Monday morning and I finally received a noisy weak reply from Barney's wife Eunice advising that Barney was in the air and would arrive soon. She asked me to send a lake trout to her with the pilot. Now it was time to do something about her request.

I went down to the stream and caught five large trout and put them into the deep cold storage of the lake until the plane arrived. I had not seen any signs of raccoons or mink along the shoreline but I was sure they were around and would thoroughly enjoy the fish if they could get at them. The water depth would not protect the fish from mink or otters but it might slow the animals down a little and get only one instead of all five. Besides, the weather had turned warm; warm enough to spoil fish. I hoped it would be like that when the machine was out of the water so it could be dried out.

Barney arrived in time to get the "A" frame erected and anchored with the winch secured in place, by late evening.

We were on the move very early next morning and in a few hours, had the seaplane above the surface of the lake. There was some damage to the pontoons but luckily, only in the small water tight compartments. The water was hand pumped from the pontoons and we soon had the plane sitting upright on the lake surface, at the shoreline, still attached to the frame and winch for safety.

We had just completed that first stage, of a water salvaging operation, that always made me feel relieved even though it was just a start with many unknown factors ahead.

While we were in the process of actually lifting the machine out of the water an aircraft arrived from Plummer's Great Slave Lake Lodge, approximately 70 air miles from our location.

A Grumman Goose aircraft was upside down on their airstrip and their Insurers, the British Aviation Insurance Co., wanted me to look after it. We were at that critical stage of the operation when, if anything is to go wrong, one expects it will probably be at that time so I could do nothing for them immediately. They were very understanding and were back again the next day. By that time we had things pretty well under way and Barney, a good self starter, could accomplish a great deal on his own.

I went to the Lodge, surveyed the scene, inspected the damage and decided that the aircraft could be safely turned back over onto its wheels without disassembling it. The notes I made, contained details that would be used in planning the salvage operation. Chummy Plummer was most helpful in offering the use of a cat and man power to turn over the aircraft. I returned to our 'plane in the dam' problem next morning.

Barney had done very well; with the two of us working hard, it was not long until the engine was ready for a run up. This was successfully completed by using proven procedures for water soaked engines.

We were, by no means, into clear sailing. A badly crumpled wing prevented us from completing the project with a ferry flight as had been done with so many other sunken aircraft. There was no way, even in the wildest stretch of the imagination, that the wing could be temporarily repaired out there.

A little later we had another surprise interruption. Sam Steele, an insurance adjuster from Edmonton, flew in with a request that I go with him, to Porter Lake, about 175 air miles north east of our camp. He had an aircraft upside down and wanted a second opinion on how and what was needed to be done in the retrieval of it. Obviously, some one had told him where I was but then again, it was a small world of business that I was in and everyone, in it, knew what was going on and who was doing what and where.

We were almost finished our project so I went with him for a few hours and laid out some plans on how the salvage job should be done. Then back to my problem. I thought, it was fortunate that Barney was an understanding and co-operative Northerner or he might have been upset over me leaving him on his own. He was an understanding fellow, ready to roll with the punches. That part of the operation was completed by pack-

ing up the instruments and radios that had been treated for the water soaking and securing the aircraft in a safe position to wait for a replacement wing.

I returned to Vancouver and in very short time, word was received that a wing was on it's way to Fort Smith. I, in the meantime, had been preparing for the salvage work to be done on the Goose at Plummer's Lodge. I arranged for replacement propellers, an engine mount and many other needed items to be shipped to Yellowknife.

The plan was to finish the Cessna by installing the wing and ferry it out, which would be a quick job, then move on to the Goose, hoping of course, that the replacements for its damaged assemblies and parts would be waiting for us in Yellowknife by that time.

I had gained considerable Grumman Goose maintenance experience at Central B.C. Air Service and later with Pacific Western Airlines but, for the job ahead of me, I thought I should have a good technician with me.

Fortunately Curly Nairn of B.C. Central Aeromotive in Kamloops was available to go. His son Rob and my son Murray completed the team.

The flight to Kamloops from Vancouver was an interesting one for Murray because he was invited to sit up in the cockpit with the well known veteran northern pilot Vern Simmons. Curly and his son boarded the aircraft and we continued on to Edmonton. Our freight, destined for Yellowknife, was checked then we left for Fort Smith to complete the Cessna job.

A Gateway Aviation Otter from Yellowknife piloted by John Bell came down to Fort Smith to transport us and the replacement wing to Monacho Lake. I was quite taken by the fact that we were using the same Otter, CF-LAP that John Longden and I had rescued from the Redstone River a little earlier.

We found that nothing had been disturbed in the camp during my short absence. The aircraft was still well secured but the water level had dropped a little and made it difficult to turn the seaplane around in the soft mud and litter of the lake bottom.

We had a couple of long days, as is usual on such jobs, up at 5 am and bed by 11 pm. The wing installation was completed without any great problem by having enough help to hold it up in place while attaching it and which, by the way, is quite a job in a hangar with ladders and work stands available.

A small amount of work was done on the pontoons while Curly installed a few serviceable instruments. The machine was given a good visual inspection and with a final successful engine run up, I signed its log book certifying it as fit for the ferry flight and it was set to go. The Otter returned with a pilot for the Cessna, then the dismantled "A" frame and other equipment was loaded into it.

Following the departure of the Cessna we left for Plummer's Great Slave Lake Camp and our next challenge involving their inverted Grumman Goose.

chapter twenty-three

Returning Single Otters

Making the Unflyable – Flyable

The calm voice of unflappable Ace Woods resonated through the telephone, "Denny, I have a badly bruised Otter up on the Dempster Highway. Your insurance folks asked me to give you a briefing on the situation. You're to call them when I've finished with you and make your usual outrageous deal."

Ace said the accident site was about 250 miles from Dawson and approximately 15 winding road miles from the Arctic Circle, near the Eagle Plains Hotel. He said there was considerable damage that included the propeller, engine mount, cabin roof and a bent up right wing and he would meet me at the site with a crane truck and tools.

Tom (Ace) Woods the maintenance manager and partner in Air North Airlines in Whitehorse. They had a very busy schedule and needed every aircraft in the fleet in the air to meet it. I was not sure just how much help they might be able to give me for the salvage job so I turned to Chris Kent of Pacific Aircraft Salvage. Chris had worked with me on other such jobs and fortunately he was ready to go.

The usual tools, repair kits,' might come in handy' materials and a disassembled propeller were air freighted to Whitehorse on the same flight we took.

We checked with Air North on arrival in Whitehorse. Ace, Darryl Stuart and Mike Stockstill were already on the road to the accident in the truck loaded with supplies and parts. Seats on tomorrow's flight to Dawson City were booked for us.

Before sunrise we were in the air. The only interruption in the flight was a stop to drop off some diamond drill bits for the silver mines near Mayo, on the Klondike highway south east of Dawson.

The Yukon River had served as the transportation link between the Klondike gold fields at the turn of the century; now a road, a real highway ran in tandem with the river. Even so, it was still a wilderness and though I was on my way to clean up a mess I enjoyed being a tourist. The view in every direction was spectacular. I was looking forward to seeing the second road; the road that joined the Klondike Highway to the Arctic Ocean; The Dempster Highway.

I had been in the Yukon when they had set the stakes for the road and I had a pretty good idea of the difficulties the road builders would face. It was completed in 1979 after several years of amazing engineering and construction work.

Now, for the first time, I was going to see some of the finished work.

The highway was named after a Royal North West Mounted Police Corporal W.J.Dempster who, in 1911, searched for and found the frozen bodies of the famous Lost Patrol near Fort MacPherson. The Dempster is the only highway in Canada that crosses the Arctic Circle.

We landed on a section of the Dempster that had been designed to function as an emergency air strip. Imagine that. A government project that delivered a "Two for the Price of One" deal. I was impressed and marked one up for the good guys.

Ace was there to meet us and take us by truck to the injured aircraft C-FSUB, which was off the west side of the road, beyond the north end of the air strip, on its side and in an awkward nose down sloping position. Ed Reimer, an experienced pilot, must have felt bad about it.

The days were rapidly getting longer and soon there would be 24 hours of daylight throughout the far north for a short few months. Ace didn't want to lose a minute and I knew he wouldn't be happy until the Otter was back at work; I was determined to make him happy soon. So no time was lost with every one pitching in on the task of preparing for the lifting and moving of the aircraft from its unflattering position. The crew was made up of aircraft technicians used to roughing it in isolated areas under trying conditions that at times, required a great deal of straight, all out, bull work with a minimum of equipment. Ace and Chris had those qualities.

It was quite late when we decided to call it a day and check into the Eagle Plains Hotel a short distance up the road. We had, by that time, with everyone sharing in the brain work, solved enough problems to set the ground work for a good start in the morning.

The ride to the hotel was well under way when we had a tire problem and SURPRISE; there was no jack or spare wheel with that rental unit. Well, the tire still had a little air in it so we continued driving until it became hot and started to burn. The fire was put out with snow then we continued with our trip. The snow procedure was repeated until we reached the hotel and a garage where a new tire was bought.

I have often thought of that beautiful hotel way up there. It was brand new and equal in every respect to any other first class accommodation I had seen. It was truly an oasis in a vast unpopulated area.

We continued with our work next morning and after reinforcing the attachment of the right main landing leg the aircraft was gradually moved until it was sitting on the road. That rough part of the work was completed by towing the machine down to a parking area at the south end of the air strip section of the highway where it would be prepared for flight.

The right wing was bent upward at a point approximately 8 feet in from its tip. The cabin roof was buckled aft of the rear centre section spar from having been crushed by the wing being driven like a battering ram when its tip jammed into the ground.

The procedures in making temporary repairs to those areas would be patterned off other previous successful jobs with similar damage. The first and perhaps the most important item was the engine crankshaft. Was it bent beyond its serviceable limits from impact of the propeller blades with the still frozen ground?

The propeller was removed and the crankshaft checked with a dial indicator that told us the shaft was well within the limits of serviceability. A reading such as that always felt good.

Ace set up a tripod to hold the engine while changing its broken mount. Chris and I set up a propeller shop and got on with assembling three blades and a hub to build up a replacement. Fred Sebus of A1 Propeller Service in Vancouver had given me crash course on overhauling propellers in the bush so we were well on our way to success.

The wing straightening and reinforcing was

Pulling outer end of wing down into position, Chris Kent.

started by placing a piece of board along the bend on the lower side of the wing. The board and some of the wing's weight was supported by a sturdy vertical pole firmly set in the ground. A small piece of wood was placed in the tip end of the wing to which a hand winch, secured to the deck of the truck, was attached. The bent up portion of the wing was then winched downward until it was slightly lower than the rest of the wing. That provided a small allowance for spring back to a level position after the repairs and the pressure was released. A very easy and simple bit of work.

The buckled points of the spars at the bend were reinforced on their smooth sides and the buckles were left as is for added strength. New metal sheeting in the damaged area of the wing top tied everything together and the wing was back to its original strength and configuration in its outer area.

Changing the engine mount under those bush conditions is time consuming and Ace was doing very well along with a number of other jobs while giving us a hand when needed.

By the time Chris and I had finished patching the cabin roof and repaired the inboard end of the rear spar of the wing, all the other work was pretty well done.

Near our working area was the remains of a hunting or trapping party camp. The skeleton of a large dog with a rope still around its neck and attached to tree was a sad sight. It had no doubt starved to death.

A successful engine and propeller performance drew our task to an end that was followed by Rick Neilsen's ferry flight down to Whitehorse and on to Vancouver for permanent repairs.

Mother Nature had been kind in sending us good weather and everyone in the crew was most compatible. What more could one ask for? The next few weeks were busy ones with several flights into the northern areas and one to Winnipeg, Manitoba following which, upon my return to Vancouver, I was presented with a problem in North Dakota, U.S.A.

A Canadian registered Single Otter seaplane, enroute to Canada, had had a landing problem that put it through a farmer's fence. George Stevenson had dispatched a couple of aircraft maintenance fellows from Springhouse, Alberta with a truck and wheel landing gear for the Otter. I left in a hurry to do the necessary in making temporary repairs to the aircraft, deal with a farmer's property damage claim and get the machine across the border.

I had an earlier ridiculous experience with the American Customs Department in a similar situation. I had not been allowed to go a couple of miles into Point Roberts, Washington to do an hour's work on a damaged Canadian aircraft to fly it back into Canada. We were forced to have a mechanic come up from 40 or 50 miles south of the border to do the job with parts I supplied then had to stand there watching him work.

That was in strong comparison to what had

often taken place in Canada with the tables reversed by allowing Americans to come up here and take their aircraft out of the country. A very one-sided affair.

I had little time to prepare against a repeat of my experience before I had to leave on the job. I phoned the pilot who was still in North Dakota, I believe it was Emil Mesich from the Smithers area, and asked him to find out if there were any mechanics around or near there who were authorities on Otters. I received a reply within a couple of hours and the answer was no, there aren't any. That was good news and I was soon on my way to Saskatoon where I picked up a U drive car and headed for the border.

I was well down the road when I had a flat tire and my first experience with a small type spare that had to be inflated by using a pressure bottle before it could be used. I was somewhat put off with that and having to drive below the speed limit.

I was at the border very early the following morning and explained to the American Authorities what I was down there for. I was surprised when the officer replied by saying. "My boss said he knew you were coming and you are to come in and take the aircraft out to Canada." The officer gave me Emil's motel phone number. That set the scene for a pleasant beginning.

I located the aircraft and did the usual note mak-

(left); Our Arctic propeller rebuild shop, Chris Kent and Denny McCartney (right); Chris Kent with gracefully formed replaced blades.

ing and photographing. There was no one else around so back across the border I went and found Emil waiting at the motel. He had, after talking to me on the phone, spoken to the American Customs and explained the situation to them, which led to them taking a practical approach to the problem.

The two of us went back to the aircraft and we were pleased to see the Springhouse men and their truck had arrived. The first thing to do was prepare for the installation of wheel landing gear. The two fellows started on that by preparing for the removal of the floats.

We were going to require the use of a crane to lift the aircraft so Emil and I went off to arrange that and at the same time purchase a standard sized wheel and a used tire for the u drive.

We were returning to the aircraft with hamburgers for the two workers when the Canadian Customs Officer came after us for taking repair parts and equipment across the border without first checking with him. We had to take the landing gear back to him so he could see it. That was no big deal because they were manufactured in Canada but business was slow and he wanted to do what would have been done later in the ferry flight north.

The fellows wanted to go out to buy a power jig saw and when I asked them what they needed it for they said that it was to be used to cut off the bent up portion of the wing. Then they would clean it up and put it back on the wing.

I couldn't believe what I had heard but I politely said "no" and that I would show them a better

Otter ready to fly south

way to make the repair. It was a certainty that they would not have been able to reposition that section so as to accurately accommodate the aileron/flap assembly. The outer mounting hinge for the assembly was on that end piece of the wing and they would have had to have been so accurate in positioning it. I had learned all about that on Max Ward's Otter up on Baffin Island when we didn't have any choice, that tip end was already off.

The crane arrived in good time and we got on with the lifting of the aircraft by using heavy rope for a sling with its ends wrapped around the wing root attachment joints. The lifting rings, normally installed on the aircraft, were missing. The fellows thought they should manufacture replacements but there was too great a chance of them failing under stress. The wheels were soon in place and secured.

I showed them how to set the wing up and position the truck to pull the bent up section down into place as we had done up on the Dempster Highway. The two were most interested in the procedure and I was pleased to be able to pass something like that on to them. Their method of reinforcing the spars and patching the torn top metal skins was good so I let them have their head on that.

I did not want anyone to feel that I was being awkward in some of the procedures because it was experience talking not just me. I had hoped they accepted it that way.

The work was completed in our final morning there and Emil checked the operation of the engine and propeller. I made a few phone calls regarding a ferry permit and to confirm that the insurance would be in full force and effect for the ferry flight to Calgary.

I signed the log books and Emil took off for a flight to the Estevan airport in Saskatchewan as a start. The wind wasn't totally in his favour and one wing came close to the ground and made our hearts pound a little.

We hadn't stopped for lunch in the last two days, just steady work and now, with the floats lashed down on their truck the boys left for Alberta. I looked up the farmer on whose field the aircraft had chosen to land and paid him the $40 he wanted for damage to 150 feet of fencing.

I was ready to head home. As I left the States I stopped and thanked the American Customs Officer for their kind co-operation and consideration then made sure that the Canadian Customs were satisfied in all regards.

The rest of the day was spent driving toward Saskatoon and the following evening I was home again. It had been a beneficial and satisfying trip although not an exciting one.

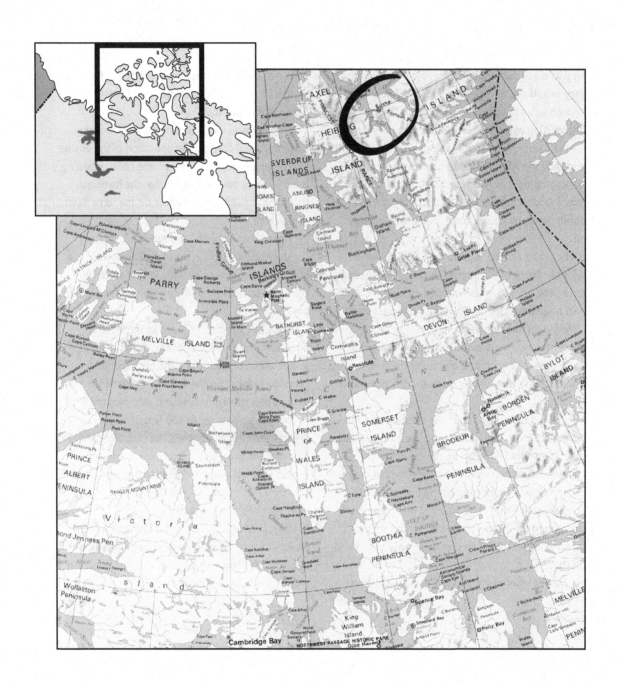

chapter twenty-four

From the Arctic to the Factory

Lockheed C 130 Hercules

The work of salvaging a damaged aircraft was very often the major part of my assignment as an aircraft insurance adjuster and engineer. However, in the case of a Lockheed Hercules aircraft, the problems involving the manufacturer on the methods and costs of permanent repairs, were unprecedented and, at times, seemed insurmountable.

A Hercules aircraft CF-PWN had slid off the edge of an air strip, at Eureka, North West Territories, as it neared the end of its landing roll.

Eureka is a J.A.W.(Joint Air Weather) site on Slidre Fjord, near the top end of Ellsmere Island and it is manned by both Canadians and Americans. Its geographic position is 80° north latitude, about 600 miles south of Geographic North Pole. That positions it at approximately 10° of latitude (about 700 miles) north of the continent including Alaska. Ellesmere Island Is the most northern part of Canada.

I was instructed by Bob Pincott of Reed Shaw Osler, insurance brokers, to proceed to the accident scene to do the necessary as an insurance adjuster and assist in making sufficient temporary repairs for a ferry flight out of there. That would be the largest aircraft I had been involved with in a salvage operation and farther north than I had previously been.

It was getting near to the middle of August 1969 when I left for that northern destination basking in its short summer. In about a month's time Old Man Winter would be knocking on the door up there and preparing to take over once again for a big portion of the year.

My first stop was Edmonton where I went to the maintenance shops of the Operators of the Hercules, Pacific Western Airlines. Their Maintenance Supervisor, Gordon Canim, briefed me on what details they had on the problem and a combined discussion took place with him and the men he was sending up to the Herc. The object of that was to pool our thoughts on what materials and equipment would be needed for the temporary repairs and ferry flight.

I was not a technical authority on the Hercules Aircraft but felt comfortable in being able to contribute a fair share by falling back on past experiences involving the airframes of other large type aircraft.

The key to being able to use that knowledge is that structures may vary in design from one aircraft to another but they have a common denominator in their useage. Therefore, it is possible to make various temporary repairs that might be similar to what was successfully accomplished on another machine. However, in using such knowledge, it is imperative that special consideration be given to its application

to various designs in order to maintain their configuration and regain the pre accident strength, while at the same time avoiding, as much as possible, changes that could build up dangerous stresses at any point.

The better part of two days were spent in preparation that included locating another nose landing gear assembly which was obtained on loan from Alaska.

Sometime after mid night of the second day we started out by firstly going south to Calgary to pick up freight for Pan Arctic Exploration. The Department of Transport Accident Investigator, Don Douglas, and a Lockheed Technical Representative accompanied us.

The flight continued from Calgary with stops at Yellowknife and Cambridge Bay, on the Arctic Island of Victoria. Then on to Resolute on Cornwallis Island, positioned on the north edge of Parry Channel, well known as the North West Passage. We arrived at Eureka in the evening.

We could see, as we flew over the waters of Cambridge Bay that there was a lot of pack ice, some of which might still be there at the start of the next freeze up.

Pack ice is formed when the winter's thick ice covering of the Arctic waters is broken up into huge chunks during the warmer periods. The force of the wind packs those pieces together, some go up on their edges and ends, forming huge irregular surfaces resembling small sharp topped mountains fifty to sixty feet high.

Immediately, upon arrival at Eureka, I had to

obtain written pilot statements. I had always looked on pilots, especially bush pilots, as doers who, in the course of their work, were continuously exposed to changing situations and conditions that often made flying a hazard. I took no pleasure in questioning any of them because I thought they must have felt a little embarrassed over an incident in which they had been involved. However, obtaining the statements was actually the starting point of an investigation for an insurance company and had to be done.

That part of my work was completed by about 10 p.m., when Don Douglas had completed his investigation, he and the pilots of the crippled Hercules left on the return flight of the aircraft that had taken us up there.

It was still broad daylight and I was anxious to get a look at the Herc. A station man offered to drive me to it. Upon returning to the station about mid night I found that everyone else had gone to bed shortly after 10 p.m. and I quickly did the same. It had been about one and a half days of steady go between bedding down times.

The following morning we were on the job early. I continued with my investigation which consisted chiefly of making notes and taking photos of the airstrip and the aircraft damage.

The airstrip had a surface consisting of silt which, when it was wet, as it was at the time of that unfortunate incident, became very slippery. The tracks and skid marks were very clear as were the deep foot prints on the edge of the runway.

Hercules with collapsed nose wheel.

That was an indication that the surface had turned into a type of gumbo with the rain and would not have provided the traction needed to control the aircraft. The Herc, when it was near the end of its landing run, had slid to one side of the strip where the nose wheel struck a runway marker and collapsed. The aircraft had then skidded on its nose to a stop.

The damage extended from the nose of the aircraft, back into the bottom area of the cargo compartment. The front end had to be raised but there was no lifting equipment available. The raising of the nose was done by lowering the cargo door at the rear of the aircraft and driving a caterpillar tractor on to it. The door was then operated from the cockpit as though to raise it into its closed position. The weight of the cat held the door down and the nose came up as the aircraft pivoted on its main landing gear. It was then blocked up in that position as a safety measure to work under.

A thorough visual inspection was done and we were relieved to find no indications of damage to any of the prime or major support structure which was a big plus for us.

The replacement nose wheel assembly was soon in place and we felt much relieved.

The damage to the hull was chiefly in its bottom or belly from the nose, extending rearward under the pilot's compartment and into the cargo or freight area.

The temporary repairs consisted of covering in a large hole in the bottom. That was done by joining up and reinforcing the bottom formers with steel plating and angle iron bolted into place. Aircraft type sheet metal was then secured to that frame work to close the openings.

The work was completed within a few days and the aircraft was ready for a ferry flight crew. Jim Brown of P.W.A. had worked hard long 16 hour days and the Lockheed Technical Representative was most helpful when we sought an opinion or advice. A friendly and co-operative atmosphere prevailed throughout the job.

During that period of time it was sunny and warm except for the wind coming off the ice pack that filled the inlet. The annual precipitation there is around two and one half inches and the ice on the inlet freezes to a depth of about 100 inches, over eight feet. Some distance out in the inlet was a tall iceberg locked into the ice and directly in line with the airstrip. It could have been used to line up for a landing from that direction. The date was August 15 and we heard that Resolute, to the south, had its first night with partial darkness that season.

The surrounding terrain is quite hilly and interesting. One day while taking a short cut walking from the station to the aircraft, I saw Arctic wolves and a herd of musk ox. Those shaggy animals had lost much of their protective winter coats and a fresh lot was growing underneath for the coming winter. They just stood there looking at me. They feed on bunch grass that grows about a foot high in that area but strangely, it doesn't grow like that in many places farther south.

I had the same thoughts and questioning mind, standing there looking at them, as I had had about the Eskimo on my first trip into their domain, some years earlier. I found the origin of names for the Eskimo to be of particular interest.

The Northern Indians gave them the name Eskimo meaning, Eaters of Raw Meat. Siberian Eskimos call themselves Yuit and North American Eskimos call themselves Inuit, both names mean Men.

It was so difficult for me to understand why they remained so far above the tree line that would have offered at least a little protection from the elements and more food. They had retained their ancient living habits their ancestors had brought to North America, from northern areas of Mongolia so long ago.

The Eskimo People apparently did not normally live that far north. Their most northern habitat is Grise Fjord at the southern end of Ellesmere Island. It was interesting to hear an Eskimo, who had been helping us, tell me that he was going south for a holiday. I soon found out that his version of south was very different to mine. I thought he meant that he was going down some where around the mainland but I was wrong. He was going to Resolute which is still about 600 miles north of the Arctic Circle. That would be his summer holidays which was good because he would be with his friends.

The Pacific Western fellows waited for pilots to come up to ferry the Hercules south. Dan McIvor came in with a Pan Arctic Twin Otter and I was able to get a ride down to Resolute with him. I picked up a flight about two in the morning and left for Edmonton via Yellowknife.

The next day I met with Frank Coulter and Gord Canim of P.W.A. to bring them up to date on the salvage operation and required repairs.

Then I had a late lunch with Dick Hicks, Phil Clayton and John Gladstone before catching a flight to Vancouver and home. Those three were the source of a lot of my work. They were always interested in my salvage jobs and the Herc was no exception.

I was steadily on the run, in and out of the Yukon until the first week of September when I was notified that the Hercules had arrived at the Lockheed Factory shops in Marietta Georgia, for permanent repairs and that I should leave for there as soon as possible.

Little did I suspect that would be the start of a new and trying experience, the like of which I never before had faced and, for that matter, never again.

I arrived in Atlanta late evening and was met by a Mr. McDaniel, a Lockheed Supervisor who drove me to a hotel where I met Joe Childs, the P.W.A. Technical Representative who had arrived a little earlier. Joe would monitor the repairs on behalf of the airline.

Next morning we were picked up and given a pleasant and informative tour around the plant and some offices to meet various department

(top) Belly damage. (above); Tractor on loading door to raise the aircraft door.

heads. We saw the large C-5A Military Transport that was indeed a giant. The freight compartment has a deck large enough to accommodate 10 or 12 Greyhound type buses and has loading doors at either end.

All the while we were informed bit by bit about the proposed repairs to our Hercules, with frequent reference to a recent repair to one with belly landing damage, costing about one million U.S. dollars.

I began to feel that we were being mentally conditioned for a big dollar proposition. It sounded as though the previous job, they were referring to, was either a one only big repair on a Hercules or one of very few they had ever done for a commercial operator.

It sounded as though it was Lockheed's practice to replace damaged parts and major assemblies rather than repair them.

Later, during a private discussion on that possibility I could see that Joe was very knowledgeable on the subject of repairing. I explained that if the restoration of the aircraft was to be based on such a procedure, I would firmly reject it. I was pleased to hear him say that he would back me 100 percent.

An insurance adjuster is always in the middle between the Insurance Company who retains him to act on their behalf and the insured who is entitled to honest compensation for his loss. It is a two way street where one has to be fair and honest to both parties. Not always easy but in that case, Joe's support made it easier for me.

I suggested that I should be the one to voice any strong objections that we might have. He could, in a quieter way, show support by expressing opinions. However, since he was going to have to remain there at the factory for a while, he should retain a pleasant relationship while not necessarily agreeing to proposals with which he disagreed.

He didn't like that idea at all but I was sure that approach would, in the long run, better service our cause over a period of time and make his stay more pleasant and productive.

Later, in the afternoon we were taken to engineering and introduced to their Chief Aeronautical Engineer, a very pleasant gentleman. It seemed that he was thinking in terms of replacing the whole front end of the aircraft which was roughly one quarter the length of the hull. Another thought was that they might replace the bottom half, including the floor of the crew quarters and cockpit that was not damaged at all. That compartment would have to stripped out completely of the pilot seats, electronics and a mass of other equipment.

Then we knew that their repair procedures consisted of replacing complete assemblies instead of the conventional standard practice of repairing. Joe and I spent the following morning in the plant familiarizing ourselves with the production and assembly line procedures especially as related to the forward part of the hull.

Several statements had been made regarding certain installations and their relationship to the hull components so we wanted to fully understand them. We frequently went back to our Herc. to see how they related to our problem.

During that time we met Harry Hearne a representative from the Maple Leaf Leasing Company in Florida that had an interest in the P.W.A. aircraft and its repair costs. Harry was present in an afternoon meeting with the Vice President, Mr. Crocket, and about 10 managers of various departments.

We were given an estimate of $700,000.00 U.S. that contained very few details, no labour breakdown, no list of parts with prices and it was not a firm figure. An estimate prepared under those conditions leaves the door wide open for price increasing. A "not to exceed figure" would have put a cap on price escalation but it would have had to have been a realistic cost to give it any consideration. I could not justify a recommendation to the Underwriters that they accept the estimate as presented.

I rejected the presentation and made it clear that an estimate must contain a complete breakdown in labour and a list of the parts with their prices. We listened to their arguments against meeting those conditions. Their procedures were totally contrary to the general practice of estimating.

Management seemed quite determined that they should be able to get a blank cheque type of agreement, so as to speak, and the more I thought about it the more I came to realize that had apparently been their practice in the past.

I expressed my concern over what appeared to

be a resistance to assist their customer, P.W.A., recover from their loss as economically and quickly as possible. I was firm in not agreeing to anything more than a repair to the forward section of the aircraft. Replacing the complete front end from a point just aft of the pilots' entrance door was not acceptable.

It was also pointed out that the chines in the damaged area were in good condition and everything from the pilots' compartment floor, upward, was undamaged and there was no need to replace it. I went on to explain that the formers in the hull's bottom were hydro press type products not unlike those in a Canso P.B.Y.-5A. It would be a simple job to install them to join up the chines with a new keel. I hadn't seen a difficult rivet to buck and told them if there was one I would buck it for them. Looking back on that remark I must admit that it no doubt sounded a bit cheeky. It was not meant to be but I had to get it across that we did not have an insurmountable problem staring us in the face.

Joe and I wanted a report on the condition of the so called black boxes (electronic equipment) but no one seemed to know where they were. Lockheed was determined to install a complete new nose landing gear. Joe and I felt sure that the original one could be recertified and accordingly, we had made arrangements via phone to ship it to the manufacturer, Menasco, in California, for a condition report and repair cost. Menasco promised we would have their report and costs

within three days of receipt of the assembly. That was excellent in our opinion. However, Lockheed refused to let it be removed from their premises.

The new one was priced out at $25,000 and I argued that for all I knew a repair could be approximately $10,000. The irony of it was that at a much later date the gear was sent out and an estimate of $10,400 was obtained to recertify it. The new one remained on the aircraft regardless.

Management then retired to another meeting between themselves and we returned to the hotel. There, we had a beer with Harry, the Maple Leaf Rep., who later paid me a fine compliment with moral support added to it. He told Joe that Lockheed had a tiger by the tail and knew that they were not talking to a fool, at the same time they didn't know what to do with him. He was very complimentary in saying he loved the position I had taken.

Quite frankly, I was not trying to be clever but I was very upset over their apparent customary type so called repair procedures.

Next day, after a brief meeting we were asked if we would go down to the aircraft to meet their Engineers and tell them how we wanted the repairs done. We met with about nine of them and explained what we thought should be done and what was wrong with the proposals thus far.

They were very interested and swarmed all over the machine. It was most interesting to note that they did not openly argue against my suggested repair schemes, just asked questions. I thought at the time, it was too bad we weren't working with them but they were not in management.

A good example for my arguments was the damaged airstair door leading up to the crew compartment and cockpit. Its frame was a riveted structure and therefore, to a degree, was flexible but it had been slightly misaligned by the crushing forces of the damaged lower structure. The sheet metal covering had been compressed and was holding the frame out of alignment.

I offered to show them how simple it would be to remove the skin, then put a new one on with the framework in the jig in which it was originally built. The challenge was not taken up but it did get attention as you will see later on.

We were informed that if the complete front section of the hull was not replaced, it would still be necessary to remove it for access in repairing the hull aft of that point. Therefore, a steel stand, needed to hold it, would have to be built.

We refused to pay for the building of a stand that we considered unnecessary because that part of the hull did not need to be removed to affect repairs. I told them that I was satisfied that they were very capable of doing the repair work in a normal, standard manner as is done in other aviation shops. It was then explained to them that the structure under the cargo flooring should be repaired first then use the frame work at the manufacturer's splice or joint as a jig and match the front end to it.

That exercise was followed by another upstairs meeting when I told them that there were very good technicians in their shops who could do much better if they were allowed to.

A state of confusion seemed to exist with the department heads as they would have to make new plans and prepare a new detailed estimate which would take a while.

I was slowly beginning to realize that Lockheed Georgia had been primarily devoted to the manufacture of military aircraft. They had definite procedures in dealing with the military that, in no way, were adaptable to commercial operations as we observed in their approach to repairs.

Lockheed may have thought of me as having only an adjusting background, but my aviation training and experience enabled me argue my case with confidence. It was in the 1930s, prior to WWII when I attended an Aeronautical College in California where I studied structure for manufacturing and major rebuilding type repair requirements. I had also worked for Boeing in manufacturing aircraft plus aircraft rebuilding after the war.

There were no signs of being able to advance any further until another estimate was prepared and that would evidently take some time. I therefore left for Vancouver.

Almost two weeks had passed before word came through that I should return to Lockheed. My employer, George Meredith, thought that I needed more support in the position I had taken. Arrangements were made to have Field Aviation of Calgary, send their Bob Corrothers down to prepare a cost figure. I returned to Marietta and the following morning Joe Childs brought me up to date on several matters as we made our way to the factory.

We had no sooner entered the shop and heading for the aircraft when a fellow approached us saying that he wanted to show us something. It was an airstair door that looked brand new and I asked him if it was. He quickly replied "No, we repaired the damaged one with a new outer skin and put on new step treads." I was quite taken by that man's enthusiasm over having repaired it to a new condition and congratulated him on doing such a fine job.

The repair had been completed by them doing exactly as I had earlier recommended. I was pleased that we had made great gains by them proving that repairing an assembly was both possible and practical.

The promised detailed estimate was received but the listed parts were not priced out and the labour was not broken down for the various operations. It also contained discrepancies in the work noted and that which was required.

A supervisor informed us that he had dropped a bomb shell on the finance department when he told them we wanted a complete breakdown on labour. It would take them another three days to prepare and it would be on a cost plus 10 percent basis. It was so exasperating.

Later, I found that for some reason that was never explained, they had put a tail on me, no freedom pass. That did not pose as a problem in any way but I thought some one wanted to know who I talked to and what I looked at.

Bob Corrothers arrived, prepared an estimate which was open on certain items because some parts prices weren't available but it was close to what we had in mind and, I might say, it was prepared without any pressure from us.

A meeting that turned out to be our final one of any consequence, took place with much discussion. We didn't seem to be getting very far in reaching an agreement on the basic methods for repairing the damaged major sections and picking up on the time lost in the meantime.

The Vice President, Mr. Crocket, went into action by announcing that they were going to put demurrage charges on the Hercules and have me escorted off the premises. That was certainly a bit of a shock and my hesitation in replying must have given them the feeling that they had nailed me down. "You are certainly in a position to do that", I replied. "However, before you proceed toward taking such drastic measures, there are a couple of conditions you should be made aware of and which you may want to seriously consider. I also have a question or two that come to mind."

"The aviation world, as a whole, recognizes that the Lockheed C 130 Hercules has no equal in its class for the work it is chiefly engaged in. Lockheed builds the best aircraft of its kind and the commercial operators through out the world know it." "However, Lockheed does not know how to repair them."

Mr. Crocket, without any hesitation, replied by saying, "Yes, we are manufacturers, not repairers." My immediate reply was, "Good, now we are getting some where." I continued. "You may or may not know that there are not more than about three Underwriters at Lloyds, in London, who are willing to provide insurance coverage for the Hercules primarily because of the very nature of their work in remote areas."

So, I had encountered another "lesson on the job". When Mr. Crockett stated that Lockheed was in the manufacturing business and not in the repair business, I realized that company policy could have a big impact on customer decision making. I told him that my underwriting clients and P.W.A. who were both interested in the cost of getting an aircraft back in the air on a cost experience basis, would be very interested in learning that Lockheed had such a policy. Remanufacturing is far more costly than repair work and in most cases is no more effective.

"If you go through with your plan I will be forced to contact those Insurers and provide them with the details of the unexpected complications that I have been faced with in this assignment. The report would not contain any opinions or personal

Temporarily repaired for ferry flight.

remarks, just straight facts that Lockheed wouldn't deny as having taken place."

I had several questions about their future plans, if they had any, to better service their commercial customers who had to depend on Lockheed from time to time.

I had a final question. "What are you intending to do for the Commercial Operator if and when your Uncle Sam quits having military conflicts around the world and business with them drops off?"

I excused myself and informed them that I would not need an escort to leave the premises. "Just let me know when I am to go and one of the friendly fellows on the shop floor will provide the courtesy I'm sure."

I had been busy discussing the repair work in progress on the Hercules for quite a while when Mr. Crocket's Aide made an appearance and I asked him if it was time to go. He replied. "No, Mr. Crocket wants you to have lunch with him." I asked. "Why? To continue with the unpleasantness?" "No." he said. "It is his way of apologizing." I didn't respond immediately and continued a discussion with a maintenance supervisor.

After a short delay I turned to him, apologized for my hesitation and asked him to please convey my regards to Mr. Crocket and tell him that I would be pleased to accept his invitation. I can still hear that fellow taking a deep breath and loudly exhaling before saying "Oh, I'm glad you said that. Thank you. I'll come down to get you later."

I was confused and tried to figure out why the sudden change. It was beyond me. On several occasions, that same young man had been very apologetic when some thing wasn't working out quite right for us. He was very likable but, of course, neither he nor we ever discussed our obstacles.

In a little while I was guided up to the executive dining room and directed to a chair at Mr. Crocket's left side. He thanked me for accepting his invitation and said. "Let us have a nice lunch and not talk about aircraft." It was indeed a pleasant luncheon with a complete change in the atmosphere.

The repair costs were still not completely set out and broken down as we thought they should be and as we were accustomed to receiving from other repair companies. However we could see that we had made our point and Lockheed was slowly responding.

All that time I was so sure that I was on the right track but even with Joe's support I did not feel easy about the delay and costs for P.W.A. Then I received a call from Bill Bryant of P.W.A. saying they were backing me all the way. That was a big relief.

It was apparent that I could not accomplish anything further in the next few days and thought it best to return to Vancouver. As we left the building, the Aeronautical Engineer, with whom we had had several exchanges of thoughts right at the aircraft, was at the door to say good-bye. I have never forgotten it along with his good wishes.

He shook Joe's hand first. I thought he was never going to let go of my hand and saying as much with his eyes as with words.

When we were on our way Joe said. "Did you ever have a hand shake like that before? So full of apology." I could only say "never" and I believe the gentleman was a very capable engineer prevented from straying from the set down military procedures of repair maintenance.

Joe had been a good supporter while I opposed Lockheed's procedures but I still felt that P.W.A. management might think I had gone too far and dragged out their down time on the Hercules. I was relieved when I learned that Don Watson, President of P.W.A., at a special board meeting said to his directors, in strong words, "Denny McCartney is doing a darn good job for this company and I am backing him 100 percent regardless of what any of you thinks."

Somewhere along the line it was thought that Air Claims, a World Wide Aviation Adjusting Firm, should be asked to investigate and submit a report on the repair procedures and costs. Mr. Ahlers of Miami was directed to do that.

I was not down there at the time of the survey but it was done in a total of 5 hours on the premises. He did have the nose landing gear sent out to Menasco as we had wanted to do earlier. His report was not totally accurate but there were no recommended changes to our proposed procedures.

There was no criticism in the report on what we

had done or proposed. It did however contain excuses for Lockheed's costing out system as related to their military practices.

The report, in short, confirmed that Lockheed had diverted from their original planning and were now in line with our thinking. It was such a relief to see them give up the idea of installing a complete new front end on the aircraft and instead, make repairs.

The work continued to a final conclusion with Joe maintaining a close watch.

I think it is quite safe to say that we were instrumental in Lockheed revamping their thinking by adopting a civilian type commercial approach they could offer airline customers.

Lockheed would soon bring on line a new type commercial aircraft, the L-1011 to compete with such companies as Boeing Aircraft. They therefore had to change their ways or get nowhere with such competitors. Mr. Ahler's report supported those thoughts too.

I was at Lloyds in London a few months later when Bob Pincott paid me a nice compliment in telling the Insurers of the Hercules that I had saved Underwriters a million dollars or better through my efforts in the claim. I added that P.W.A. Management and their Technical Representative, Joe Childs, played a big part in that achievement. Which was a fact.

That claim had been finalized for some time when I received a call from Bob Pincott with instructions to leave for Edmonton on another problem. It was near the end of February, 1970 and I was to determine whether or not the repair costs to another Hercules would exceed the insurance deductible. The aircraft was up in the Arctic at Resolute and would arrive in Edmonton next morning.

Upon arriving at the PWA shops I was directed to an aircraft with damage to the roof of the pilots' compartment.

The nose wheel, during a landing on an upsloping northern airstrip, had been driven upwards with sufficient force as to develop a vertical loading that caused a bending action in the roof, leaving creases in the metal skins.

Upon entering the crew compartment I could see that sketches had been made on the inside of the roof metal covering for some type of repair.

I jumped to a conclusion, before making any inquiries, that they were making temporary repairs and in turning to Gordon Canim, asked why. He informed me that they were permanent repairs recommended by the Lockheed Technical Representative.

That did it and without stopping to think I said "Excellent idea and good thinking but I didn't think anything that practical and intelligent would come from Lockheed." Within the next few seconds Gord said. "It sure did and the Rep. is standing right behind you, I'm sure you two know each other."

I had to say no which was the truth. However, the Rep. said "Oh, I know who you are Denny from when you were down at our plant in Georgia." Just

imagine how I felt with having rudely opened my mouth then trying to apologize and being told it was not at all necessary.

I asked him if he would have a coffee with me, on our own, later and without any hesitation he said "yes." In the coffee shop I asked him what I could say to apologize for opening my big mouth as I did. His reply was a simple one. "An apology is not at all necessary because what you do not know is that I was fired while you were down at our plant." I replied, "It was common knowledge what I was doing but what did you do to deserve that?"

He came back with a quick and startling reply. "I was supporting you and my immediate bosses didn't like it so I was let go. I knew who you were from reading articles in trade magazines on your work. I warned others that you were a capable person. Later, I was rehired by higher authority, mainly because I was needed for military repairs."

It almost blew my mind when he said, "your remarks and questions have been steadily bouncing and ricocheting off all the buildings around the Lockheed plant with meeting after meeting on them."

"What on earth could some one like me from way up north, have said that a company, as large as Lockheed, would take any notice of and have such meetings?" "Well, for one thing, you suggested that it might be interesting for Underwriters to hear about the problems you had with Lockheed."

"Another thing. You asked them what they were going to do for the Commercial Operator if and when Uncle Sam's military work drops off. You have not gone unnoticed or forgotten and you have left a lot of echoes in Lockheed."

He explained that he was enroute to Viet Nam to lay out some repair plans for several aircraft and was asked to dogleg up to Edmonton first, for the same purpose. I had met an Aeronautical Engineer with a practical background and experience with an approach to repairing as compared with assembly line repetitive procedures.

As I looked back over the exercise I had been through with Lockheed, it was quite plain that the system used to deal with the military was well ingrained and it had taken me a while to realize it. I had broken into that pattern in rather an abrupt fashion with my thinking based on the normal, standard type repair and estimating procedures used throughout the commercial aviation industry.

Boeing has always been a fine example of co-operation and their technical representatives go out of their way to make practical repairs and keep both costs and down time to a minimum. In the long run perhaps no harm was done with the action we took but it was a nervous exercise at the time in 1969.

I had never been involved, previously or for that matter since then, with a military type repair pro-gramme where costs didn't seem to be a consider-ation. It must have been difficult for them to even consider our request for a standard type commer-cial repair approach after so many years of having what seemed to be an open, blank cheque style contract with the people of The United States.

There were no grounds to criticize the quality of Lockheed's shop work.

I was recently out to an International Air Show at Abbotsford, B.C. and had an interesting conver-sation with a Hercules Maintenance Chief from Alaska. He spoke very well of Lockheed's practi-cal approach and co-operation in regards to repairs of all dimensions with parts and technical advice being made readily available. I was very pleased to hear him speak so highly of Lockheed.

chapter twenty-five

D.E.W. Line Confrontation

It was October 1958 in the early years of the Distant Early Warning Line operation and the site was Cambridge Bay, Victoria Island, N.W.T. The D.E.W. Line consisted of a string of airstrips and radar stations every 50 miles across the north coast of Canada and Alaska, the bulk of which were on Canadian soil. It was constructed by the American Government for their military forces in keeping an eye on Russian flying activities etc.

The various bases were serviced by Canadian civilian operators such as Pacific Western Air Lines in the western section.

A rush call had me up at Cambridge Bay in a big hurry with P.W.A. representatives. A C 46 cargo aircraft registration CF-PWD had had a problem at the end of its landing roll and was now on its belly with the main landing gear damaged and its nose sticking over the end of the runway. That model aircraft was one of the largest twin engine freighters at that time.

I was immediately faced with an awkward situation that I later realized had been developed by an individual from his close association with the U.S. Army and its procedures of doing things their way, regardless of the consequences.

What we saw, called for immediate action without firstly going through the normal channels of checking in at the base office. Two large cranes, each with their winch cable secured to an engine, had the front end of the aircraft lifted well above its normal level position. At the same time I caught sight of a very long flat bed truck with a couple of flat topped trailers attached to it.

I asked the nearest person, who turned out to be the crew chief, "What are you doing?"

He replied. "We are going to haul the aircraft down beyond the other end of the airstrip and dump it there."

It raced through my mind that the place, he was referring to, was their graveyard for damaged equipment including military aircraft. I had previously heard about the existence of such dumps. It appeared that the military placed little value on damaged equipment and considered it more expedient to replace than repair. The same procedures were followed in the construction of the Alaska Highway where many tractors were left in sunken positions and the road was built over them.

It was more of an order when I said, "Have the crane operators lock their winches and stand by." That was done without any hesitation by the crew chief, then we introduced ourselves. I asked, "Who ordered the removal of the aircraft?" He said, "The station supervisor had given him the orders."

All the damage was photographed and a very rough mental calculation indicated that repair costs would be only a portion of the amount for which it was insured. It was carefully explained to him that if they continued with their plan the aircraft would be destroyed. The weight of the aircraft would crush its belly on the trailers which would be forced up into the aircraft until the sides of the fuselage touched the ground. I told him that the aircraft was not owned or came under the con-

(left); An unhappy finish to a landing. (right); Aircraft moved forward and ready for ferry flight patching up.

trol of Federal Electric and therefore continuance with their plan would lead to a legal action against them. Photos would be taken of the additional damage for a full report to the Insurers at Lloyds in London. Then the operators of the D.E.W. Line would find out that they were up against a much larger organization that would not back off.

He remained calm and polite then left as he explained he had to report to the supervisor.

It was not long before the crew chief returned to saying, "It is our procedure to clear the airstrip of anything that would interfere with its use. However, the supervisor wants to know what we want to do with the aircraft."

My reply was simple. "Move it forward off the airstrip and down the slight incline to the level area where it would be blocked up and secured and ready for a repair crew. It would be off the strip and below it, clear of any aircraft coming or going."

The crew chief made another hurried trip to their offices and upon his return, informed me that the supervisor agreed to our suggestion. He then said to me. "I'm glad you did that because I didn't want to do as I had been ordered." He then told me that he was from Alaska.

The task of facing up to Federal Electric was made much easier through the support and help I received from the Pacific Western Airlines fellows.

The aircraft was very gently rolled forward on its tail wheel to a level area with no added damage. It was such a relief when the station supervisor

agreed with our suggestion. Had we had been delayed to any extent in our arrival, there was little doubt but what the aircraft would have been destroyed. We could see no reason for them to have rushed into action as they did because the crippled machine didn't interfere with the arrival and departure of aircraft and we had landed without a problem. It was simply a case of military thinking and unnecessary hurried follow up action.

Our thoughts turned to plans for temporary repairs. It was farthest from my mind to consider asking for hangar space which was limited so I went in another direction and laid out plans to do it right where the aircraft sat, independent of the station as much as possible. I had in mind a canvas type shelter for each engine with a closed in passage way between them. That could be extended back a bit for work on the belly and wheels with heated comfort from Herman Nelson heaters. I was sure I knew where such equipment or the plans would be found.

Canadian Pacific Airlines had built themselves up from bush flying and had found it necessary to do some on the spot bush repairs from time to time.

Upon my return to Vancouver I went out to see Bill Wiskin in the engineering department of Canadian Pacific Airlines and described my needs. He had exactly what I wanted and it was available. That was a good start and I was ready to go in with a C 46 familiarized crew and get the job going. An adjuster, for whom I was doing the work, changed things around and appointed Field Aviation of Calgary to take over the salvage operation.

Field had very capable technicians and I suggested that they not move the aircraft but use the C.P.A. portable design shop and Herman Nelson heaters. Instead, they talked their way into the use of hangar space, only to be moved out into the open again before the job was finished. I received word that they were most uncomfortable but completed it and the machine was flown to Calgary for recertification.

chapter twenty-six

Adventure in the High Arctic

The entries in my diary for the year 1961 support my thoughts that it was the busiest year I had ever had. My destinations ranged in latitude from the high Arctic to South America, entailing long hours of flying in slower aircraft, not the jets of today.

Any time I had, between out of town trips, was spent on rebuilding De Havilland Beavers at the Vancouver Airport. On a Sunday in late June I had been working all day on a Beaver. A phone call in the evening contained instructions to catch the next flight to Edmonton.

The next two days were taken up with insurance problems that adjuster Dick Hicks and underwriter Bill Meyers had, as related to several damaged aircraft. At the end of the second day I was sent to Calgary on some technical work for Frank Enderton, an Insurance adjuster.

Following that, Frank and I left for the Nahanni area in Yukon via car to Ft. Nelson BC. A Beaver seaplane to Heatherbell Lake and a helicopter completed our trip to site of a damaged helicopter.

Upon completion of our inspection and assessment of the damage, arrangements were made to sling it out to a road. We left for Wrigley on the MacKenzie River down stream from Fort Simpson where a Cessna 210 took us to Fort Nelson. I remember, while waiting on the Wrigley airstrip, seeing a lady standing in front of me. She had two streams of blood trickling down the back of one of her bare legs. The large horseflies can make quite an incision with a bite that involves removal of a piece of flesh.

We drove all night straight through to Edmonton, arriving there about 11 A.M. During that trip the road was often alive with rabbits. The car lights seemed to hypnotize them as they sat straight up in the roadway looking directly at us. Several times we heard thump, thump, thump as the car bumper struck their heads. Using the horn didn't move them. The ravens would have had a big feed as soon as it was daylight.

Well, up to that point we had been extremely busy but now Bill had two more trips set for us. One was in Yukon and the other was in the High Arctic. It was then the first week of July but I knew that it would still be cold up up on the North West Passage so I phoned home to have clothes, parka and my down filled sleeping bag flown to Edmonton.

We left that same afternoon and flew to Watson Lake, Yukon in a Cessna 310 through very stormy weather. Next morning we flew with Don Douglas and Mac McCubbin two very capable and well like Department of Transport Accident Investigators, south to Dease Lake and from there, via helicopter, to the accident scene of another helicopter.

Following our inspections, arrangements were made to sling the machine out to a road for transport to its base. That trip was an exception. It was not all work. We had a short session of rainbow trout fishing in that remote lake. A few trout were given to the exploration crew camped there and a couple to our pilot, Walt Forseberg.

I met Bud Harbottle again in Watson Lake and helped him with small problems on his MK.V Anson. Mac Sanderson, whom I knew quite well, was with Bud. It was always nice to see familiar faces so far away from home.

We flew to Edmonton next day and gave the Government men a ride out with us.

The following day was a busy one. My northern gear had arrived and I purchased miscellaneous items including, of course, several newspapers for people I would meet in Resolute

We left Edmonton in the Cessna 310 about mid afternoon on, approximately, a 2000 mile N.E. flight. We were on our way to Resolute, which is positioned on the south end of Cornwallis Island, at 75° north latitude. Resolute is on the north side of Parry Channel, often referred to as the North West Passage. It is about 160 miles South East of the North Magnetic Pole. We had supper in Yellowknife, refueled in Cambridge Bay on the south end of Victoria Island and arrived in Resolute about 3 a.m.

Ice still covered all the Arctic waters but there were large Leads (open cracks) that are the first signs of the ice starting to break up. Keep in mind that it was the month of July. Strong thunder storm winds had made that last portion of our flight very rough.

I found Resolute very interesting but had no time to explore it as I would have liked. As soon as we were set up in quarters that were similar to a military setting we contacted the pilot and engineer, Ron Sturgess, about the helicopter accident we had been were sent up to investigate. The location was on Lowther Island, a short distance south west of Resolute.

Most of the day was taken up in trying to get an aircraft to fly us to the island the next day but no luck. A storm with rain had grounded the aircraft that day but they all had bookings for the following day, just when we needed one.

As usual, I contacted the Royal Canadian Mounted Police detachment to advise them of our plans. They told us that it could be dangerous for us to go onto the island because the edges of the many leads in the ice around the island had large numbers of seals on them. They attract polar bears which would present a danger to us. We were not permitted to take any firearms into the Arctic areas for our own protection. The RCMP were very restrictive about who was given such privileges.

There are very strict laws there to protect the wild life, which was the result of very advanced thinking for those early years. The Officer resolved the issue by offering to accompany us and provide the needed protection. That suited us fine.

While discussing that matter with the Officer I noted that he had a terrible cold and mentioned that he didn't look at all well. He hadn't complained about it either and still, was ready to go with us. He replied that he felt rough and needed some rest and a hot rum at bed time would help immensely but he didn't have any. Well, it so happened that I had brought such an item with us and told him that he could have it. That surprised him and he seemed to show a marked improvement almost immediately.

I had found the Police Officer on his way to check on something in the Police cold storage locker and he invited me to go along with him while we talked. He must have sensed that I was rushing around on our project. When we entered the locker I could see that it contained a large number of Eskimo carvings, furs and other interesting things. However, what attracted me the most was the beautiful skin, of what must have been a very large polar bear, hanging on the wall, minus its head.

I wanted to know why someone would butcher a beautiful hide like that. He said that there was an interesting story on how that happened. He explained that three government men were out on the ice doing survey work some distance from Resolute about one month earlier. At the end of one day, they bedded down on the ice in their sleeping bags for some sleep. Sometime later, two of them were jolted out of their sleep by the agonizing screams of the third man. A polar bear was dragging him (in his sleeping bag) across the ice at quite a pace. The two of them advanced toward the bear while screaming, shouting and waving their arms, in an attempt to frighten the bear into letting go of their friend and taking off out of there but that didn't work. The bear wasn't about to be scared off. He must have thought he had hit a jackpot and there was more for the taking because he dropped his planned meal and ran towards the other two. Fortunately, the government men were allowed to have a rifle with them and the bear was shot.

The Officer said that both the bear and the unlucky man or should we say, in one way, lucky fellow, were brought into Resolute. He was flown down to Winnipeg because of bear teeth injuries to his shoulder and the bear's head was shipped out for a rabies check. That disease was prevalent in those northern areas, especially with foxes.

I thought that story could be classified a unique one.

Now, back to our problem. We continued our hunt for a fixed wing aircraft or a helicopter as a few were still coming and going but we were having no luck. We preferred a helicopter, especially if it was large enough to haul the damaged Bell 47 helicopter into Resolute. We rushed to the airport

Beaver on Tundra tires.

every time we heard a machine come in, only to be disappointed because they had a tight schedule for a short season. There was a great deal of exploration work going on at that time including the Continental Shelf Project.

I decided to get some sleep to end a long spell without any. I hadn't been asleep very long when Frank and a pilot who said he had a helicopter that would solve our problem awakened me.

He was not one known to me and and I was not familiar with the name of his employer. He didn't mince any words in coming directly to the point by saying he would do our job for $500 and that it would be a simple operation.

It sounded great and he had a positive approach that was encouraging so I suggested that he get in contact with his employer to obtain their approval. I also wanted to know what insurance coverage they carried for slinging operations. He refused to contact his employer and kept saying that $500 was a good price. I then wanted the name and address of his employer so that a cheque could be sent to them for their services. He refused to provide that information and insisted that the payment be made directly to him.

I then knew that he was out to cheat his employer and that didn't please me one bit. I also wanted to make sure that the load would be covered by an insurance policy in the event he dropped it. Bear in mind, we were desperate to get the job done but we weren't going into it blindfolded. We had a responsibility to both those who had

sent us up there and the owners of the helicopter. I questioned him about his experiences on that type of work, had he ever slung out another machine and how could he be so certain that it would be a piece of cake as he put it. He was insulted that I should question the ability of a former Colonel of the United States Army Air Corps who could guarantee a safe slinging job with no problem at all.

I said, "O.K., if you do the job I will rig and hook up the load for you." He shot back in a loud voice, "Do you know how to do that?"

I supposed that he thought it was his turn to ask a direct question. I replied that I most surely did and the load would be very securely attached to his machine. He replied by saying he would expect it to be secure or else - I interrupted him at that point and assured him that the sling would be perfectly secure.

"Where ever that load goes you will stay with it because you have guaranteed there will be no problem." He asked me, "What do you mean?" My reply was, "When I do the hook up I will make it permanent with a piece of lock wire. You will not be able to jettison the load. Simple as that." He jumped up and shouted at me saying, "You can't do that, you can't do that!!!" I ended the discussion by saying, "Just as I thought, you want to cheat your employer, you are not concerned about our position, you say it's a cinch of a job and yet you want the opportunity to drop the load if it turns out that you don't know what you are doing.

You have a lot to learn and your military rank doesn't impress me in the least. You are a bull sh- - artist and a cheat."

He stomped out of the room talking to himself. Frank was not happy about the turn of events and that was understandable but my feeling was that the helicopter would be safer there on the island for the moment than in the hands of that pilot. He may have done a satisfactory job for us but he was thinking too much about his own concerns for us to take a chance. I went back to bed to get some much needed sleep.

Next day we were again looking for a machine to charter and ran across Ron Wells, a well known and highly experienced pilot. Ron was all set to help us with his Otter, but he was sent in another direction. Finally, we were fortunate in meeting Dick Dublique who flew a Beaver for Barkley Air Services and arrangements were made for us to go. His aircraft was mounted on Tundra wheels and tires, an adaptation for which Barkley Air was well noted.

I had never seen anything like them before and was fascinated by them. The tires were similar in size to those used on a DC3 but with less air pressure that allowed the tires to absorb a rock instead of bouncing off it. That modification enabled the aircraft to operate on some very rough surfaces that would be impossible with the smaller original wheels and tires with higher air pressures. It was a very clever installation and gave the aircraft greater mobility in moving people and equipment

in those early days of heavy exploration in the North.

The flight to the island was most interesting. There were a large number of seals resting on the edges of the leads and as we passed over them they just did a roll over, into the water.

We landed not far from the helicopter and taxied up close to it. We could not have done that with conventional wheels and tires.

We didn't think we would be able to take much of the helicopter out of there but Dick had a safe way to load the disassembled machine. Thus our project started to take shape.

It was quite a sight to see the Beaver take off with a short run slightly downhill and as I remember, and with three small bounces on those large tires it was in the air.

The temperature was between 38° and 40° F. (summer average) and with a light breeze. So parkas were certainly needed. I was told that the average winter temperatures were around -40° to -50° degrees F. and a yearly rainfall of about 2.5 in.

We finally completed our task and were thankful that Dick had such a positive attitude and could back it up with a true northern approach. What a comparison he was to that egotistical clown who thought we should not question a U.S. Army Colonel.

Preparations were made for our return trip south. I would have liked to have been able to see more of that area but that would have be at another time, I hoped.

I had a little hobby of collecting pieces of mineralized rock such as galena (lead silver and zinc) from various exploration camps I got into. My two trips into the Yukon just prior to going up to Resolute netted me a few pieces.

When I first rolled out my sleeping bag to get some badly needed sleep, the chunks of ore fell on the floor. A fellow sitting on a bed nearby, as it turned out, was a geologist, and of course was most interested until I told him where they came from. He then showed me a good sized piece of coral which, he said, was like some that can be found in Hawaii. He went on to say that there was lots of it in the Resolute area.

He gave me a good sized piece and it is now in the face of our recreation room fireplace that was built with mineralized rock that I carted home in my sleeping bag.

The Arctic, to me, has been most intriguing and it is mind boggling to be up in the Arctic snow and ice while trying to imagine it as having been tropical at one time. How long ago? In 1986 the ice receded enough to expose the remains of large trees and stumps on Axel Heiberg Island. That High Arctic island is west of Eureka which sits at 80 degrees north latitude. The trees are Sequoia and similar to those found in Northern China today. The root formations resemble the root structure of the trees of the Florida Everglades, which could suggest that it was once very swampy. The experts have estimated that the tree remains are about 40 million years old. An interesting part of our old and ever-changing world.

I arrived home after two of the busiest weeks I can ever remember. I was in Vancouver for the next three days, working on a Beaver. Little did I know at that time, that I would be back to the High Arctic and it would be Eureka.

chapter twenty-seven

Sunken Helicopter Rescue from Fraser Canyon

The year 1961 was indeed a busy one for me. In January and February I was on the Yukon River re the Aero Commander, up in the high Arctic for a helicopter, then a helicopter in the upper canyon of the Fraser River and finally to South America to ferry a Single Otter to Calgary. There were also many smaller problems that I took care of, in between those jobs, for three different insurance adjusting offices.

The retrieval of most damaged aircraft is a challenge to say the least but this one was unique and one of a kind.

A helicopter had struck a cable strung across the Upper Fraser River at the river's upper canyon a short distance east of Sinclair Mills. The pilot had escaped but his machine had sunk in the river.

It was common practice for logging and construction companies to string cables above rivers from shore to shore as an assist in moving equipment and men across fast flowing waters. In those early days, little or no thought was given to marking them to warn pilots of their existence.

I arrived in Prince George, with Dick Bolding, on an early C.P.A. flight that took my work boots on to Whitehorse, Y.T. No time was lost in getting a U drive car and leaving for the accident site in the company of an R.C.M.P. Officer. The road was a rough one consisting of gravel and mud with lots of frost boils, all of which made driving difficult. The Officer took over and showed me how to deal with the road.

We arrived at Sinclair Mills and met Mr. Ray Mueller, a river boat man who provided the transportation via boat, to the crash site.

The river was in its Spring flood stage and still rising. The cable that the helicopter struck had been strung across from one rock face to the other at the end of the canyon.

The helicopter was in a wider pool like stretch of

Helicopter lifted from upper Fraser River bottom. This rig shot the upper Fraser Canyon rapids.

quieter water with its narrower down stream end forming a long run of fast white water. It appeared that the helicopter had been flying down the canyon at the time of the accident. We estimated that the helicopter would have possibly gone about half way down the length of the pool before settling to the bottom. Later, we would find we had made a close guess.

We returned to Prince George. The next two days were spent with a boat trying to locate the machine by dragging for it with a large four pronged hook. Divers couldn't hang on to a rope as they worked, logs and trees came out of the canyon and nearly turned the boat over. We finally gave up the thought of finding the helicopter while the water was so high at 9 feet above normal.

My attention was drawn to another problem in the Quesnel area.

I had just returned from a High Arctic trip when a call came with word that the river at Sinclair Mills was back to normal. Back I went with the family station wagon and the flat deck trailer.

I arrived back at Ray Mueller's home unannounced because of no phone, and was made welcome. We had a short discussion on the problem and decided we would need two river boats. The boats were similar to those used in Yukon, they were quite long with flat bottoms and high sides for maximum water clearance.

A second boat man was needed so we had to locate Ray's son who was out working in the woods. The equipment and tools for our plan were loaded into the boats then early next morning back up the river we went.

It was a very different scene that time with the water level so much lower.

We got on with our dragging and it was mot long before we hooked onto the helicopter. Then a rigging was needed to lift it out of the water.

A plan, mostly Ray's, was set in motion by nosing the two boats up onto the beach approximately 10 feet apart. They were then lashed together, by securing long poles across the rear and front sections. Next, 4 long poles were set up on end in the boats and lashed together at their top ends to form a quadrapod with a hand winch at the top. The helicopter was raised to the surface and the winch line was secured to the stubs of the main rotor blades and head. The helicopter was slowly winched up and when its bottom end was above the sides of the boats pole were placed under it and across the boats to form a deck to rest it on.

When the machine was securely lashed in place and everything else was double checked for safety, we were ready to leave for Sinclair Mills.

Down through the white water we went at a great clip with Ray and his son, each controlling an outboard motor. It was quite an exciting trip down the fast water, through what is known as the upper canyon of the Fraser River. That was no doubt the first and last excursion on the river with a rig up such as we had. I often think of it and admire those River Men.

At Sinclair Mills a crane was used to load the helicopter on my trailer and I left there about 9 p.m. on a very slow, rough drive at 15 miles per hour for 60 miles, arriving in Prince George about 2 a.m. It had been another long day but a successful one, thanks to Ray and his son. I was in Vancouver the following night.

I think I mention a point of interest that I spotted while we were searching for the helicopter. It is associated with the history of our early development in B.C.

There were pieces of railroad rails sticking up at the side of the river, near the canyon mouth. Apparently, when the Grand Trunk Pacific Railroad (later, named the Canadian National Railroad), was being built, much of the materials such as rails were transported by river rafts. The story I heard in the Prince George area led me to believe that men, chiefly Chinese Immigrants, manned such rafts and were also lost in those accidents.

My wife's father, Mr. Murray, was the civil engineer in charge of much of the construction for the railroad at that time. My information did not come from him because he had passed away before I first met my wife Dot.

chapter twenty-eight

Owikena Lake Retrieval

This story illustrates that getting to the scene of a crash was, on occasion, an adventure in itself.

Owikena Lake provided the setting for the most exasperating experience I can ever remember. It was near the end of May, 1965. The lake is a short distance beyond the head of Rivers Inlet, into which it drains, and is approximately 150 miles up the coast from Vancouver. It has a beautiful setting in a long valley with heavily treed hills on either side that graduate up into mountains 2900 and 3500 meters high, crowned with glaciers and snow fields.

A Triway Air Cessna 180 seaplane, an air charter company, was upside down at a logging company's booming grounds.

I was flown to the accident site in another of the charter company's seaplanes with a pilot whose name, I believe, was Charlie We were at quite a good height when we arrived over the accident scene. Rather than using a normal procedure to gradually lose altitude for a landing he rolled the aircraft over on its back and dove like a fish hawk down to the water.

I do not scare easily but that smart aleck maneuver made me angry and I wasn't short in telling him so.

During WWII I frequently flew in torpedo dive bombers of the Royal Navy Fleet Air Arm when rapid descents were started with a wing roll over and dropping down to within a few feet of the ocean surface. Those actions didn't bother me because the aircraft were built to withstand the resulting high stresses and the pilots were well trained. But in a light commercial machine and a strange pilot I had my doubts.

If my memory serves me correctly, Charlie was killed in a flying accident at a later date a short distance north of Vancouver, near Sechelt, B.C.

Oh, I must mention that one of those Navy flights took place right after I had had a hearty breakfast of kippers (smoked herring) that I enjoyed. During the maneuvers that followed our take off the kippers wanted to get out. I fought them for the full flight and on completion of the trip one of the armourers had the nerve to say that I looked a little green around the gills.

We tied up to the C.& L Development camp dock and optained the use of a small boat and its operator Bert.

The pontoon noses of the sunken plane were well secured to a log that was part of log booming ground enclosure in which logs were sorted and made into booms for transport to a saw mill.

I set about to upright the aircraft by using past experiences but it would be a first in using a log sitting in deep water. A rope bridle was secured to the rudder posts of the floats and this was attached to a tow line from the camp's tugboat

(left); **Pontoons lashed to a large log.** (right); **On its way over.**

operated by Captain Grant. I would use pre arranged hand signals from my position in a small boat to guide Grant in pulling the aircraft up and over the log.

The tail of the aircraft came up a little, then one wing went too high in the air and the other one was even deeper in the water. The aircraft would be twisted if that continued so I signaled the tug to slack off and with an axe in hand I ran down that slimy log and cut the one float free. The aircraft settled back into the water and we started over again.

Grant, in the next attempt, watched for any unfavorable movement and maneuvered the boat to counter it. The tail came up as the nose of the floats and the log sank deeply into the water when the aircraft was in a vertical position, tail high. Suddenly, the seaplane dropped down onto its floats and the major part of my problem was done. Grant had done it with his superb mariner's ability.

The aircraft was towed to a dock with a small shack on it in the bay containing the booming grounds. I worked until late evening then suddenly realized that the floats had slow leaks, and had to be pumped out every three or four hours. Several compartments were leaking, probably old damage, as there was no damage to the floats but, regardless, it was one more problem. That first night I pumped them at midnight and the camp fellows did it for me at four a.m. on their way to work.

I slept fitfully with my mind on the aircraft sitting on 1200 feet of water.

A proven procedure in preparing the engine for flight included three lots of oil, the first of which was used for only a two minute engine run then the milky coloured oil was drained out. The next lot was used a little longer before draining and the final lot was for the ferry flight.

The electrical units were opened and exposed to the air while being sprayed with a water absorbing lubricant.

The fuel tanks were a different matter. They were completely drained but there are always pockets of water remaining in the bottoms of the tanks and a water film coats the tops and walls. I might add that I never, at any time, drained engines or fuel tanks into a body of water. It was always caught in containers and made a lot more work but I couldn't have done otherwise.

During the retrieval of several sunken aircraft, over a period of time, I developed a very successful method for getting rid of that moisture. Clean fuel is put into the tanks that are not completely filled, leaving a little space for the fuel to slosh around in them. The aircraft is then taxied around on the water for a while, cutting through its wakes to rock and roll it.

The rough movement of the fuel washes the moisture down to the outlets and drained off at the filter upon return to the dock. Sometimes that had to be repeated but I never had a fuel/water problem in any ferry flight.

Owikena Lake, because of its position in a deep, long valley of the coast mountain range, is at times, subjected to strong winds coming off the ocean to replace warm, rapidly rising air in the interior of the country, east of the mountains.

We were, at the time, enjoying warm spring weather and by about 10 a.m. strong winds every morning produced rough water with white caps. Those were the conditions we were faced with when the aircraft was finally ready for the taxi work on the water.

A pilot, named Ted, whom I had never met before, had been sent up the previous day to ferry the aircraft to Vancouver. I asked him to take the aircraft out for the taxi work but he was to stay in the fairly large sheltered bay where we were. I

was most emphatic about him not going out on the main body of the lake because by that time it was too rough and dangerous with three foot swells. He was reminded that there was water in the fuel system and out on the open lake was no place to be if he had any engine trouble.

The pilot had been expressing a desire to get going for home and objected to me saying we would do just that but only in the early morning before the winds started. I also wanted to leave as soon as possible but safety and common sense were top considerations.

I helped him away from the dock and watched him operate the aircraft until I was convinced was

The aircraft left for home after engine and instruments were cleaned up plus some metal work.

being done satisfactorily. I then turned my attention to my typical bush work bench consisting of a couple of up ended fuel barrels. The shack provided a shelter from the wind and with my back to the water I became deeply occupied with the preservation of the instruments and radios. Fortunately, the most important instrument, oil pressure, was sealed and connected to the engine by oil filled tubing and didn't need any special servicing.

It seemed like only a few minutes had passed when I heard the speed boat approaching the dock at full speed and, I couldn't believe my eyes, with the soaking wet pilot in the bow screaming hysterically at the top of his voice. "I did it again. I did it again."

I saw in a flash that the aircraft was missing and asked Bert what had happened. He out shouted the pilot while saying "the aircraft is upside down again and I happened to be near when it happened and saved the pilot from drowning."

Now, all that had been said in about 20 seconds and in utter disbelief it suddenly dawned on me that he had sunk the aircraft again. I was too stunned for words and perhaps just as well because there shouldn't have been any need for me to explain my evil thoughts. I couldn't give him credit for having any intelligence but surely he must have been able to at least imagine what I was thinking.

The pilot went into the shack and stayed there for the rest of the day. He wanted to go home. I don't remember checking to see if there was any heat in there to dry him out because I had no time to lose in getting to the aircraft and safeguard it against being driven onto rocks or otherwise damaged.

The wind was very strong and the lake had rolling swells.

Bert and a fellow named Bill helped me in trying to turn the aircraft back up onto its floats but we failed and with darkness setting in, the aircraft was secured for the night.

I was in for another restless and worrisome night.

I decided that the turning over of the aircraft would be done at a beach farther down the lake, using a system that had been proven successful in a number of previous salvage operations involving seaplanes upside down in water. I had not earlier, wanted go that route if I could avoid it because the aircraft would have had to have been towed quite some distance down the lake in its inverted position.

Next morning, Grant and I used a small power boat for the towing. I had not previously towed a machine any distance in that position and for that matter I never found it necessary to do it again.

We started out slowly in a smooth fashion then increased the speed a little. The aircraft started into a glide to the bottom of the lake. Grant cut back on the speed and the aircraft came back up to its level position.

The wings are designed to lift the aircraft as it is

pulled through the air by the engine powered propeller. They had been performing in the same manner with water substituting for air and boat power in place of a propeller, taking the aircraft downward.

We finally reached a sheltered beach where the aircraft was nosed up on a sloping sandy bottom of the lake but still a short distance from the shore which was ideal for our purposes. We did not have a hand winch to pull the aircraft up and over on to its floats and besides, there was no high ground on which to set a winch for a needed upward type pull.

A shiv (pulley) was secured high up on a tree. A rope bridal was attached to the water rudder posts of the floats then a line was run out from the tug, through the shiv and down to the bridal.

The propeller was forced into a horizontal position to prevent it from being bent on contact with the lake bottom.

A signal to Bill, the tug operator, and the turn over was started. The tail of the aircraft slowly and steadily rose up until all the weight was on the nose ends of both floats.

I can tell you that I always had a feeling of relief when that point was reached whether it was in water or on dry land. The aircraft reached its apex, tail high and vertical. Then, with a slight encouragement from the tug it made a smooth cushioning drop as the float bottoms settled into the water. The seaplane was once again sitting in its normal upright position.

It was then turned around and pulled up as far as possible, nose first toward the shore until it grounded out on the lake bottom with a small strip of water between it and dry land.

I got started on the engine, electrical and fuel system servicing and preserving work for the second time and I suppose, as I went along, it could be said that I muttered a little about having to do it twice.

The next two days were busy ones working on the aircraft alone and added to that was the discomfort of having to wade to the aircraft in ice water coming down from a glacier with the spring freshet.

I had the use of a small boat which was fine until the inner spring of the clutch broke. Grant took me to a camp called Van Dell where more fuel and oil was procured. It wasn't long until the engine was ready and the fuel from a drum was in the tanks. The usual cautious procedures were used and soon the machine was ready for taxing which I did myself that time.

It had rained hard that day and I was very wet from it and wading up to my hips as the level of the lake rose. The aircraft, because of the leaking floats, had to be pulled up closer to shore to keep it out of deep water.

I helped Grant move out a boom of logs after dinner for him to be towing all night. I then had a most pleasant hot shower that took the chill out of my bones.

A phone call to the office in Vancouver informed

me that a Beaver seaplane owned by the British Columbia Government was upside down in Lac la Hache, a lake near 100 Mile House alongside the Cariboo Highway.

There was nothing more to do on the Cessna so when Charlie, who was on his way, showed up, we left to look into my next job. Our destination was in a general direction of east, well into the interior of the Province.

We had a beautiful day for our flight that began with a slow climb up the valley, through the mountains and up over their tops. We passed low over large expanses of glacier/snow fields including part of Mt. Waddington sitting there in all her majestic glory.

I have always enjoyed flights over the mountains and that one was spectacular. Time slipped by so quickly and soon we were preparing for a landing and the beginning of another challenge.

The Beaver had been flipped over by a sudden strong wind direction change during a take off attempt from the lake. It appeared to be in good condition structurally and was floating high in the water. It was always a relief, in that type of accident, to find that the floats and their attachment struts were undamaged. That reduced the salvage job to a minimum by comparison.

Equipment and various materials would be needed after its removal from the water to preserve and prepare it for a ferry flight.

Experience dictated that, if it was practical and convenient, it was better to leave a seaplane submerged, as was the Beaver, until it could be serviced immediately in all respects, after it was removed from the water. Exposing the engine, instruments and electrical systems to the air for a prolonged period could cause much deterioration. The quality of the water is always a big factor in determining just how long an aircraft can be left in it.

The Beaver was anchored in deep water for safety. We returned to Vancouver and the next morning I was back to Owikena, rechecked the Cessna and with another pilot, brought it down to Gordy Peters at West Coast Air Services in Vancouver for recertification.

Late night paper work was completed at the office and I was on my way again to get the wet Government Beaver back to its Victoria base.

the Revenge of a Grizzly Bear

Max Ward and Canada Tungsten to my rescue

This story goes back to February or March 1961. The local was in an area known as Tungsten in the south side of the Mackenzie Mountains, not far from the South Nahanni River and directly north of Watson Lake, Yukon.

Canada Tungsten Mining Corporation, better know locally as Cantung, was establishing a mine that was still in the developing stages of construction when CF-JGI, a Piper PA18 (Super Cub) flown by Walt Foresberg, went over onto its back during a landing on a snow covered airstrip.

The air craft was however further damaged by nature, to the extent that it was declared a total loss for insurance purposes and was advertised for sale on an "as is where is" basis.

I was not acting in the capacity of an adjuster on that loss and was therefore in a position to bid on it which I did. I remember so well having my wife Dot type up a bid late one evening then I asked her to change it by increasing the amount by $50.00. She was tired and angrily tore the bid out of the typewriter while saying "make up your mind!" I know very well how she felt because it was around 11 p.m. and I was about to leave on another road trip that night.

As it turned out later, I was the highest bidder by $50 fair and square, much to the disgust of an individual in Watson Lake who was sure I had had an inside track in the bidding. He was known to have a questionable business back ground that guided his evil thinking.

I left for the Cub with a trailer to haul it to Vancouver and on arrival in Watson Lake I flew into the Cantung Site to prepare the aircraft for a flight out to Watson.

The story about how the post accident damage to the Cub turned into a major loss was fascinating and very original. Walt, with help from the camp, had managed to turn the aircraft back over onto its wheels and move it off to one side.

As I remember the story, Walt was alone and preparing to move the aircraft when suddenly he heard a loud roar and angry grunts from some animal. Looking over the rear section of the aircraft he saw a bear approaching at great speed, heading straight for him. He turned and ran toward a tool shed near by with the bear continuing in a straight line after him. It didn't waste any time going around the aircraft but instead, attacked it as though it was a stack of brush in its path, crushing the rear section of the fuselage to the ground.

The aircraft must have slowed the bear down a little, at least enough for Walt to get inside the shed and close the door.

The bear vented its anger on the shed by tearing off the corner boards then turned to boxes con-

taining drill rods and broke them up. Walt did not know if the bear returned to the aircraft or not, I would suggest that having failed to get Walt, it took a final swipe at the aircraft as it went off and that was probably when the fabric on the bottom side of the wing was shredded. In any case the damage to it was substantial.

Later on, an ex RCMP officer named Archie Currie, then working for Cantung, shot the bear. It was a Grizzly with a bad wound from a previous shooting by someone who didn't have the nerve to track it down and finish it off. No wonder the animal was a raging mass of anger looking for revenge.

I have to think I was most fortunate in the time I spent out in the wilderness over the years without having to face something like that. I rarely took a rifle with me but there were occasions when the RCMP thought I should do so and offered to lend me one. That was chiefly for the purpose of survival.

There was no road into the mining site at that time so aircraft were busy freighting in equipment and construction materials. Heavy equipment , including Catterpillar shovels and bull dozers, were taken in by firstly cutting the units into sections that could be put into an aircraft. Each piece of equipment was reassembled at the camp by welding crews spaced out from each other with wood fires between them for a little warmth (with smoke) for the workers.

Max Ward, whose Otter Karl Frisk and I had rescued from Baffin Island in 1958 , was using his Bristol Freighter for much of the freighting. A couple of times I stood by for him to make sure the fork lift operators didn't accidentally abuse his machine in the process of unloading, while he tended to business at the mine office with Roy Lambert.

I had been working on the Cub, with slow progress, for about 3 days. I was startled one afternoon by hearing my name called several times from the direction of the mine office, a couple of hundred yards away. It was Max running toward me hollering, GOT A DEAL FOR YOU, GOT A DEAL FOR YOU! I started toward him and he, short of breath, said, "Knock the wings off the Cub and when I'm back here again I'll take it out on a back

haul to Watson. You do have a trailer there don't you?" Max continued, "Both Cantung and I have been thinking we should do that for you but we both thought the other would not agree to it, that is, until we stumbled onto it a few minutes ago." Talk about a surprise! A question raced through my head! "They would do that for me?" It took me a bit to come down to earth and express my thanks. I should have thought about trying to make such arrangements and pay for it but I hadn't. Costs were a big factor for our company and so I did some things the hard way. Both Max and Roy were pleased with the plan and while it was never mentioned, I'm sure that Cantung managers Jack Crowhurst and Len White had had a hand in it too.

A grizzly bear's revenge.

It seemed that Max might not be in there again for a while so I left for Whitehorse on an Aero Commander problem and from there to Vancouver.

Jack Crowhurst was not long in sending a telegram advising that the Bristol would transport the Cub about April 18 so back north I went. I arrived at Cantung in a Beaver they had chartered, then removed the Cub wings. It was loaded into the Bristol and out it went to Watson Lake where it was stored in Cantung's building at the airport as I had to rush up to Whitehorse again.

Not long after that I hauled the Cub to Vancouver and rebuilt it in our shop. Shortly after that it was put out on short leases for needed revenue. On one of those contracts it disappeared on a flight up the coast of B.C. along with the pilot. No trace of them was ever found.

Strangely enough, it would be 20 years later at a golf club Happy Hour party in Guaymas, Mexico that I would run into Roy Lambert again.

Switches Off

As the chief diaper changer in the nursery said, "I'm just going from mess to mess; there has to be an end to these ends."...I have taken you on a fireside tour of selected sorties into Canada's inhospitable "outback". Nobody will ever do it again on a full time basis. That chapter is closed, over, done with; the insurance companies no longer find it economically viable to go after a bent bird. Too bad in a way; we did some wild and risky things but the work was loaded with job satisfaction. I had a good time. - Now it is time to ask, "What's next?"

"Next" for Dot and Denny is some non-business travel. This time around we are going to stop and smell the flowers. London, Paris, Rome, Berlin, Moscow, Athens, Odessa, Tokyo...all those places and more are going to be checked to confirm that there is more to them than a hotel room and a hangar.

I hope this "digest" of crash and carry events meets the expectations of those who persuaded me to tackle the project. I felt like a blind umpire making the call on which story was in and which was out. For sure,

some with personal involvement will think that choices could have been improved. So be it, I'm stuck with what you see.

For young readers who swerved into exposure or were steered there, I want to encourage them to be interested in aviation. Although the glamour and glory days of goggles and slipstream whipped silk scarves are below the sunset, there is much more adventure to come in every facet of the industry. If it captures your interest and sets you to dreaming, go for it and you'll have as good a time as I did.

To those who didn't grow old in the business and took off too soon for the heavenly hangar, I salute you and your contribution. To those who stayed the course, who built and polished the many facets of the flying business, I say, "Thank you."

Now for the last time:
Block the control surfaces
set the chocks
and confirm..
SWITCHES OFF